the latin american kitchen

elisabeth luard

Elisabeth Luard is an award-winning food writer who has written many books on Spanish and Latin American cuisine. Both this, *The Latin American Kitchen*, and her most recent book for Kyle Cathie, *The Food of Spain and Portugal* were recognised with Gourmand International awards, for best Latin American cookbook, and best foreign cookbook respectively. She is a regular contributor to various magazines and newspapers, including the *Scotsman*, the *Sunday Telegraph*, *Waitrose Food Illustrated*, *Decanter* and *Gourmet Magazine*.

the latin american kitchen

a book of essential ingredients
with over 200 authentic recipes

elisabeth luard

photography by francine lawrence

Kyle Cathie Limited

**For my New World granddaughter,
Sophie Francesca Patricia**

First published in Great Britain in 2002 by
Kyle Cathie Limited
122 Arlington Road
London NW1 7HP
general.enquiries@kyle-cathie.com
www.kylecathie.com

This paperback edition published in 2006
ISBN (13-digit) 978 1 85626 686 4
ISBN (10-digit) 1 85626 686 9

10 9 8 7 6 5 4 3 2 1

Project editors: Helen Woodhall and Caroline Taggart
Design: Geoff Hayes
Text editor: Robina Pelham Burn
Editorial assistance and picture research: Esme West
Home economy: Elisabeth Luard
Styling: Susi Hoyle
Production: Lorraine Baird and Sha Huxtable

A Cataloguing in Publication record for this title is available from the
British Library.

Printed and bound in Singaporeby Kyodo Printing Co.

Half-title page: Mayan girl, San Lorenzo, Chiapas, Mexico
Title page: 'Fruits of Brazil', Rio carnival
*This page: New Year's Day festival in Mexico – teenage boys re-enact
the story of Mary and Joseph*

contents

introduction

My earliest childhood memories are of a cool house shaded by mimosa trees on the shores of the River Plate, the broad river that takes its water from the Parana, which drains southwards from the Mato Grosso, the tropical highlands of Brazil.

I was seven years old when my family took passage on the HMS *Andes* for the month-long journey to the southern tip of South America. We steamed steadily across the Atlantic, putting in at the Canary Isles, crossing the equator by way of Rio, sailing on in stately splendour till we arrived at our destination, Montevideo, my stepfather's first diplomatic posting among the Latins. As the capital of Uruguay, Argentina's little sister – cattle country settled by Scots as well as Spaniards – Montevideo was held to be suitable for diplomats with families.

We – my brother, mother, stepfather and I – waited on the quayside while mountains of luggage were unloaded. My mother, the daughter of a considerable fortune, saw no reason to economise on life's small comforts. Our family possessions included a motor car – a brand new silver Jaguar, which, winched from the hold, dangled precariously over the waters of the harbour. Customs officers appeared. Accommodation was reached. Money changed hands. Released, we made our way to our new abode.

My brother and I – our father had been killed in the war, my mother, a young widow, remarried – rapidly discovered that life among the Latins was far more colourful than the somewhat dismal life we'd led in post-war London. Passers-by admired our curly blondness and gave us sugar cane to suck. We learned Spanish almost overnight. My brother acquired a fishing rod and a posse of urchin friends. Most of my time, when I wasn't at school, was spent in the kitchen, since my mother employed a cook and enough maids to staff a small hotel. Fortunately for our freedoms, my mother embarked on a new family, making adult supervision even looser.

Every evening, after school, I would sit on the back porch sucking a mate gourd through a straw, accepting sweets from strangers, my nostrils filled with the delicious scent of vanilla-flavoured cookies, or roasting chickens, or caramelising garlic – all equally exquisite.Then, if there was a party to be catered for, Esperanza, the cook, would open the door and call me in. I was needed in the kitchen. Really needed.

Actually, it was probably the first time I'd ever been needed in my life. Certain tasks were mine: rolling out the meatballs till they were perfectly spherical and no bigger than marbles, each flecked with green parsley. Mine, too, to peel the shrimps and pack them into avocado boats. On ordinary days I'd be allowed to sift through the lentils for tiny stones, or pick over the rice for insects, or allowed to use a small sharp knife to scoop out the creamy hearts of zapallitos, small round marrows perfect for stuffing. At weekends, my mother being busy with her own affairs, my presence was not much required in the household. Happily, as children often will, my brother and I took advantage of what was, to the outside world, a degree of neglect. My brother overnighted with the fisherboys, while I would go home with Esperanza to the *barrio*, a row of tumbledown shacks full of people, chickens and flea-bitten cats where, after a supper of maté tea sweetened with condensed milk and spiked with brandy, curled up on an old mattress on the earth floor among the sleeping babies and mouse-hunting felines, I slept soundly.

Those were the good times. Less good came when I was sent 'home' to boarding school in England, a cold and dreadful place on the Welsh borders, where my strange foreign ways, ability to speak languages and weird holiday destinations – my family continued on the Latino circuit, taking in Spain along the way, and the summer holidays were all I was permitted – ensured I remained an outsider. Later, as a young adult almost – though not quite – engaged to be married, I took employment in the embassy in Mexico City, a hardship post for my parents but not for me, since I took advantage of my stepfather's seniority to attach myself to expeditions organised by Mexico's Sociedad Indigenista – Society for Indigenous Peoples. We travelled by bus, bumping through badlands, the Chiapas, where the natives spoke no Spanish and everyone carried guns. On the river Uxumazintla I learned how to pluck and roast a parrot, on the plains of Guerrero I was shown how to ferment the juice of the maguey cactus by passing it through the mouth in a straw.

Sounds exotic? Indeed it was. And yet there was much which was familiar. Still more so when I took the decision that my own children should have the benefit of life among the Latins, though the land of my choice was Andalucia, Spain's southernmost province. Perhaps I chose it because it made me feel at home – certainly there was no other reason, only that I had an instinctive feeling that four children (I was a young mother, and all were at one time under six) would be happy where I was happy.

I did not know it at the time, but there was reason for me to feel at home. The culinary habit as well as the speech patterns of my Uruguayan childhood were unmistakeable. It was from the impoverished rural populations of Andalucia that the early colonisers of the New World were drawn.

The glittering port of Seville, a day's donkey journey from our valley, held the great library of the Indies, and it was here, in the writings of Bernal Diaz and the companions of Columbus himself, that I found the written record of what I already knew by instinct.

The culinary habit of Latin America – a shotgun marriage, the result of the fusion of two entirely different cultures and larders – dates from 1492, the year in which Christopher Columbus made landfall in what he declared to be the New Indies. That this voyage took place immediately after the fall of Granada – the final battle of the fight to regain the lands of southern Iberia held by the Moors for seven centuries – was no accident. The victory claimed by the combined might of the Catholic Kings, Isabel of Castile and Ferdinand of

Aragon, closed the route to the Orient, the source of so much pleasure to the cooks who learned their trade from the Moors. Hunger might be appeased by the wheatfields of the Guadalquivir, but man cannot live by bread alone. With her population clamouring for spices, Isabella pawned her jewels to fund the wild dreams of a Genoese seaman who promised a new route to the East.

From the moment the Old World's fragile ships made landfall in the New, a two-way traffic began. This trade, a process known as the Columbian Exchange, was in men and women, in ideas and philosophies, in gold and silver, in spices and oddities valued for their rarity – but above all in food, the raw material of life. The process of integration was surprisingly rapid, leading to an interweaving of culinary habit which, through the use of unfamiliar ingredients in familiar ways and of familiar ingredients in unfamiliar ways, makes the gastronomy of Latin America an edible history lesson. By the time Granada fell to the Catholic

Kings in 1492, the cooks of Spain and Portugal used spices liberally, had acquired pastrymaking skills as well as learning the confectioner's art, and understood sophisticated culinary techniques such as the use of pounded nuts to thicken sauces, the art of rice cooking, the use of delicate flavourings such as saffron and coriander. Along with these Moorish tastes, they had acquired a willingness to sample new and unfamiliar ingredients.

The early colonialists – Spanish and Portuguese, mainly from the south and therefore poorer and more Arab – imported the meat and milk animals of the Old World: pigs and chickens throughout, cattle to the Argentinian pampas and sheep to Patagonia. They set about subduing the indigenous peoples – the Aztec and residual Mayan civilisations in Central America, the Inca empire of Peru as well as other less well-organised tribal groups. Some, such as the Caribs of the Caribbean, defended their territories fiercely,

Colonial architecture in the historic district of Salvador, Brazil

Ploughing near Pucón, Chile

manner of citrus fruits, as well as grapevines for the winemakers of Chile and Argentina.

Although the ingredients themselves, both flora and fauna, can be clearly defined in naturalist's terms as being of native or alien origin, culinary habit is far less easy to distinguish. Who's to say if the seviches of Mexico are more closely related to the escabeches of Spain and Portugal than they are to the marinated fish dishes enjoyed by the Maya, whose taste for raw fish is shared by the inhabitants of the islands of the Pacific, including Japan? It would be a brave ethnologist indeed who could trace the descent of the dried-shrimp dishes of Bahia to the salt-cod traditions of Portugal without acknowledging the use of dende oil as part of the conservation process, an ingredient and method of purely African origin. Or who could claim exclusivity for the use of the earth-oven or pit-barbecue, a method of cooking which, as it happens, is common throughout South East Asia as well as among the aboriginal shore-dwellers of Australasia?

To generalise (always a dangerous exercise), the basic culinary habit of the native peoples of the southern lands of the Americas was and remains vegetarian, with much attention paid to nutritional balance and digestibility. A little opportunist meat-eating was mainly confined to tribal gatherings – and even today, meat is considered festive food. There were exceptions, naturally. Coastal dwellers of Chile and Brazil depended on fish augmented by sea vegetables, while the jungle-dwellers of Amazonia and the highlands of central America depended on river fish, berries and roots.

By the time the Europeans appeared, the indigenous inhabitants – those who had settled down as farmers rather than those who had simply continued as nomadic hunter-gatherers – had already developed and refined the food plants on which they depended, exchanging and

others treated the newcomers with more circumspection – indeed among those with an expectation of divine visitation, they were greeted as gods.

As the indigenous population declined or, less willing to take the consequences of defiance, retreated to the less hospitable interior, the European colonisers began to import slave labour from Africa, adding another layer to the culinary as well as the social pile-up. More recent gastronomic colonisation has taken place for economic reasons: coffee grows well in Brazil, bananas thrive throughout the tropical and sub-tropical zones, while additional botanical riches – though scarcely needed to swell the indigenous coffers – include pineapples, mangoes and all exporting between themselves. Tomatoes, for instance, are found in their wild and unpalatable form in Peru, but were cultivated in their modern form by the Aztecs of Mexico; Mexico, too, is the homeland of the avocado, a tree which remains sterile unless grafted with a fruit-bearing branch, indicating human intervention at an early stage in its food-supplying career. At the same time, a system of intensive cultivation was developed which suited the climate and the natural fertility of the soil. Some of the crops were simultaneous: rows of maize corn providing a climbing frame for a crop of haricot beans – lima, pinto, black or

Decorated pig at La Taconga festival, Ecuador

brown; acting as a weed-suppressant between the rows were pumpkins and marrows – winter and summer squashes. These three vegetables are often cooked together, providing a perfectly balanced meal in a single pot.

The indigenous population quickly accepted Europe's domestic animals – the cow as a milk-producer, egg-layers in the form of chickens, the mighty sty-pig as the principal meat animal, sheep and goats for cropping marginal lands – as useful additions to the New World's fauna. The Europeans had much to learn from those they colonised, including sophisticated skills in the preparation of ingredients which, in their untreated state, ranged from the indigestible to the inedible to the downright toxic. Ingredients as varied as cassava, maize, chocolate and vanilla all fall within the categories of foodstuffs which need special preparation to achieve their potential. Added to these was a profligacy of roots, tubers, fruits and vegetables – among them potatoes, tomatoes, peppers, squashes and pumpkins, legumes of the haricot family including all the storecupboard beans, pineapple, avocado – whose taste and culinary virtues were completely unknown to the world beyond their native territory.

Although these unfamiliar foodstuffs were slow to gain acceptance in the Old World, not so among the early colonisers of the New, who, naturally enough, were rarely accompanied by their wives. Contemporary accounts of the Conquistadores as provided by the evangelising monks who followed close behind describe the surprising palatability of the dishes prepared by their hosts. Once the colonisers brought their wives, the emphasis shifted. The ladies – women in their own kitchens being notoriously conservative – demanded the introduction of food plants and domestic animals of the Old World, establishing a process of overlay rather than

outright replacement. Wheat was planted to provide the raw material for yeast-raised breads (maize corn being relegated in many areas to animal fodder), which were served, and still are, in tandem with the maize-corn flatbreads of the indigenous inhabitants.

In the gardens of the homesteads – *estancias* built to the Hispanic pattern – were planted familiar Mediterranean pot-herbs, onions, carrots, brassicas and leaf vegetables in the form of lettuce and spinach; in addition, citrus groves were established, and salt, vinegar and sugar were introduced as methods of conserving fresh foodstuffs. Commercial interests established banana, sugar cane and coffee plantations where the climate and soil were suitable. During this time, the missionaries had already planted vineyards and were busy replacing pagan hallucinogens with reliable Christian wine (as well as introducing the process of distilling in the form of brain-addling Christian brandy). Meanwhile, the Africans transported as slave labour to work the new plantations in the Caribbean and Brazil took advantage of the white man's leavings by developing a sophisticated repertoire of offal dishes.

Pioneers, whether intrepid explorers or iron-clad armies, must live off the land or die – a necessity which can be turned to good account when the sun shines and the land is fertile. A culinary habit that is born of hardship – hammered out in response to the need for the taste of home, not simply to satisfy hunger but to render the exotic not only familiar but pleasurable – becomes doubly precious. When this is allied to the desire, once the colonial yoke is removed, to reconcile two alien cultures, culinary habit can be transformed into a

Old world meets New: a woman offers fabric for sale in front of the highly decorated façade of La Merced church, Antigua, Guatemala

declaration of national identity, an expression of something which might not find outlet in any other way. The exile not only longs for the taste of home, but is sure of exactly what he longs for – seasonings and all.

The territory is vast, the climate and geography bewilderingly diverse: all these factors contributed to the development of a sophisticated regional cuisine long before the imposition of colonial power.

Officially, there are twenty-six sovereign nations in Latin America, more if you include the islands of the Caribbean which, though some are French-, English- or Dutch-speaking, nevertheless can be said, culinarily speaking, to belong to the Latino tradition. The official Latin American rollcall, according to the US Board of Census which uses the term to identify its immigrant citizens, is, in rough geographical order starting in the north: Mexico, El Salvador, Nicaragua, Costa Rica, Guatemala, Belize, Honduras, Panama, Venezuela, Colombia, Ecuador, Peru, Bolivia, Chile, Argentina, Uruguay, Paraguay, Brazil, the three Guianas (Suriname, French Guiana, Guyana), Cuba, Puerto Rico, the Dominican Republic, Jamaica and Haiti.

Although all these nations share the New World larder, there are differences of climate and geography which allow one foodstuff to thrive in one place and not in another. Of the staples, maize – Indian corn, sweetcorn – is grown throughout Central America (including Mexico) and by the Andean nations, Colombia, Chile, Peru and Ecuador. In the Caribbean and the lands of Amazonia the staple is cassava root, a tuber whose most important characteristic is its rib-sticking starchiness. The potato is widely grown throughout, although it achieves the status of a staple only in the Peruvian highlands, where its cultivation ensured the survival of the Inca Empire in a region which yielded no alternative crops.

Quiche Maya Indian market in Guatemala

In addition, it's possible to divide the culinary habit of the territory into groups which reflect the way in which food is prepared and served. The nations of the Pacific coast prefer spoonfoods – soupy combinations which can be eaten from a bowl; the tortilla-eaters of Mexico and Central America have a preference for scooping-foods – salsas, bean purées, meat and vegetables chopped small in order that they may easily be conveyed to the mouth without cutting. The gaucho nations – Argentinians and their neighbours of southern Chile, Uruguayans, Paraguayans and the cowpokes of southern Brazil – are meat-eaters: they like their meat on the bone and roasted over an open fire, don't care much if it comes with bread or vegetables, and they like plenty.

Brazilians and Caribbeans of African origin developed a taste for offal not simply because it was the cheapest meat in the market, but because innards and lights – oxfoot, pig's tripe and all the other odds and ends the butcher might otherwise be unable to sell, or which make up the leavings from the salters and barrellers who victualled ships for the Atlantic crossing – can be subjected to long, slow cooking in a closed pot, the method used to tenderise wild-gathered game of uncertain age. Pepperpot, the Caribbean's famous all-in stew, is a collaboration between the hunters of the New World who used cassareep, an extract of bitter cassava, to tenderise their game, and the home cooks of the sugar plantations, searching for a way to feed their families and finding in the method and flavourings a little of the taste of home.

Of the Latino nations which can claim a distinctive culinary identity, that of Mexico is probably the most widely recognised – though not necessarily for the right reasons. Much of what is believed to be Mexican is actually northern borderlands cookery, Tex-Mex, the chilli-con-carne and the taco-wrap, a bowdlerisation of what is in reality a highly sophisticated culinary tradition traceable back to the Mayas, the civilisation which predated the Aztecs. The staple foodstuffs are store-cupboard beans and lye-treated maize flour, with avocados and tomatoes providing a nutritional balance; the chilli is the most important flavouring; chocolate and vanilla, both prepared by a complicated process of fermentation and sun-drying, are the luxuries. The presentation puts the emphasis on choice: chillis and salsas are presented separately, the diner being left to make his or her own decisions on how to eat the various elements, the degree of pepperiness or sweetness to be added.

Three distinct traditions combine in Brazil: indigenous, Portuguese and African. Among these, the indigenous inhabitants had, and continue to maintain, a sophisticated understanding of what might or might be done with forest foods and a preference for earth-ovens and barbecues. The Africans brought ingredients from their homeland – black-eyed peas, dende oil, okra, coconuts – to add to a natural willingness to eat what nature provided, however unpalatable or unfamiliar it might seem. The Portuguese brought a taste for sailors' one-pot stews and saltfish and an appetite for meat expressed in the churrascos – barbecue pits – of Bahia and Rio. Their wives were blessed with a light hand with the frying pan and that peculiarly Catholic taste for egg-and-sugar confections acquired from the Moors. Add to all this the traditional Mediterranean skills of cheese-making, ham-salting and the art of spicing store-cupboard sausages, and the result is a distinctive gastronomic tradition as inventive as it is exuberant.

Throughout the region, a distinction can be made between the food of the towns and country cooking. While rural households make little distinction between mistress and maid – both consume the same foods cooked in the same way, the master simply eats more than the servant – the food of the urban poor is the rich man's leavings, offal and the cheaper cuts of meat which must be tenderised by chopping or mincing. For this reason, and because country people are more resistant to change, it's among the pots and pans of the old haciendas that the conservative cooks of the old tradition can still be found. Among the specialities of these rural

A couple perform the quintessential South American dance, the tango, in Plaza Dorrego, Buenos Aires

kitchens are rich bean stews fortified with salt-cured sausages; roast meats made with fiery chilli; egg-custards made with pineapple juice; ices perfumed with vanilla and chocolate, desserts made to Old World recipes with New World fruits – papaya, pine-strawberry, guava, passionfruits; instead of wheat, cakes and cookies made with cassava-meal or maize ground to a fine polenta flour; as soon as the Hispanic housewife had access to milk-beasts – cows or goats – she made cheeses of the homely sort, junkets for children, milk porridges for invalids; in addition she stocked her cellar with home-made wines, jams, jellies – all the good things which any rural housewife took pride in putting by against the changing seasons.

The tradition is practical, the rules flexible – frontiersmen must adapt or die. There's little of what might described as *haute cuisine*. Elaborate presentation is left to commercial confectioners – caramel and cream fantasies are strictly for cake-shops, to be sampled Spanish-style, held in the hand in a scrap of paper, consumed at the counter as the high spot of the morning's marketing. The everyday cooking, the salsas and sauces of the Latino kitchen, require a subtleness of palate, but very little in the way of culinary tricks. There's no mystery – unless it's in the skill with which the tortilla-maker pats out her circular flatbreads in a Mexican market, or the swiftiness with which a Chilean fisherman shucks an oyster or slips the top off a prickly sea-urchin to expose the sunny corals.

This is not a cuisine of trickery – you'll find no low-fat, slim-as-you-eat solutions to compensate for your willingness to come to table. To eat without appetite, or consume good food in the expectation that it won't do what it's meant to do – satisfy and fortify – is to insult the cook, or, worse, make mockery of the gods. The food itself – flavours, scents, textures, colours, the pleasure of profusion – is what matters in the Hispanic tradition, in the New World as well as the Old. That's not to say it's dull. The Latino temperament is famously contrary: fiery and earthy, romantic and homely, conservative as well as inventive. Domestic traditions which evolved from necessity rather than choice – exile, captivity, isolation – are a product of compromise.

Macaws – the most colourful of South American birds – photographed in the Amazon region of Brazil

Latin America – the phrase itself a marriage of Old and New – is exactly that.

An understanding of the spirit of the recipe matters more than the correctness of the ingredients – some of which may be hard to find, or even when findable, not in perfect condition. This is true of any culinary tradition whose integrity is based on limitations – season, geography, a common well-spring of inherited knowledge. Few of us these days keep a household cow, or have the possibility to walk down the road and buy fresh fish directly from the fisherman or even catch our own fish, or pull vegetables straight from the earth, or pick fruit from the tree, or – even rarer – slaughter and salt down the family pig for winter stores.

Yet Latin Americans who have settled elsewhere – and the US has a huge population of immigrant Latinos – don't throw up their hands in despair if they can't find the right ingredient. If what they need is not available at the right price and quality, they find something else. That's easy enough if you know what you're trying to substitute, less so if you've never tasted the original. With this in mind, I have suggested ingredient alternatives throughout: it helps to know that the small plump Mediterranean cucumbers make an acceptable substitute for chayote; shredded celeriac has the look and texture of jicama; chilli flakes plus a handful of raisins deliver a fair copy of the sweet syrupy flavour of *chile pasilla*. In addition, botanical information makes it easier to select fruits or vegetables which, though they may only be available locally, have close relatives commercially grown elsewhere.

Lifestyle largely dictates what we will and won't cook, with time the most important factor in our busy modern lives. The everyday recipes of the region are usually quickly prepared – even the slow-cooked bean dishes need little preliminary

Garlic offered for sale in typical Brazilian wrapping

preparation and no elaborate finishing. Admittedly, festive dishes such as the mighty Brazilian feijoada, black beans and pickled pork, are labour-intensive – but that's because at family gatherings, the preparation is part of the pleasure. While few of us can call on an extended family to share the labour of pounding and grinding the chillies and spices which make the Mexican *mole negro* one of the world's great dishes, such tasks can be performed in minutes by modern machinery. The food-processor has revolutionised home cooking: recipes which would otherwise be dauntingly time-consuming – particularly salsas and sauces which depend on the chopping knife – are easy and quick.

While no special equipment is required, some of the techniques and cooking processes can be startlingly unfamiliar. The use of lye as a preparation process, the earthenware comal used as a

A few of the processes might seem too exotic to be considered at all. Where's the sense in recommending, to someone cooking on a one-ring gas-burner in a bedsit in Birmingham, say, the exquisite fragrance imparted to the meat of a wild turkey by wrapping it in banana leaves and burying it in an earth-oven? Then again, why not? The earth-oven is simply a response to the same lack of choice: a single heatsource, limited ingredients and the need to cook food economically without losing any of its goodness. A chicken, when slow-roasted in a covered pot on a single flame with aromatics easily obtainable at the corner store – while not quite up to the romantic standards of the Brazilian rainforest – delivers the right stuff to the taste-buds, and without the spade-work. And if the alternative to a pot-roast fowl is a fistful of unidentifiable meat patty basted with a chemical copy of hickory smoke – ancestor-nostalgia gone crazy – how much more delicious is a casserole of creamy white beans gently cooked on the lowest possible flame, finished with pumpkin, sweetcorn and a flavouring of sweet basil?

The Latin American kitchen, in a nutshell, is reactive rather than recipe-led: what's right for the dish matters more than a slavish attention to authenticity. It's the spirit which counts – and just as well, since no recipe, however detailed, is infallible. No two cooks, provided with same ingredients and identical cooking-instructions, produce exactly the same dish, not even in a professional kitchen. The way food reacts to the application of heat depends on more variables than there are parrots in the Guatemalan jungle: among these, fuel source, shape and construction of the cooking implement – whether the pan's made of iron or earthenware or teflon-coated steel; the raw materials – freshness, ripeness, sweetness, sourness, juiciness, wateriness; the temperament of the cook, even the

Something for everyone – flowers and beer on the same Brazilian stall

bakestone, the meticulous attention paid to the blending of dried chillies. While culinary manners vary from culture to culture, even from kitchen to kitchen, stepping outside a familiar cultural framework – forebearing, say, from frying the meat before adding the liquid to make a stew, or learning to pat an arepa rather than roll it, even the addition of a coloured oil or aromatic lard as a finishing flavouring – takes confidence.

weather. When it rains, maize flour needs less liquid to make a tortilla dough. When the sun shines, ripe tomatoes need no more than a sunny windowsill to melt into a salsa; a raw-fish seviche is made in minutes rather than hours.

While cookery can never be an exact science, the culinary habit of this diverse region is more inexact than most. It has no secrets – unless it be a light hand and an open heart. What it does have, and in abundance, is soul. Beyond this, no special equipment is required. Bring your favourite pan, the pot of your choice and your sharpest knife. The reward, as I hope you'll discover for yourself, is a culinary tradition which is simple yet sophisticated, robust but subtle, which reflects the beauty of the land, the sunny nature of the people and the profligacy of a fertile earth. This – as the Incas explained to their disbelieving conquerors – is a treasure far more valuable than gold, the gift of the gods, the food of the sun.

Festive masks on sale in Chichicabtenango, Guatemala

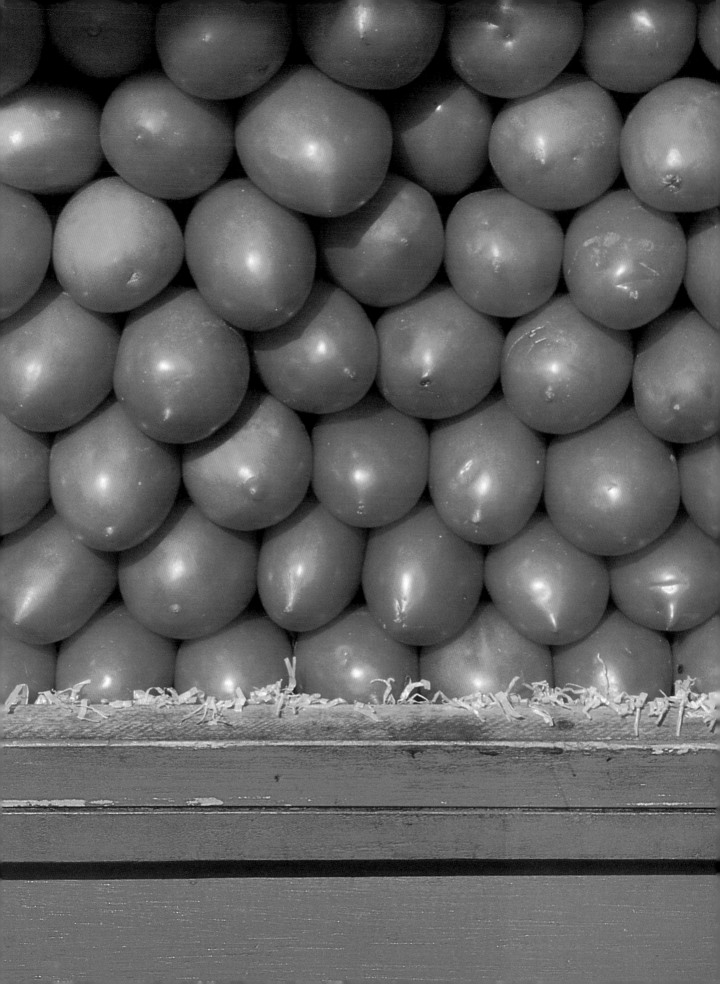

vegetables

The geography of this vast continent – a landmass which stretches from the Arctic to the Antarctic – combined with the relatively late appearance of man there has led to an astonishing diversity of habitats. This diversity – from the most inhospitable rocky uplands to the lushest of tropical floodplains, thousands of miles of coastline, innumerable islands – allowed the development of a vegetable kingdom without equal anywhere else on earth. Not all its secrets are yet revealed: the flora of the equatorial forests of Amazonia have yet to be fully explored, as have parts of the Andean uplands and riverine landscape of Central America. Nevertheless, long before the arrival of chemists and botanists, the indigenous inhabitants of the Americas were already cultivating sophisticated strains of edible plant-foods totally unknown anywhere else, developing ways of processing foodstuffs which, in their untreated state, were at best unpalatable, at worst, deadly.

While the most useful and easy to prepare – maize, beans, potatoes – quickly became staples to fill the world's store-cupboard, others – chillies (modified to produce the mild sweet pepper), tomatoes, avocados, the mighty family of squashes – became widely popular because they tasted good, filled a need and were remarkably easy to grow. Many of the vegetable-foods of the region remain relatively unexploited – though appreciated in their land of origin – sometimes because they occupy a specific botanical niche which cannot be reproduced elsewhere, but more often because their preparation and usefulness is little understood.

tomato

or tomate, jitomate (Mexico, from the Nahuatl xitomatl) (*Lycopersicon esculentum*)

A vine-fruit native to the Americas, the tomato is a member of the nightshade family. Slow to gain acceptance in the Old World – where it was initially classed as a fruit – it was in the Mediterranean vegetable-patch that the tomato found what can be considered its spiritual home, and it is in this new form, often combined with garlic and olive oil, that it re-appeared in Mediterranean recipes.

How it grows

Small fruited and hardy in the wild, the form in which it's still found in the Andean uplands, the tomato was described by a botanist who travelled with Pissaro in Peru as a weedy, aggressive little plant of minor gastronomic interest. The Aztecs of Mexico thought otherwise, cultivating the vines in the irrigated gardens of their holy city and offering the fruits in their temples as food for the gods: blood-red juices to satisfy blood-hungry deities.

Appearance and taste

Modern tomato hybrids come in every shape and size, from the fragrant little cherry to the rich-juiced plum to the big meaty beef-steak. While most varieties ripen to scarlet, some produce fruits which ripen to cream, yellow, orange, a deep crimson, all the way to almost black.

Buying and storing

Look for firm fruits with a plump unwrinkled skin and strong fragrance (the best pointer to flavour). Colour is not necessarily a guide to sweetness and ripeness: some varieties are deliciously sweet when still streaked with green. Field-tomatoes which have been allowed to ripen on the stem are always superior to any other. While the tomato takes well to the greenhouse – hence its popularity as a year-round salad-vegetable – glass-grown tomatoes, unless left to mature in their own time, are watery and tasteless, particularly if grown for looks rather than flavour. When buying fresh store at room temperature – never in the fridge. To preserve for longer, cook down to concentrate and bottle under oil. In cooked sauces (mostly of Mediterranean origin) tinned plum tomatoes are preferable to out-of-season fresh fruits.

Medicinal and other uses

Tomatoes are a good source of vitamin C, most of which is found in the jelly round the seeds; vine-ripened tomatoes have twice as much as fruits picked green. Naturally antiseptic, tomatoes are useful in the treatment of cirrhosis of the liver, hepatitis and other complaints of the digestive organs. The tomato is reputed to be a neutraliser for skunk-spray – invaluable when you need it, no doubt.

Culinary uses

Plum tomatoes are meatier and less juicy than the round varieties – good in sauces and for oven-drying. To prepare, halve vertically, sprinkle with salt and set to dry in the lowest possible oven (the temperature should be roughly that of a summer's day in Acapulco). Cherry tomatoes have a concentrated sweetness perfect for salsas; beef-tomatoes are good for stuffing and baking. Recipes of the region concentrate on presenting the tomato in its raw form – sliced, chopped or pulped as a salad or salsa. To separate the flesh from the rest, cut off the top and scoop out the seeds; holding the body of the fruit firmly in your palm, rub the cut surface down the coarse holes of the grater, peeling the skin back as you go, until you're left with nothing in your hand but a flattened circle of skin.

Tomates rellenos con granos tiernos

(Tomatoes stuffed with corn-kernels)
Serves 4

An Ecuadorian dish of tomatoes filled with a delicate stuffing of fresh corn-kernels, finely diced courgette and Andean yellow carrot – *zanahoria amarilla* – whose replacement is parsnip or celeriac.

4–8 tomatoes (depending on size), ripe but firm
1 cup fresh corn-kernels, sliced off the cob
1 parsnip or thickly sliced celeriac, diced small
1–2 courgettes, diced small
4 tablespoons olive oil
Juice of $^1/_2$ lemon
1 garlic clove, crushed
1 teaspoon salt
Pinch sugar
1 tablespoon chopped parsley
1–2 fresh chillies, de-seeded and finely sliced

Scald and skin the tomatoes. With a small spoon, hollow out the interior, saving the pulp and discarding the seeds. Dice the pulp.
In a small pan with the lid on, cook the corn-kernels with the diced parsnip and courgette in a very little water (no salt) until tender – about 10 minutes – and drain.

Meanwhile, use a fork to mix the oil with the lemon juice, garlic and salt and a little sugar. Toss the drained vegetables with the dressing. Allow to cool a little before you fold in the reserved tomato flesh, parsley and chilli. Spoon the filling into the tomato shells and finish each with a curl of lemon zest.

Mermelada de tomate

(Spiced tomato marmalade)
Makes about 1.3k (3lb)

A Cuban way with a fruit which hasn't quite decided if it's a vegetable or is more at home on the dessert-trolley – here, it's neither a jam nor a pickle, but something in between. Served in Old Havana as a membrillo, a fruit-paste eaten with cheese.

900g (2lb) ripe but firm tomatoes, chopped
  small

Tomatoes stuffed with corn-kernels, dressed with chilli and coriander

6 allspice berries
Short length cinnamon
3–4 cloves
1 lemon, zest and juice
About 900g (2lb) granulated sugar

Put the chopped tomatoes in a roomy pan with the spices and zest, add half a glass of water, bring to the boil, turn down the heat, put the lid on loosely and simmer gently for 20–30 minutes, stirring occasionally, until completely pulped.

Push the pulp through a sieve. Weigh it and return it to the pan. Stir in the same weight of sugar as pulp, add the lemon juice and bring gently to the boil, stirring until the sugar dissolves. Let it bubble, stirring to avoid sticking, until it reaches setting-point – it's ready when a drop on a cold saucer wrinkles when you push it with your finger.

Bottle up in warm sterilised jars. Seal or tie down under paper hats when cool.

tomatillo

or tomate verde, miltomate, tomate de capote
(Mexico), green tomato (*Physalis ixocarpa*)

A smallish tomato-
like vine-fruit about
the size of a hen's
egg, the
tomatillo is
native to Mexico
and Guatemala,
and belongs to the same family as the physalis or cape
gooseberry (see p.216 for the other members). Used in the
cookery of the Aztecs, it is much valued in Mexico as a
sauce ingredient – essential in green sauces, to which it
imparts a gluey texture and lemony flavour – and to a
lesser extent in Guatemala.

Buying and storing

Choose firm, hard, dry fruits whose calyx
shows no sign of mould or blackening, with a
clean, sweet, well-developed gooseberry scent.
They can be stored unhusked in a single layer
in a cool place for several months.

Medicinal and other uses

The tomatillo is high in fibre with plenty of
vitamin C. In its land of origin, a tea brewed
from the calyces is said to cure diabetes.

Culinary uses

To prepare, remove the papery covering and
rinse (don't worry about scrubbing off the
sticky substance round the stalk-end) and
chop. It is usually eaten cooked, though in
Central Mexico it is sometimes used in a raw
salsa as a dip for barbecued meat. The skin is
very fine – no need to remove it.

How it grows

A bushy perennial with tomato-like leaves,
usually grown as an annual, the tomatillo has
downward-pointing, lantern-like fruits enclosed
in the green exterior husk or calyx – mildly toxic
– which are common to all *Physalis* species. As
the fruit swell, the husk becomes brittle and
papery and bursts.

Appearance and taste

The fruit is green even when ripe, though it can
progress to yellow or purple. The flesh – crisp
and juicy when raw, soft and glutinous when
cooked – is solid all the way through, sprinkled
with seeds tender enough to crunch between
the teeth. The flavour is that of gooseberry and
apple sauce, with a touch of lemon zest.

Market place, Mexico

Salsa verde de tomatillo, Mexico's favourite dipping-sauce

Salsa verde de tomatillo

(Green tomato salsa)
Serves 4

A deliciously fragrant, rather gluey-textured salsa – one of the truly nostalgic flavours of the Mexican kitchen.

8 tomatillos (green tomatoes), hulled and
* wiped*
2 green chillies (jalapeno or serrano),
* de-seeded and chopped*
1 garlic clove, finely chopped
1 teaspoon sugar
Salt
1 tablespoon chopped coriander

Cut the tomatillos into chunks and put them in a small pan with just enough salted water to cover. Bring to the boil and simmer for about 10 minutes until perfectly soft. Stir in the chopped chilli and garlic, mash to soften, season with sugar and salt and leave to cool before stirring in the coriander. Serve warm or cool with anything with which you would serve a red tomato sauce. Delicious spooned over a fried egg, excellent with cold chicken.

Tomatillos gratinados

(Gratin of green tomatoes)
Serves 4

A Mexican specialty, very rich and delicious. Serve as a party dish, with freshly baked bolillos, bobble-shaped bread rolls no bigger than can comfortably be held in the hand, slow-risen to give a dense-textured crumb, baked in a wood-fired oven to give a thick golden crust, and sold fresh in the bakery every morning.

900g (2lb) ripe tomatillos
300ml (1/2 pint) cream
2 tablespoons olive oil
1 garlic clove, skinned and chopped finely
3 tablespoons fresh breadcrumbs
1 tablespoon chopped parsley
1 teaspoon crumbled oregano
1 tablespoon grated white cheese
Salt and pepper

Preheat the oven to 425°F/220°C/gas mark 7. Slice the tomatillos thickly and overlap them in a single layer in a gratin dish. Pour the cream over and sprinkle with salt and pepper. Bake for about 15 minutes until the cream is boiling. Meanwhile, warm the oil in a small frying pan, add the garlic and let it fry gently until it softens. Sprinkle in the breadcrumbs and let them crisp up in the hot oil. Stir in the herbs and tip the contents of the pan all over the tomatoes. Finish with a sprinkle of grated cheese.

avocado

or acuacate (Mexico), abacate (Brazil), palta (Chile),
alligator pear (US) (*Persea americana*)

Technically a fruit but treated as a vegetable, the avocado is
pear-shaped to perfectly spherical, ranging in size from as
small as a hen's egg to as large as a cantaloup.

Sorting recently picked avocados beside Lake Atitlán, Guatemala

How it grows

A magnificent, glossy-leaved, semi-tropical tree
native to Mexico, the avocado is infertile unless
grafted with a fruit-bearing branch. The fruits
don't begin to ripen until they drop (or are
harvested) from the branch.

Appearance and taste

Hundreds of different varieties are grown. Skin-
colour varies from frog-green to purple-bronze;
the skin-texture varies from tender, smooth and
fine, to pock-marked, tough and woody. The
flesh when ripe is buttery and soft, varying in
colour from pale green to clotted cream – when
hopelessly overripe, it becomes fibrous and
dark. In Mexico, only the superior large, round,
thick-skinned, creamy-fleshed fruits are
considered suitable for eating whole, either
sliced or scooped directly from the shell; the
inferior, smaller, thin-skinned varieties are
considered more suitable for
guacamole – the Aztec word
for pulp.

Buying and storing

The larger the avocado, the better
the ratio of stone to flesh. Look for an
unblemished exterior, preferably with 'ready-
ripened' on the pack. If you buy hard
avocados, you won't know if they've
been bruised or not until they
ripen. Once ripe, keep them in
the fridge: being very rich in oil,
they go rancid.

Medicinal and other uses

The avocado is as close as any fruit gets to the
perfect food: remarkably high in protein, rich in
fibre and carbohydrates, endowed with all
essential vitamins and minerals and easily
digested; it is good for babies, the elderly and
all stages between. High levels of copper and
iron in easily assimilable form make it ideal for
the treatment of anaemia, and invalids and
convalescents will find it improves hair and skin
quality. It is not recommended for anyone with
liver-trouble since its high fat-content (largely
mono-unsaturated) makes it hard to digest. An
infusion of the leaves is used as a diuretic in
Brazil.

Culinary uses

Don't do anything until you must. Once cut, the
flesh quickly discolours, a process which also
affects the flavour: if you have no choice but to
prepare ahead, leave the stone in the hole, or, if
mashing, pop the stone in the middle and keep
covered with clingfilm – there's no logical
explanation, but the presence of the stone
does delay the darkening. An unripe avocado
can be ripened by popping it in a paper bag at
room temperature for 2–3 days – less if you
include a ripe banana. Avocado oil – bland and
odourless, qualities which make it sought-after
by the cosmetics industry – has a remarkably
high burn-point: 520°F.

Crema de palta

(Iced avocado soup)

Serves 4

A sophisticated green soup in which the rich flesh of the avocados provides the thickening as well as the flavour. To serve hot, blend with boiling stock and serve immediately – it goes brown very quickly. The smooth-skinned green avocados are best for this dish: the flesh is creamier and smoother than the rough-skinned Hass.

2 perfectly ripe avocados, skinned, stoned
* and diced*
600ml/1 pint cold chicken stock
2 tablespoons lime or lemon juice
Salt

To finish:
1 tablespoon diced cucumber
1 fresh green chilli, de-seeded and sliced
A few fresh coriander leaves

Process all the ingredients thoroughly to a smooth purée. Dilute with water if too thick. Taste and salt lightly. Ladle into bowls and finish with cucumber, slivers of green chilli and a few coriander leaves.

Guacamole

(Avocado dip)

Serves 4 as a starter

A chopped salad in which all the ingredients are separately identifiable – a preparation known to the Aztecs. To serve as a sweet relish, combine with pomegranate seeds and dress with honey and lemon juice.

2 large ripe avocados, diced
3 tablespoons diced mild onion
3 tablespoons diced tomato
2 tablespoons chopped green pepper
1 small green chilli, de-seeded and chopped
* small*
2 tablespoons chopped fresh coriander
Juice of 1–2 limes
Salt

Mix everything together lightly with a spoon, adding lime-juice and salt to your taste. If you don't mean to serve it immediately, to prevent browning pop one of the avocado stones in the middle to fool the avocado it's still in the shell – sympathetic magic. Serve with cos lettuce leaves and crisp tortilla chips for scooping – fry your own, the commercial ones are far too salty.

Dolce de abacate

(Avocado whip with rum)

Serves 6

The Brazilian housewife treats the avocado as a dessert fruit, serving it with cream and sugar. Here, it's finished with pomegranate seeds, tart and crunchy. All the ingredients should be cold before you start.

2 small, perfectly ripe avocados (Hass,
* for preference)*
2 tablespoons lime juice
4–6 tablespoons caster sugar
1 tablespoon rum
About 300ml (1/2 pint) single cream

To finish:
Seeds of 1 ripe pomegranate

Skin and stone the avocados, put them in the liquidiser with the rest of the ingredients and process to a purée, adding the cream gradually until the mixture has the consistency of thick yoghurt. It'll keep in the fridge for a day or two – or you can freeze it and serve as an ice cream. Pile in individual glasses and finish with pomegranate seeds.

Clockwise from top: avocado soup, avocado and pomegranate relish, guacamole

jicama

or yam bean, Mexican potato
(*Pachyrhizus erosus, P. tuberosus*)

The tuberous root of a member of the pea family, the jicama is a native of Central America and the lands of Amazonia. The name comes from the Nahuatl *xicama*, meaning 'storable root'.

How it grows

The jicama is a garden plant, grown for the beauty of its trumpet-shaped flowers which turn themselves into inedible pods. The edible part is the subterranean tuber, storage system for the plant in winter, which looks rather like a large brown turnip.

Appearance and taste

When young and fresh, the skin is fine, almost translucent, and the flesh is snowy white and a little sweet, very like a water-chestnut in flavour and texture – crisp and delicate. Older specimens develop a flavour rather like raw potato, so are best cooked, when they become starchy and bland but retain much of their crispness.

Buying and storing

Pick medium-sized tubers which are firm and free of blemish, with fine, tan-coloured, smooth skin; elderly tubers are rough-skinned and dry-looking with fibrous and starchy flesh, only suitable for cooking. Store in a plastic bag in the fridge for up to 3 weeks. To prepare, just pare off the fine potato-like skin and the fibrous layer immediately beneath, and slice or dice. Once peeled, keep in cold water with a squeeze of lemon.

Medicinal and other uses

Low in fat, high in fibre: perfect for slimmers.

Culinary uses

The jicama can be eaten raw when young, cut into chips or slivers and dressed with citrus juices, the form in which it's sold as a quick snack in Mexican market places. When included in a fruit salad, it can be mistaken for apple. Mature roots are suitable for inclusion in spicy stews, or for cooking in combination with other root-foods.

Pico de gallo
(Rooster's-beak salad)
Serves 4 as a starter or side-salad

This salad takes its name from the dressing – pico de gallo or rooster's beak – the sharpness of the citrus juices balancing the blandness of the raw root, while the softness of the fruit complements the vegetable's crispness.

1 jicama, about 450g (1lb), peeled and cut into matchsticks or ribbons

The dressing:
Juice and finely grated zest 2–3 bitter (Seville) oranges or lemons or limes
Salt

To finish:
2 sweet green oranges in segments (or 1 large eating orange in segments)
1 tablespoon pine-kernels, toasted
Chilli flakes or finely chopped fresh red chilli

Toss the prepared jicama with the orange juice and salt and leave for an hour or two in a cool place. Combine with the orange segments and finish with the pine-kernels and the chilli.

Fruit and vegetables on sale in Buenos Aires

Pico de gallo, a refreshing summer salad finished with pine-kernels

Manchamantales con jicama

(Jicama and chicken hot-pot)
Serves 4–6

**Food for the greedy – hence the name
tablecloth-stainer. Wear a bib and eat with
your fingers.**

900g (2lb) jicamas, peeled and cubed
4 tablespoons oil
2–3 garlic cloves, slivered
1 large mild onion, finely sliced in half-moons
4 chicken joints or 450g (1lb) cubed pork
4 chile poblanos or 2 green peppers,
  de-seeded and cut in strips
4–5 large ripe tomatoes, chopped
A handful dried apricots, chopped

A handful prunes, stoned
1 tablespoon raisins
2–3 chile pasillas, soaked and torn
2–3 dried chillies, de-seeded
1 short stick cinnamon
1 teaspoon powdered cumin
1 tablespoon dried oregano
Salt and pepper

To finish:
1 tablespoon powdered sugar mixed with
  powdered cinnamon

Put the jicama to soak in lightly salted water.
Heat the oil in a roomy pan and fry the garlic
and onion. Push aside as soon it softens and
add the chicken or pork and the poblano or

green pepper strips. Fry until it all browns a
little. Add the tomato pulp, fruits, chillies,
spices, oregano, salt and pepper. Add enough
water to cover, bubble up, put the lid on and
leave to simmer until the meat is tender and the
juices well-reduced – an hour or so.

Halfway through the cooking, add the jicama –
you'll need more water.

To finish, take off the lid, turn up the heat and
let the sauce bubble fiercely for a few minutes
to evaporate extra moisture and thicken the
sauce. Pile into a big bowl and finish with
cinnamon sugar. Serve with thick slices of fried
plantain and green papaya dressed with lime-
juice.

winter squash

or pumpkin, calabaza, abóbara (Brazil)
(*Cucurbita* spp)

Edible gourds of the storable varieties – in varying sizes, shapes and colours – are among the most venerable of the continent's cultivars. Ethnobotanists suggest it was the first of what has been called the American Triad: beans, squash and maize – food plants still grown in association and prepared in recipes which feature all three.

How it grows

A vine-fruit, storable once harvested, winter squash swell through their long, slow growing season, accumulating sweetness as the vine withers.

Appearance and taste

A very variable bunch – spherical, squashed-oval or pear-shaped – winter squash have hollow hearts which contain a great many small, edible seeds. Most develop hard, warty, inedible outer skins, though the butternuts and some of the green-skinned winter squashes are exceptions.

The texture is hard when raw, soft and melting when cooked. The flesh varies from pale gold to a deep orange and is very sweet, though some squash are sweeter than others.

Buying and storing

Pick healthy gourds with no sign of bruising. Buy whole for storage, or cut into chunks or in pieces for immediate consumption, in which case it will need to be wrapped in clingfilm and kept in the fridge for no more than 3–4 days. Whole pumpkins can be overwintered on a beam or on top of a cupboard, even in a centrally-heated kitchen. Varieties popular in the region include the bottle-shaped butternut, which has a fine, tender, almost translucent gold to ivory skin and dense orange flesh, very sweet and almost spicy. Largest is the mighty pumpkin – tough-skinned, with rather watery flesh, but making up in quantity what it lacks in quality – which is particularly popular in the Caribbean, where it can be spherical or squashed, and the skin can be any shade between pale ivory to deep orange, to speckled ivory to deep green. The Brazilian pumpkin is more fibrous and denser-fleshed than the Caribbean variety.

Medicinal and other uses

Very digestible, winter squash are packed with easily-assimilable sugars and carbohydrates, and are low in calories and high in vitamin A and potassium. The juices are highly alkaline – useful in the treatment of acidosis of the liver and blood and recommended as an anti-inflammatory. The raw seeds are eaten to get rid of tapeworm.

Culinary uses

The denser-fleshed squashes – butternut and other small to medium-sized varieties – are delicious in desserts or cut into chunks and roasted, or baked with cream. The larger, watery-fleshed pumpkins make excellent soups and stews; as a pie-filling, they need to be cooked down to evaporate excess moisture. The flowers are also eaten, particularly the males which can be picked without damaging the fruits. Related ingredients include *pepitas* – toasted pumpkin seeds – and pumpkin-seed oil (nutty and delicate but it goes rancid rapidly unless kept in the fridge).

Sopa de calabaza

(Dominican pumpkin and orange soup)
Serves 4–6

Spiced with ginger and sharpened with orange, this is the most delicious of the Caribbean's many pumpkin soups. It is best made with one of the dense-fleshed pumpkins such as butternut or banana squash. If you are using one of the large watery-fleshed Hallowe'en-type pumpkins, you'll need a little sugar and a squeeze of lemon.

1 small pumpkin or a wedge weighing 900g (2lb)
A nugget of butter
1 yellow or white onion, finely chopped
1/2 teaspoon ground ginger
1/2 teaspoon nutmeg
850ml/11/2 pint chicken stock
300ml/1/2 pint freshly squeezed orange juice
Salt and pepper

To finish:
Pumpkin seeds, lightly toasted

Preheat the oven to 400°F/200°C/gas mark 6. If using a whole pumpkin, slice it in half, scoop out the seeds and place it face down on a baking sheet lined with foil. If using a wedge, de-seed, cut into chunks and arrange on the foil. Bake for 40 minutes or so, until perfectly soft and a little caramelised. Slip off the thin skin, but don't get rid of the little brown bits. Meanwhile, melt the butter in a roomy pan and fry the chopped onion gently until it softens and takes a little colour – don't let it burn. Sprinkle in the ginger and nutmeg and add the pumpkin, chicken stock and orange juice. Bring to the boil, turn down the heat and simmer for 20 minutes to marry the flavours. Purée in a food processor until perfectly smooth. Reheat when you're ready to serve. Finish with a sprinkle of toasted pumpkin seeds.

Sopa de calabaza, sweet and spicy

Dulce de calabacín

(Candied pumpkin)

Very sweet, sticky preserves such as this are traditionally served as a welcome to visitors. They can be offered in little dishes with a glass of water; but are nicest served on a small spoon over a glass of chilled coconut-water or fresh orange juice.

1.3k (3lb) pumpkin, peeled, seeded, and cut into large, chunky strips (the size of a Mars Bar cut lengthwise in half)
225g (8oz) sugar
6 tablespoons water (less if pumpkin is watery)

Layer the pumpkin and the sugar in a heavy saucepan. Add the water. Set the pan on a very low heat, cover tightly, and simmer for 50 minutes or so, until the pumpkin is tender and the syrup thick and shiny. You may need more water, or you may need to boil the syrup down with the pan uncovered – it all depends on the pumpkin. Leave it to cool in the pan in its syrup. Put in a pot, making sure the pumpkin pieces are completely submerged.

summer squash

or vegetable marrow, calabaza, courgette, zucchini, calabacín, zapallito (*Cucurbita* spp.)

This pepo – the name given to the fruit of a member of the gourd family – is grown to be harvested in spring and summer, and harvested green: hence, summer squash.

Marrow ready to be harvested

How it grows

A bushy, tendril-forming annual herb with yellow flowers, the courgette has rough hairy stems and deeply-pinnate leaves. It is often grown in association with maize and beans, when its rambling habit and broad, shady leaves serve both as a weed-suppressant and moisture-preserver. Traditional recipes reflect this association.

Appearance and taste

When young it is bright green and shaped like a small cucumber, with creamy yellow mild-flavoured flesh; when older and larger, the soft skin darkens and hardens, the roundness develops into flat planes and the flesh becomes more watery and fibrous. There's also a round, pale green or speckled ivory-green variety, sapallito, specially grown for stuffing. It's the perfect size for eating when it sits comfortably in the palm of the hand.

Buying and storing

Young, immature fruits should feel firm and have no soft patches or flexibility. Store them in the salad-compartment of the fridge and eat them as soon as possible. Mature marrows should also be clear-skinned with no bad patches. They keep well and can be stored at room temperature.

Medicinal and other uses

Digestible and easily assimilable, but, being 90 per cent water, their nutritional value is limited.

Culinary uses

To prepare when tender and young, simply wipe and slice; older specimens should be skinned and the woolly middles and seeds scooped out and discarded. Quickly-cooked when young or old, it is best steamed or cooked in a covered pan with as little liquid as possible. Young squashes are firmer and more delicate than older specimens, which need to be skinned and de-seeded before cooking. The flowers are also eaten: they are delicious shredded and included in a stuffing for an empanada, or stuffed, dipped in batter and deep-fried.

Budín de zapallitos

(Courgette cheese-pudding)

Serves 4 as a main dish

A dish I remember from my Uruguayan childhood: rich, creamy and flavoured with lots of cheese.

3–4 large courgettes (zucchini), grated
2 tablespoons butter or oil
1 large mild onion, finely chopped
2 large eggs
300ml (1/2 pint) creamy milk
2 tablespoons grated parmesan

4–6 slices white bread, crusts removed
4 tablespoons freshly-grated hard cheese –
  gruyère or cheddar
Salt and pepper

Preheat the oven to 375°F/190°C/gas mark 5. Salt the grated courgettes and leave in a colander to drain for half an hour. Rinse and shake dry.

Heat the butter or oil in a frying pan and fry the onion gently until it softens. Add the courgettes, put the lid on loosely and shake over the heat until the flesh turns transparent.

Mix the eggs in with the milk, stir in the parmesan and season with salt and pepper. Lay half the bread in the bottom of a buttered gratin dish, cover with the vegetables and top with the remaining bread. Pour in the egg-milk mixture, and sprinkle the top layer of bread with the grated cheese. Bake for 20–25 minutes, until deliciously golden and bubbly.

Tortillitas de calabacín

(Courgette fritters)

Serves 4 as a starter

The crispness comes from the pre-salting – necessary to draw excess moisture – as well as the use of textured flours. Stoneground is best.

6–8 courgettes, sliced lengthways
1 tablespoon fine salt

Batter:
3 tablespoons coarse bread flour
1 tablespoon roughly-ground cornmeal
1 teaspoon rough salt
1 tablespoon olive oil
300ml (1/2 pint) water
1 large egg, separated

To cook:
Oil for deep frying

Salt the courgettes slices and leave in a colander to drain for half an hour. Whisk all the batter ingredients together, reserving the egg-white.

Heat a panful of oil until you can see a faint blue haze rising.

Rinse the courgette slices and pat dry. Whisk the egg-white until firm and fold it into the batter. Dip the courgette slices – one at a time – into the batter and drop into the oil, only as many as will bob comfortably about on the surface. Allow to brown, turning to fry the other side – they will take 3–4 minutes. Remove with a draining spoon.

Eat them as they come out of the pan, with a squeeze of lemon.

Budín de zapallitos, a creamy gratin of grated courgettes

chayote

or christophene, chocho, custard marrow, mirlitón (USA) (*Sechium edule*)

A summer squash which looks rather like a large green pear, the custard marrow is marked from stem to stern with deep irregular ridges. Classed as a pepo – the name given to fruits of the cucumber type – it is native to Central America and was first cultivated in Mexico by the Aztecs, who gave it its name. The colour varies from dark to pale green; the pale green flesh has more or less the texture and flavour of cucumber with a touch of kohlrabi.

How it grows

A perennial vine which draws its nourishment from large, subterranean tubers, it is astonishingly prolific: a single seed planted in a pot in sunny conditions with plenty of water can produce enough leaves and fruits to shade a whole verandah.

Appearance and taste

When young, the skin is pale green and soft (only older specimens need be peeled) and the flesh is crisp and firm. The female fruits have smooth skins while the males are prickly – the former are fleshier and preferred to the latter. All parts of the plant are edible: leaves, shoots, tubers and the nut which develops within the fruit.

Buying and storing

It is best eaten in infancy – no bigger than a hen's egg – when the flavour will be more concentrated and the flesh juicy rather than watery. Choose clean, clear-skinned chayotes which feel firm in the hand. Store them in the fridge and use while still fresh – they go mouldy after a week.

Medicinal and other uses

Bland, delicate and digestible, it is suitable for invalids and babies, particularly when given additional food-value by being cooked in a broth or in combination with dairy foods.

Chayote for sale, Mexico

Culinary uses

The fruit is bland and almost tasteless – a blend of cucumber, kohlrabi and courgette – so perfect as a vehicle for other flavours. It can be grated and eaten raw in salads, stir-fried, steamed, or stuffed and baked (there is no need to skin it). To boil the chayote, rinse and remove the single seed before cooking. The kernel is edible and has a delicate, rather almondy flavour. The tuberous root looks and tastes like a yam, and young shoots are picked in the spring, to be eaten like asparagus, or stirred into soups.

Buttered chocho
Serves 4 as a side-dish

This is the Jamaican way with this most delicate of summer squashes – butter and mild sweet onion form the dressing, with a touch of chilli to excite the taste buds.

900g (2lb) chayote, cut into small cubes
1 sweet yellow onion, finely sliced
A generous knob of butter
Salt

Buttered chocho – classic, simple and delicious

Salt the chayote cubes lightly and leave in a colander to drain. Rinse and transfer to a saucepan with the sliced onion. Add a splash of water – there's plenty of liquid in the vegetable – put the lid on tightly and steam in its own juice over a medium heat for about 10 minutes, until perfectly tender but not collapsed. Pile on a dish and drop the knob of butter on top.

Chancletas
(Chayotes baked with cheese and cream)
Serves 3 as a main dish, 6 as a starter

A Puerto Rican dish, known as old slippers – no doubt as much for the delectable scent of the stuffing as the shape of the container. Pattypan squash is an acceptable substitute as a container.

3 chayotes – each weighing about 350g (12oz)
Small knob butter
150ml (¹/₄ pint) single cream
225g (8 oz) grated white cheese such as mild cheddar or gruyère
3 tablespoons raisins or sultanas
1 teaspoon vanilla extract or a knife-tip scrape from a vanilla bean
1 tablespoon sugar
Salt

To finish:
6 tablespoons fresh breadcrumbs
2 tablespoons grated hard cheese – mature cheddar, parmesan

Cook the chayotes in enough boiling, lightly salted water to cover until perfectly tender: 45–50 minutes. Drain, allow to cool a little, then cut in half lengthways. Scrape out and discard the woolly middle and seeds. Scoop out most of the flesh, chop roughly and reserve. Arrange the shells in a buttered baking dish.

Preheat the oven to 375°F/190°C/gas mark 5. Drop the reserved flesh in the liquidiser and process to a puree with the cream. Transfer to a bowl and mix in the cheese, raisins, vanilla and sugar. Spoon into the shells and sprinkle with the breadcrumbs mixed with the grated cheese. Bake for about 20 minutes, until the top is crisp and golden.

okra

or ladies' fingers, gumbo (West Indies), quiabo (Brazil) (*Hibiscus esculentus*)

A pod-vegetable, okra is an ancient cultivar of the hibiscus family, known to the Ancient Egyptians, imported from Africa as part of slave-culture, and established in the Caribbean and Brazil in the 17th century.

A small tree-like annual with pretty yellow trumpet-shaped flowers, it is a member of a family which includes the cotton-plant and the roselle (raw material of sorrel, a refreshing drink popular at Christmas in the Caribbean).

Appearance and taste

The part of the plant of interest to the cook is the immature seed-pods – ridged, finger-shaped with one pointed end and one capped, about the length of a thumb – though the young leaves are also edible. Two varieties are grown, one longer than the other. In cross-section, it looks like a miniature wheel with tiny seeds sticking to the spokes. The flavour is pleasantly pea-like, while the juices are naturally gluey in texture (mucilaginous), its chief attraction as a soup-thickener.

Buying and storing

When fresh, the pods have a glow to them. To choose, look for bright green pods with no sign of browning or withering. Inside, the seeds should still be pale and pinkish – if dark and hard, the okra will be old and stringy. To store, treat as green beans: keep them in a paper bag in the fridge and use as soon as possible.

Bundles of okra in Castries market, St Lucia

Medicinal and other uses

Although high in protein and well-endowed with vitamin C, okra is chiefly valued for its mucilaginous qualities, and is invaluable as a soothing lubricant for irritated intestinal membranes.

Culinary uses

Cook like green beans or in any recipe which suits the summer squash. To avoid bleeding out the mucilage, trim the stalk without cutting into the pod and leave the tail in place. Some – not me – don't like the glueyness: to minimise this, cook the okra with a little lemon juice or vinegar; for the same reason, some cooks don't add salt during the cooking. To reduce the mucilaginousness still further, sprinkle with salt and leave in a warm place to dry for an hour. Okra flour, milled from dried okra pods, can be used to thicken and add nutritional value to soups and stews.

Okra and potato salad with green mango

Serves 4–6 as a starter or side-dish

A West Indian salad which combines soft okra with the crisp, tart flesh of unripe mangoes. In the West Indies, green mangoes are eaten in the street, straight from the hand, like apples.

450g (1lb) okra
450g (1lb) small new potatoes, scrubbed
4 tablespoons olive or sunflower oil
2 garlic cloves, finely chopped
1 small onion, finely chopped
1 small green chilli, de-seeded and chopped
Juice 1 lemon
2 tablespoons chopped fresh coriander
Salt and freshly-ground black pepper
1 unripe green mango, chopped (skin on – but slice out the stone)

Top and tail the okra by removing the hard caps and trimming off any hard little tails, rinse well and shake dry. Boil the potatoes until tender – start them in boiling salted water – and drain well.

Warm the oil in a shallow frying pan or wok. Toss in the chopped garlic and onion and let it sizzle gently until it softens – 3–4 minutes. Don't let it take colour. Turn up the heat, add the chilli and the okra and stir it over the heat for 5 minutes or so, until the okra has softened a little, but is still fresh and green.

Turn down the heat and stir in the potatoes and lemon juice, turning to mix everything thoroughly. Add the coriander, season with a little salt and plenty of pepper, put the lid on and leave to simmer gently for 5 minutes to marry the flavours. Leave to cool before combining with the mango. Serve at room temperature, with plantain chips (see patacones, p. 207).

Quiabo con tomate

(Okra with tomato)
Serves 4–6 as a starter or side-dish

A Brazilian way with more mature okra pods, which require slow, gentle cooking.

700g (1 1/2lb) fresh okra pods
2 tablespoons oil
1 onion, chopped
2 garlic cloves, chopped
3 large tomatoes, chopped
1 chilli pepper, de-seeded and chopped
1 teaspoon sugar
Salt

Prepare the okra by trimming the stalks close to the pod. If you don't enjoy their glueyness – though lots of people do – don't hull, just trim off the stems, toss the pods with salt and a little vinegar and leave in a colander for an hour or two, by which time they will have yielded up their gloop; rinse well before using. Chunk.

Warm the oil in a heavy pan or casserole and gently fry the onion and garlic until soft – don't let it brown. Add the tomato, chilli and sugar and bubble up, squashing with a wooden spoon to encourage a rich little sauce. Stir in the okra, add a glass of water, and bubble up. Turn down the heat, put the lid on loosely and simmer for 30–40 minutes, until the pods are perfectly tender and the sauce deliciously rich and sticky. Or bake in the oven at 300°F/ 160°C/gas mark 2. Serve at room temperature, with quartered limes and chilli-pepper sauce on the side.

For a more substantial dish, include slivers of beef or pork tossed in the hot oil when you fry the onion and garlic, or finish with a handful of fresh prawns or shrimp.

Quiabo con tomate, okra pods cooked gently in a rich tomato sauce

palm-heart

or palmito, pupunha (*Euterpe edulis*)

The palm-heart is the growing tip of a young palm tree which springs up with remarkable rapidity in the Amazonian rainforest whenever a clearing becomes available. A seven-year-old palmito produces a heart about 5cm (2in) in diameter. Luxuriously large hearts – 8–10cm (3–4in) in width – are the product of a tree which has already been growing for twelve years or more.

How it grows

The removal of the heart kills the tree – a form of cropping perfectly acceptable when the jungle could renew itself virtually overnight, less so when there's not enough to go round. New plantations supply the canning factories which satisfy the increasing demands of gourmets in other lands.

Appearance and taste

When sold fresh in the market, palm-hearts appear as a tightly packed bundle of leaf-bases about the thickness and length of a man's arm. When tinned, the palm-heart is ivory-coloured and tender, a little like a short length of bamboo, with layers of outer covering enclosing a soft inner heart. Very delicious, even when preserved in brine – like artichoke-flavoured asparagus.

Buying and storing

Palm-hearts are hard to find fresh, but when available, choose pale, plump hearts with no sign of dehydration or browning. They are available in cans or bottled – find a brand which suits you.

Medicinal and other uses

The palm-heart has all the virtues of young vegetables when fresh: it is a laxative and well-endowed with vitamin C. When tinned, it is of little nutritional or medicinal value.

Culinary uses

The palm-heart can be eaten aw and fresh, and is also delicious roasted or as a creamy soup. When canned, it is best combined with seafood in a salads, to which it contributes texture as well as taste. Related palm-tree products include dende oil, a frying oil of African origin extracted from a relation of the coconut palm and much prized in Brazil. In its untreated form it is high in beta-carotenes and is almost 100 per cent saturated fat. Palm sugar, known in Mexico as piloncillo, is the cooked down sap produced by tapping one of the sugar palms – date or coconut.

Palmito asado

(Roasted palm-hearts with butter and honey)
Serves 4

Freshly roasted palm-hearts, drenched in butter and sweetened with honey, are served as an appetiser in the estancias of the farming districts of São Paolo: a rare delicacy, presented glistening on a banana leaf with justifiable pride.

2 large palm hearts (about 700g/1 1/2lb each)
225g (8oz) unsalted butter, clarified
Salt and freshly ground pepper
Honey for a sauce

Preheat the oven to 160°C/325°F/gas mark 3. Run a sharp knife down the length of the palm-heart and remove the outer layer. Leave the next layer in place, even though it's a little tough. Place the hearts on foil, brush with butter, sprinkle with salt and pepper, seal tight and place on a baking tray. Bake for an hour and a half, until perfectly tender, soft and buttery. Unwrap and serve with its juices, with melted honey handed around separately.

Young palm trees in Peru, grown for their delicious hearts

Salata de palmito e cangreijo

(Palm-heart salad with crab)

Serves 4

Shore crabs scuttle around among the palm trees which line Brazil's beautiful white beaches. The sweetness of the crabmeat provides a perfect counterpoint to the delicate flavour of the hearts of palm. To prepare canned palm-hearts (perfect for the dish), cut off any tough outside pieces and use a potato-peeler to cut tagliatelli-like ribbons – also a good technique should you manage to lay your hands on fresh palm-hearts.

1 can palm-hearts, sliced into fine ribbons

The dressing:
6 tablespoons olive oil
2 tablespoons lime juice
Shake of malagueta pepper sauce (see p.51) or Tabasco
1 teaspoon rough salt

To finish:
1 cos lettuce, shredded
About 350g (12oz) crab meat (save the carapace for serving)
Shredded fresh coconut

Combine the palm-hearts with the dressing ingredients, leave to marinate for an hour or two, toss with the shredded lettuce and crabmeat and finish with finely shredded coconut.

Salata de palmito e cangreijo, a delicate salad of crabmeat and ribbons of palm-heart

sweet potato

or batata, boniato
(*Ipomoea batatas*)

A tuber-bearing member of the morning-glory family, a New World native grown by the Mayas in Mexico and the Incas in Peru, the sweet potato was brought back by Columbus from the West Indies. It was one of the first of the New World tubers to make the Atlantic crossing and is now established as a food-plant in tropical parts of the world where the ordinary potato cannot thrive.

How it grows

The sweet potato is planted out as shoots which develop into a rambling vine, producing a thick mass of heart-shaped leaves and a few trumpet-shaped purple flowers. The leaves are sometimes cooked and eaten in times of famine, since the tubers take about 8 months to mature underground.

Inca ruins at Machu Picchu

Appearance and taste

Literally hundreds of different varieties are grown, ranging from long and slender to short and globular; the skins vary from ivory to rose to russet to deep chestnut, the flesh from cream to a deep orange. Pale-skinned varieties are likely to have ivory-coloured, dry, mealy, mildly honeyed flesh; those with dark skin are likely to have orange, very sweet, juicy flesh and are sometimes labelled yam – although the true yam is an entirely different species.

Buying and storing

Look for fresh, bright skinned tubers with no sign of blemish or shrinkage. Store at room temperature for up to a fortnight or in a cool dry store for up to a month, but never in the fridge – as a tropical tuber, they hate frost and develop an oddly musty flavour.

Medicinal and other uses

Digestible and nutritious, the sweet potato is mainly a source of starch but has enough protein to serve as a sole foodstuff; yellow-fleshed varieties are particularly high in vitamin A. Most of the nutritional value is stored in and near the skin. It is good for the diseases of the digestive tract – ulcers, inflammation of the colon – and is de-toxifying thanks to the presence of phytochelatins, which attract heavy metals. If you feed mashed sweet potato to a child who has swallowed a metal object, the potato will stick to it and allow it to pass through the colon more easily.

Culinary uses

The sweet potato can be roasted, steamed, baked or fried. Cooked and mashed, it can replace up to one quarter of the weight of flour in cakes and bread. Some varieties are starchy and bland, some sweet and spicy: sweet is the most popular. The flesh is dense – a modest helping will satisfy even the heartiest appetite.

Boniatillo

(Sweet potato purée with orange and cinnamon)
Serves 6

This is usually made with the white-fleshed boniato which, though less sweet than the orange-fleshed varieties, is considered to have a finer flavour. Either will do. At Christmas, the same recipe, without the eggs, is prepared as a festive treat. The trick is to cook it right down to a paste.

450g (1lb) boniato or sweet potato, peeled and sliced
350g (12oz) unrefined caster sugar
8 tablespoons water
1 orange, juice and zest
½ lemon, juice and zest
1 short stick cinnamon
1 tablespoon butter
2 eggs, separated
Salt

To finish:
Cream
Powdered cinnamon (optional)
A few curls orange zest

Cook the potatoes until tender in enough lightly salted water to cover – they'll take about 40 minutes. Drain, allow to cool a little, and peel. Or bake in the oven and skin. Mash the flesh to a purée.

Meanwhile, melt the sugar in the water with the orange and lemon zest and juice and cinnamon, and bring to the boil. Simmer for 5 minutes and set aside. Remove the zest and stick-cinnamon, and combine the hot syrup with the mashed boniato. Return the mixture to the heat and beat it with a wooden spoon until it thickens to a soft purée which holds its shape on the spoon.

Remove from the heat and beat in the butter. Allow to cool a little and beat in the egg-yolks. Whisk the egg-whites and fold them in. Allow to cool and pile into pretty glasses. Finish with a lick of cream, an optional sprinkle of powdered cinnamon and a few curls of orange zest.

Boniatillo, a delicious sweet-potato dessert flavoured with orange and cinnamon

Batata frita

(Sweet potato chips)
Serves 4

Perfect with a seviche, for dipping in a guacamole or with a chilled soup – in fact, with anything which benefits from a touch of crispness and sweetness.

1 medium-sized sweet potato, peeled and
   thinly sliced
2–3 tablespoons cornflour
Oil for deep-frying
Salt

Rinse the potato slices, drain and pat dry. Spread the cornflour on a flat plate. Heat the oil until lightly hazed with blue.

Dust each potato-slice lightly through the cornflour before dropping it in the hot oil. It should immediately acquire a jacket of small bubbles. Continue with dusting and dropping until the surface of the oil is covered.

Fry until crisp. Remove with a draining spoon and transfer to kitchen paper to drain. Continue until all are done.

jerusalem artichoke

or sunchoke, topinambur (*Helianthus tuberosus*)

The tuberous root of a member of the sunflower family, the Jerusalem artichoke is a North American native, one of that vast store of edible roots and tubers well known to the indigenous population, but which has never achieved the same popularity universally. Although rarely seen in the markets of Central America, it is popular in Chile and Peru.

Jerusalem artichoke foliage

How it grows

A tall leafy annual with yellow daisy-like flowers, its many creeping roots produce numerous tubers which, in unhybridised form, are about the size and appearance of a ginger-root, long and slightly flattened. Many varieties are now grown.

Appearance and taste

Jerusalem artichokes are knobbly little tubers with pinkish to coffee-coloured skin and crisp ivory-coloured flesh; they look a bit like an exotic variety of potato. Their shape is against them: peeling is a bit fiddly. The flavour is earthy, delicately sweet with a hint of fennel.

Buying and storing

Choose tubers with firm, bright skins and no signs of withering or green patches. Store in a cool place away from the light, as you would do potatoes.

Medicinal and other uses

Fat-free, the Jerusalem artichoke is an excellent source of nutrients much valued by the Huron in its land of origin. It is a brilliant source of iron – almost as good as meat. Its notoriety as a flatulence-promoter is due to the form in which the root stores carbohydrates: as inulin, a form of sugar which can be eaten by diabetics.

Culinary uses

The Jerusalem artichoke can be eaten raw, grated or slivered in a salad or served as a nibble with a dip It is good for boiling, steaming, mashing and makes delicious pancakes: grate, mix with a little flour, bind with egg, and fry. The peel is edible, although it rather spoils the look of a mash. For ease of peeling, boil for 10 minutes in salted water and then drain under the cold tap, when the skins can be rubbed off. The flesh remains firm and slightly translucent even when perfectly tender.

Guiso de topinambures con champiñones y olivos

(Jerusalem artichokes casseroled with mushrooms and olives)
Serves 4–6 as a starter

An easy one-pot dish – all you need is a little patience.

900g (2lb) Jerusalem artichokes
1 lemon
4 tablespoons olive oil
2 large onions, finely chopped
2 garlic cloves, finely chopped
225g (8oz) mushrooms, diced
1 teaspoon dried thyme
1 wine-glass white wine
2 tablespoons green olives, stoned and
* chopped*
2–3 tomatoes, skinned and chopped (optional)
1 red pepper, deseeded and diced (optional)
1 leftover arepa or stale bread, crumbled
1 hardboiled egg, chopped
Salt and pepper

To serve:
Crumbled white cheese or hardboiled egg
Crisp lettuce leaves for scooping

Peel the knobbly little root-artichokes carefully and divide into bite-sized pieces. As you peel each root, drop it into a bowlful of cold water into which you have squeezed a little lemon juice.

Heat the oil in a roomy casserole and fry the chopped onion and garlic until soft and golden (don't let it brown). Push aside and add the mushrooms. As soon as they yield up their juices, add the artichokes, olives, and the optional tomatoes and red pepper. Let them sizzle for a moment. Stir in the thyme, season with salt and pepper, pour in the wine and the same volume of water and let everything bubble up.

Turn down the heat, cover loosely and leave to simmer very gently for an hour, until the roots are perfectly tender. Stir in the coriander and the crumbs – they'll soak up all the aromatic juices, leaving the tubers bathed in a deliciously fragrant dressing. Hand crumbled white cheese or chopped hardboiled egg separately, with crisp lettuce leaves for scooping.

Chupe de topinambures y elote

(Jerusalem artichoke and sweetcorn soup)
Serves 4

A Chilean way with the knobbly tubers – convenient since you don't have to worry about removing all the skin. The fresh corn-kernels underline the natural sweetness of the roots.

450g (1lb) Jerusalem artichokes
1 onion, finely chopped
2 tablespoons butter or corn oil
850ml (1 1/2 pints) chicken or vegetable stock
6 allspice berries
300ml (1/2 pint) sweetcorn kernels
Salt and pepper

To finish:
A handful basil leaves, shredded
1 garlic clove, finely chopped
1 yellow chilli, de-seeded and chopped

Scrub and roughly chop the roots. In a roomy pan, fry the onion gently until it softens – don't let it brown. Add the chopped roots and let them feel the heat for a moment. Add the stock and the allspice, bring to the boil, turn down the heat, put the lid on loosely and simmer for 20 minutes or so, until the roots are perfectly tender. Liquidise the contents of the pan, reheat and stir in the sweetcorn. Bubble up, turn down to simmer, replace the lid loosely and cook gently for another 10 minutes. Taste and season. Ladle into bowls and finish with a sprinkle of shredded basil, chopped garlic and chilli.

Guiso de topinambures con champiñones y olivos, a fragrant artichoke and mushroom casserole

edible fungi

Many of the familiar market-place fungi – chanterelle, boletus, oyster, russola – are found throughout Latin America, as well as a great many edible varieties unknown outside the territory. Less familiar cap-mushrooms include the tecomate, a large, firm-fleshed mushroom with a brick-red cap and yellow gills. Most unusual, but acquiring a gourmet reputation, is the cuitlacoche or corn-mushroom, a fungi which transforms its host into a fragrant mush.

How it grows

All the copraphiliacs – fruiting bodies which take their nourishment from decaying vegetable matter – acquire most of their flavour and their chemical composition from their host-plant, making them an unpredictable bunch. Even if they look familiar, gather from new habitats only if accompanied by a knowledgeable local guide.

Appearance and taste

While the usual cultivated mushrooms are available throughout, members of many of the edible fungi families, including gill-mushrooms, sponge-caps, puff-balls and morels, are gathered and eaten with relish. The maize-mushroom has a powerful morel-cepe fragrance allied with the sweetness of the corn. Notable exotics include the *huitlacoche* – an ink-black fungus which appears on sweetcorn kernels, turning them silver; and the Haitian black mushroom used in a rice-and-bean dish, *djon djon*, found nowhere but Haiti; the woody stalks produce a deep black dye used to colour the water in which the rice is cooked;

after draining, the stalks are discarded and the rice tossed with the sliced caps along with an equal volume of ready-cooked lima beans.

Buying and storing

When selecting fresh fungi, whether cultivated or wild, choose dry, unblemished specimens which smell fresh and are bug-free. While many of the wild varieties are available in dried form, the maize-mushroom – actually, a mush made from the affected kernels – is exported in cans since it has a short shelf-life and cannot be preserved by dehydration.

Medicinal and other uses

To confuse the issue, both pharmaceutical and hallucinogenic fungi are sold alongside the non-mind-altering varieties. Make sure you understand exactly what you're buying.

An autumn haul of wild fungi includes chanterelles, horn of plenty and russolas.

Culinary uses

Fungi are usually cooked simply – grilled or roasted with a little oil. In a stuffing for an empanadilla or tamale, they're treated as a meat substitute, included for flavour rather than substance.

Salsa de cuitlacoche

(Corn-mushroom purée)
Makes just under a litre (1^1/$_2$ pints)

The basic method of preparing corn-mushrooms and their host kernels – cuitlacoche – produces a dense, fragrant paste which can be used as a flavouring. It is particularly good as a sauce for chicken, stirred into boiling cream. It'll keep for 3 months in the freezer.

750g (about 6 cupfuls) cuitlacoche
3–4 tablespoons oil
1 tablespoon chopped onion
1 chili poblano or green pepper, de-seeded and cut into ribbons
1 tablespoon chopped epasote or leaf-coriander (optional)
Sea salt

In a roomy frying pan, heat the oil and fry the onion and chile poblano, stir in the cuitlacoche, season with salt and cook gently for 15 to 20 minutes, then stir in a little epasote or fresh coriander for extra flavour. The mixture should be moist but not wet: if the crop was picked on a dry day, you may need to add water; if the weather was damp, you may have to boil rapidly for a minute or two to evaporate excess liquid.

Empanadas de cuitlicoche o champignones

(Mushroom and sweetcorn pasties)
Makes about a dozen fist-sized pasties

Tortilla-dough turnovers stuffed with corn-mushroom salsa is one of the great dishes of Mexico. Failing the real thing, substitute cornkernels processed thoroughly with powdered porcini – 4 tablespoons corn to 1 tablespoon mushroom. Or use fresh mushrooms, chopped, lightly fried and mixed with their own volume of corn-kernels.

Empanadas de hongos con maíz

450g (1lb) salsa de cuitlacoche or substitute as above
4 tablespoons soured cream
3–4 poblano or green pimento peppers, charred and cut into strips
110g (4 oz) grated cheese
Salt and pepper
Oil for deep frying

The casing:
12 ready-rolled uncooked 12cm (5in) tortillas (or ready-cooked)

Warm the cuitlacoche in a small pan. Put the cream in the blender with the peppers, process to a purée, and stir into the cuitlacoche. Bubble up for a moment to blend, stir in the cheese, season, remove from the heat and allow to cool.

Drop a tablespoonful of the mixture in the centre of each tortilla. Dampen the edges and fold in half to make semi-circular pasties, pinching the edges together to seal.

Heat a panful of oil. When it's lightly hazed with blue, slip in the pasties, a few at a time, and fry until golden and crisp – 3 or 4 minutes. Transfer to paper towels to drain. Delicious with a green-tomato salsa – very *mexicano*.

exotics

Edible leaves and shoots

A remarkable variety of leaf-vegetables and shoots, variously textured with different degrees of mildness and bitterness, are used throughout the region – many of them peculiar to the area in which they're gathered. The leaves of the edible roots, tubers and gourds whose use is widespread throughout the region are the most commonly encountered, including the Trinidadian callaloo, the name given both to the stew and the leaf with which it's cooked. As a general rule, any edible leaf can be substituted for any other – failing these, chard, spinach, and the more tender members of the cabbage family will do.

Couve con maní
(Wild greens with peanuts)
Serves 4

A Brazilian dish of African origin, this is made with a wide variety of edible greens including spinach of the tough evergreen variety, the young leaves of pumpkin, cassava and sweet potato, chard, spring greens and cabbage. Serve as a vegetarian dish with soft polenta or rice.

700g (l¹/₂ lb) spinach greens or other leaves
½ teaspoon salt
450g (1 lb) tomatoes, finely chopped
6–8 spring onions, finely chopped

To finish:
4 tablespoons pounded roasted peanuts

Cook the spinach in a tightly lidded pan in the water which clings to the leaves after washing. Sprinkle with salt to encourage the juices to run.

As soon as the leaves collapse and soften, remove the lid and add a layer of chopped tomatoes and chopped spring onion. Sprinkle with the powdered peanuts, but do not stir. Turn down the heat, put the lid on loosely and simmer for about 15 minutes, until the tomato flesh has softened. Stir, put the lid on loosely again and simmer for another 15 minutes. Remove the lid and bubble up to evaporate any excess juices. Reverse the contents of the pan onto the serving dish, and finish with a sprinkle of whole roast peanuts.

Andean roots and tubers

Of the many root-vegetables grown by Andean farmers, though largely unknown outside the territory, the most notable – already gaining popularity among the gourmets of North America – is the Peruvian white carrot, *zanahoria blanca*, a celery-flavoured parsnip-like root which cooks like carrot and combines particularly well with seafood.

Two others waiting in the wings are the *melloco* or butter-potato, and the *oca*, a sweetish tuber similar to the Jerusalem artichoke. Both can be substituted for potatoes in any recipe, though the former is more suitable for savoury dishes – include it in bean soups, as a side-dish dressed with garlic and chilli; while a purée of *oca* – the tubers steamed in their skins and pushed through a mouli - works well as the starchy element in cakes and desserts.

Couve con maní

Edible thistle

Edible thistles/
wild artichokes

Of the local varieties available in the markets of
Chile's Alta Plana, two – chagual and penca –
are of particular interest. The first is described
by Ruth Gonzales in *The Chilean Kitchen* as a
cone-shaped rosette of tightly-packed leaves
which can be served as a salad. The second is
a long, juicy stem which has to be stripped of
its thorns before it can be eaten – like the
chagual, the penca should be dressed with oil,
lemon and salt. The taste, Ruth Gonzales says,
is much like celery.

Seaweeds

Sea-vegetables were important as a source of
protein to the indigenous inhabitants of Chile's
long coastline in pre-columbian times. All
seaweeds are edible, though some are too
tough to be palatable, and some taste better
than others. A wide variety used to be gathered
by the shore-dwellers who lived mainly on the
prolific crops of razor-shells. People still
understand what to gather and when, and
know how to name the various stages of
development – evidence of a sophisticated
culinary vocabulary. The fresh roots are called
ulte, while the leafy parts are known as luche.
When dried, they are known as cochayuyo, the
name by which they are sold, tied up in neat
bundles and offered in the markets as the
poor-man's steak. To prepare in the Chilean
way, reconstitute in the same way as other
seaweeds by soaking; then chop finely and
include in the stuffing of an empanada instead
of fish or meat. Any edible seaweed can be
substituted. It is good in combination with
yellow chillies and crumbly white fresh cheese.

The Pacific batters the seaweed-clad coast at Mirasol, Chile

chillies

All the capsicums, the pepper of the New World, are descended from the same pair of ancestors, *Capsicum annuum* and *C. frutescens*. *C. annuum*, a native of Mexico, is, as its name suggests, a bushy annual whose fleshy, lantern-shaped fruits hang down like Christmas baubles. *C. frutescens*, a Peruvian native, is a perennial shrub with torpedo-shaped, upward-pointing, thinner-fleshed fruits. Both are fiery in their natural state, though the Peruvian is hotter than the Mexican. The two species are inextricably entangled through hybridisation, deliberate or accidental, since the earliest times, making it impossible to untangle lineage.

The chilli's heat, the peppery element, triggers the production of endorphins, excitement-inducing chemicals manufactured by racing drivers and mountaineers in response to danger. The substance which delivers the message is capsaicin, an alkaloid with all the characteristics of poison, which, though present in both flesh and seeds, is found mainly in the white membrane which attaches the seeds to the interior ribs. Test for fieriness with caution: cut off an end and lick rather than chew since the really hot ones are pretty explosive. Don't rub your eyes when handling, and rinse your fingers in cold water afterwards.

Chillies – fiery or mild – are hard to slip into a culinary slot, falling somewhere between a condiment, a vegetable and a spice. Nevertheless, for culinary purposes, they can be divided into three groups: fresh flavouring chillies (including pickled), frying chillies (including salad peppers) and dried or store-cupboard chillies (including powdered and flaked).

flavouring chillies

or chile picante, ají (Peru)
(*Capsicum annuum/C. frutescens*)

These small chillies are eaten fresh or pickled, in the form of a condiment or as flavouring, much as freshly milled pepper, (although the inclusion of one by no means precludes the other). The chillies can be lantern- or torpedo-shaped and are picked at any stage of maturity. All chillies mature from green to varying shades of scarlet; some varieties stop at yellow, others progress to a purple so dark it's almost black.

Buying and storing

To choose fresh chillies, look for a shiny, firm, stretched-looking skin – once a chilli wrinkles, it's past its best – and check there are no little black patches, particularly around the stem. A chilli harvested when green and immature, though it will certainly change colour, will wither and rot. But a chilli harvested when fully ripe will progress, just as nature intended, to dehydration – the stage at which it can be kept in a clean dry jar and stored for later. Do remember that a chilli will lose fragrance and colour (though not its heat) if kept too long on the shelf.

Medicinal and other uses

Fresh green chillies are high in vitamins A, B and have up to six times as much vitamin C as oranges (although this decreases as they ripen and disappears completely as they dry). Chillies are anti-scorbutic, disinfectant, insect-repellent and fever-reducing – virtues which can be ascribed to capsaicin, the hot element in the chilli, which promotes sweating. All these virtues were known to the ancient civilisations of the Aztecs and the Incas. To counteract chilli-burn – that moment of truth when you know you've bitten off more than you can chew – take a glass of milk or yoghurt. Reaching for the water-jug will just compound the problem since capsaicin, like oil, does not dissolve in water and swamping it simply spreads the problem.

How it grows

The chilli grows as a crouching annual or upstanding bushy perennial, depending on ancestry and habitat. Mexico alone accounts for more than a hundred named varieties, each with a different shape, fragrance and degree of fieriness.

Appearance and taste

Flavouring chillies vary in appearance but are all small. Neither colour nor shape is a reliable indication of heat, which varies within the species, even within fruits from the same plant. The flavour of green immature chillies is grassy, acidic and lemony; as they ripen in sunshine, it matures to sweet and fruity. Two of the most popular Central American varieties for eating green are the thick-fleshed jalapeño, an elongated blunt triangle of middling fieriness, the chilli of choice for a guacamole and to flavour maize-foods such as tamales; and the *chile serrano* or mountain-grown chilli (the pickling chilli) which is thinner-fleshed and very hot. The habanero or Scotch bonnet, a quadrangular thin-fleshed lantern-shaped fruit, is the Caribbean favourite. Andean chillies – *ajíes* – are triangular, short or long, of varying degrees of fieriness, with yellow varieties the most esteemed. The Brazilian favourite is the long, thin malagueta pepper, which ripens to scarlet and is very fiery.

Capsicum annuum **on the plant**

Culinary uses

Stimulating to the digestive juices, chillies make anything taste good. However, too much makes a dish inedible – hence the wisdom of serving raw or pickled chillies on the side. The hot element, capsaicin, is present in both flesh and seeds, but is concentrated in the white woolly fibres which attach the seeds to the ribs.

Pimenta malagueta

(Brazilian pepper sauce)
Makes: a bottleful

The true flavour of Brazil, this seasoning sauce – condiment, pickle – is as fiery as the temperament of the ladies of Copacabana beach. The liquor is a little milder than the chillies, but both are relished.

Hanging bunches of chillies from a hook is an effective and eye-catching way of drying them in a current of air

450g (1lb) malagueta peppers or bird's-eye chillies
300ml (1/2 pint) white rum or vodka
300ml (1/2 pint) olive oil
150ml (1/4 pint) wine vinegar

Pick over the chillies, discarding any which are blemished. Be careful not to touch your face or rub your eyes while you're working. Rinse the chillies with the rum or vodka – washing in water makes them rot – and shake them dry. Pack the chillies in a clean wine bottle and pour in enough oil and vinegar in proportions of 2:1 to submerge the peppers completely. Jam in the cork and store for a month. The preparation keeps indefinitely.

Ají de maní

(Chilli peanut salsa)
Serves 4–6

Typical of Peruvian ají – the name given to the sauce as well as its main ingredient – which rarely include tomato. Peruvian *ají* are long, thin, torpedo-shaped yellow or orange chillies, thin-fleshed and fiery, with a distinctively fruity flavour. Yellow bird's-eye chillies or habaneros will do instead.

150ml (1/4 pint) beef-bone broth (or any well-flavoured stock)
225g (8oz) roasted, pounded peanuts (coarse peanut butter will do)
Juice of 1 lemon
6 yellow chillies, de-seeded and finely chopped
3–4 spring onions, finely chopped
1/2 mild red pepper, finely chopped
1 tablespoon chopped coriander
1 hardboiled egg, finely chopped
1/2 teaspoon salt

Heat the broth until just below boiling, stir in the peanuts and lemon juice and blend thoroughly, until an emulsion forms. Stir in the remaining ingredients. Serve at room temperature as a dipping sauce for the little, yellow-fleshed, perfectly spherical criollo potatoes, the caviar of the crop. Or with Colombian empanadas or tamales stuffed with pipian potatoes: criollos mashed with a tomato, red pepper and peanut sauce.

frying & stuffing chillies

or *chile para freír, para rellenar*

A frying chilli can be any of the larger capsicums which, lacking the heat of their smaller sisters, can be treated like a vegetable: fried, stuffed, roasted, grilled or included in rices and stews for colour and flavour rather than fire.

Appearance and taste

The *poblano* is the most popular Mexican frying pepper: a long, torpedo-shaped, thin-fleshed pepper usually eaten green. The alternative is the thick-fleshed salad-pepper: a mild, sweet hybrid developed during the nineteenth century in Hungary, exported to Spain and later re-exported to its land of origin.

Buying and storing

The colour should be bright and the skin shiny and stretched. Check for bad patches and signs of wrinkling: there should be no soft dimples – a sign of impending rot. Store in the salad compartment of the fridge for no longer than a week. Unripe fruits – picked green and immature – will probably ripen to red, but will become wrinkled and soft. It is best to buy at the stage of ripeness that you need.

Medicinal and other uses

There's no loss of vitamins when a pepper is bred for mildness, although its antiseptic properties will not be as strong. Fresh green chillies are higher in vitamin C than ripe red ones; they're rich in Vitamin A, which boosts the body's immune system, protecting against colds

Culinary uses

Capsicums have a remarkably high sugar content when ripe, which is why they roast or fry so deliciously, caramelising just before they burn.
To peel fresh peppers, hold in a flame until the skin blisters black, then drop in a paper bag and leave to steam for 10 minutes, after which the skin will peel off in neat little rolls.

Empanadillas colombianas
(Colombian chilli pasties)
Makes about 12

These little bite-sized turnovers, crisp and fragrant, are made with arepa dough stuffed with green chillies and white cheese. Street-food, they are sold in every bar in town by spotlessly aproned, arepa-sellers, wearing their magnificent hand-woven wraps, making the rounds with their baskets.

The dough:
450g (1lb) masarepa or tortilla dough (see p.81)

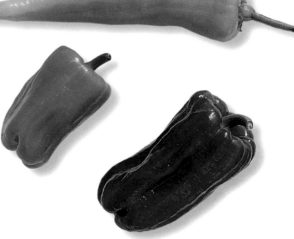

The filling:

3–4 fresh ají (chillies), de-seeded and finely
chopped

2 tablespoons chopped flat-leaf parsley

2 tablespoons chopped basil

4 tablespoons crumbled white cheese (feta-
type)

A little milk or egg to bind

To cook:

Oil for deep-frying

To serve:

Pickled chillies, puréed with oil to make a
dipping-sauce

Knead the dough into a ball and cover with clingfilm. Mix the filling ingredients together.

Break off a small piece of dough about the size of a walnut, roll it into a little ball and flatten it in the palm of your hand to make a small round disk – the thinner the better. Use your hands rather than a rolling pin or the dough will crack. Drop a little of the stuffing in the middle of the disk, paint the edge with water and fold one half over the other to enclose the filling. Continue until all are ready.

Heat enough oil to submerge the pasties completely. Slip them into the hot oil one by one – the edges should acquire a fringe of small bubbles. Fry, turning once, until crisp and golden. Cornmeal dough takes a little longer than wheatmeal dough. Drain on kitchen paper.

Chile poblano en nogado

(Stuffed frying chillies with walnut sauce)
Serves 6, with accompaniments

Mexican wedding-food suitable for a celebration because the preparation is laborious – many hands make light work. Very delicious and very Latin.

6–12 chilli poblanos *or green salad peppers*
(depending on size)

The picadillo for stuffing:

700g (1¹/2lb) minced pork

1 onion, finely chopped

2 garlic cloves, finely chopped

Chile poblano en nogado, a celebration dish of stuffed peppers with a creamy walnut sauce

2 tablespoons oil

450g (1lb) tomatoes, skinned and chopped

2 tablespoons raisins, soaked in a little orange
and lemon juice

4 tablespoons diced papaya or peach

2 tablespoons slivered toasted almonds

1 teaspoon powdered cinnamon

Salt and pepper

The walnut sauce:

100g (4oz) freshly-crushed walnuts

4 tablespoons cream cheese

350ml (12fl oz) soured cream

A pinch of sugar and a little powdered
cinnamon

Toast the peppers by holding them on a long fork over a naked flame or by placing them under the fiercest grill until the skin chars and blisters. Drop them in a paper bag and leave for 10 minutes to loosen the skins. Slip off the skin, slit neatly lengthways and remove the seeds. Reserve.

Prepare the picadillo: gently fry the meat, onion and garlic in the oil until all is soft. Add the tomato and bubble up to evaporate excess juices – the mixture should not be too wet. Add the fruits and nuts. Season with salt, pepper and cinnamon and set aside to cool.

Make the finishing sauce by whisking all the ingredients together. Chill and set aside to serve separately.

when a faint blue haze rises. Stuff the peppers with the picadillo and arrange in a baking dish. Heat through in a low oven.

If serving at a betrothal – a family feast – dip the peppers in egg-and-flour batter and fry to give a crisp coating: richness expresses hope for future prosperity. For a wedding – a feast for the whole community – prepare as for a betrothal and finish with pomegranate seeds – for fertility, of course, though no doubt you worked that out for yourself.

store-cupboard chillies

or cayenne, chilli powder, pimentón, paprika (*Capsicum* spp.)

Dried chillies, small and fiery, are the peppercorn of the New World. In their land of origin, fieriness is considered secondary to fragrance, flavour and colour. It is this variability, the subtle differences – which make this one of those rare ingredients which, in the hands of a skilled cook, is capable of gastronomic greatness.

Manufacture

Chillies of all varieties are picked when fully mature and allowed to dry naturally, providing the raw material of all dried-chilli preparations. Chilli-blending is elevated to an art in Mexico, where cooks often make basic blends or pastes to recipes handed down since the days of the Mayas. It is on the sophisticated combinations of different chillies, each contributing to the balance of the finished dish, that much of Mexico's formidable culinary reputation rests.

Appearance and taste

There are hundreds of chillies, many of them place-specific, drawing not merely from genetic inheritance but from the soil itself. Differences between one kind and another are as evident to devotees as, say, to a Tuscan chef making a choice between olive oils or a coffee-connoisseur judging the virtues of a bean.

Buying and storing

When choosing whole chillies, check for powderiness, a sign of insect-infestation; the colour should be deep and rich with no sign of fading. If buying in powdered form, a clear bright colour is the best indication. As for flaked chilli, my own preference is for seedless flakes – the flesh has all the flavour. If these are unavailable, prepare your own from whole chillies. The *chile ancho* – *chile poblano* in dried form – is the most useful of all the dried chillies, providing the basic flavouring for stews and sauces such as Oaxaca's exquisite mole negro (see p.177). In dehydrated form, chillies and paprika peppers can be stored almost indefinitely, whether whole, powdered or flaked, so long as you keep them in a cool dry place away from direct sunlight.

Medicinal and other uses

Curative when applied topically to wounds, dried chillies provide the active ingredient in many cold-treatments, hangover-remedies and cure-alls – they are particularly good for clearing the sinuses. Stimulating, disinfecting and anti-bacterial (bury a chilli in the beanpot to keep insect predators at bay), chillies make one less prone to the digestive upsets which afflict travellers. The paprika-loving Hungarians discovered its anti-malarial properties when they were employed to dig the Suez Canal: only the Hungarians were immune. Capsaicin, the hot element in the chilli, is actually a defence-mechanism against insect-predators and is not destroyed by cooking, freezing, drying or any other attentions including, to put it daintily, human digestive juices.

Culinary uses

Dried whole chillies of the larger bell-shaped varieties should be de-seeded, torn into pieces, then soaked to reconstitute the pulp so that this can be scraped off the tough skin. The pieces can also be lightly toasted in a dry pan before soaking, a process which caramelises the sugars and deepens the colour. When adding to slow-cooked stews, you can omit the preliminary soaking. Although recipes may stipulate certain chillies – sometimes three or four in the same recipe – once the principal of their inclusion is understood, variations are possible. *Chile pasilla* – raisin-chillies – add sweetness; if unavailable, add a handful of raisins to the blend. If you have only one or two, a pinch of the 'sweet' spices – cinnamon, cloves, allspice – will add complexity and depth. Dried sweet peppers of the newer, fleshier breeds – *pimentos dulces* – provide colour and flavour as well as varying degrees of fieriness, and are milled for *pimentón dulce* (mild paprika) and *pimentón picante* (chilli-powder). In powdered form, capsicums burn very easily – they are best added to wet ingredients rather than dry. *Pimentón dulce* can also be used as a sauce-thickener – the ground-up vegetable swells and absorbs moisture when added to a liquid. Don't try it with *pimentón picante*: it's far too fiery to add in sufficient quantity.

Enchiladas de San Cristobal

(Stuffed tortillas with chilli-cream)
Serves 4

The enchilada is really an excuse for eating as much chilli in as many ways as possible. This is how they make them in San Cristobal, a pretty colonial town in the Chiapas, Mexico's mountainous southern region, where the revolutionaries come from. Perhaps the fierceness of the inhabitants can be ascribed to their fondness for fiery foodstuffs.

Enchiladas de San Cristobal

450g (1lb) cubed, boneless pork
2–3 mild frying peppers, de-seeded and cut into strips
1 small onion, finely chopped
1 garlic clove, sliced
Salt

The sauce:
4-5 chiles anchos (or your chosen blend of dried chillies)
450ml (³/4 pint) cream

To finish:
8–12 corn tortillas
Oil for shallow frying
2 tablespoons grated or crumbled white cheese

Cook the pork in a tightly lidded pan with very little water and a pinch of salt for about 30 minutes, until perfectly tender. Allow to cool in its own juices, shred with a couple of forks, and reserve. Gently fry the pepper strips, onion and garlic in a little oil until soft but not browned, season and combine with the shredded pork.

Prepare the sauce by opening up the dried chillies and shaking out the seeds. Tear into large pieces and toast lightly by placing skin-side down on a heated griddle, pressing down for about 30 seconds until the upper surface is a rich brown. Remove and soak in a cupful of boiling water for 15 minutes to swell. Transfer to a blender with the soaking water and process till smooth. Add cream and process again. Transfer to a small pan, bubble up and simmer till the cream thickens a little, then taste and add salt.

To assemble the enchiladas, fry the tortillas briefly in pairs in shallow oil, flipping once, until the edges curl. Transfer to a paper towel to dry. Dip each tortilla in the cream sauce, inner side only, and roll it round a tablespoonful of the pork filling. Continue until all the tortillas have been filled. Finish with the remaining sauce. Serve with pickled or fresh green chillies.

Salsa picante mexicana

(Mexican hot sauce)
Makes about 1.2 litres (2 pints)

A sauce to waken the dead.

3.6kg (8lb) tomatoes
300ml (¹/2 pint) vinegar
4 tablespoons brown sugar
1 tablespoon crushed allspice berries
1 teaspoon salt
1–3 tablespoons powdered or flaked chilli

Wash and roughly chop the tomatoes. Put all the ingredients except the chilli into a large saucepan and leave to infuse for half an hour.

Bring the pan to the boil, turn down to a gentle simmer and leave to cook over a low heat for at least an hour. It shouldn't need much attention as the tomatoes produce plenty of liquid at this stage, so there's little danger of sticking. Push the tomato mixture through a fine-meshed wire sieve, leaving skin, pips and spice debris behind. Return the purée to the pan. Unless the tomatoes are field ripened in full sunshine, it'll probably be far too liquid.

Bring back to the boil and simmer vigorously, stirring until the sauce is as thick as you like it – it may take 40 minutes. Stir in the chilli – as much or as little as you like. Adjust the seasoning. Bottle in empty tequila bottles and cork tightly.

starches
pulses
& grains

Roots and tubers, known in the Caribbean as 'ground provisions' – food which cannot escape the gatherer – are treated as soulfood in Latin America, as elsewhere. The traditional diet of the indigenous peoples of the Americas was almost entirely vegetarian, based on the mighty trinity – maize, beans and potatoes – with cassava (manioc) grown wherever none of these three could survive. This simple but nourishing diet was balanced by a wide variety of gourds and greens, usually cultivated in association with the main staple-food, with fish and shellfish when available. Meat, barbecued or cooked in an earth-oven as part of the celebrations, was only consumed at festivals and on days when offerings were made to the gods.

cassava

or manioc, mandioc, yuca
(*Manihot utilissima/M. esculenta*)

Cassava is an edible tuber of the euphorbia family, a group which includes the toxic milky-juiced spurges and the Christmas poinsettia. Native throughout the warmer zones of the Americas, it was cultivated by the Mayas in the Yucatan, and considered a staple in Brazil and the Caribbean, where its starchiness and blandness makes it ideal for mopping up spicy stews.

A basket manioc press in French Guiana

Cassava, sealed under wax to preserve freshness

How it grows

A herbaceous semi-tropical plant, the cassava is sun-loving, tall – as much as 3 metres (10ft) – with indented fan-shaped, edible leaves and a long, fibre-covered, dark brown tuberous root, which can weigh several pounds. Actually a node, this looks like a large hairy yam.

Appearance and taste

Two types exist, one bitter, one sweet. Bitter cassava is toxic unless subjected to lengthy preparation during which two by-products, tapioca and the meat-tenderising agent cassareep, are produced. Sweet manioc (the only one on sale fresh) has ivory-white flesh which when boiled or steamed becomes almost translucent, with a deliciously buttery taste. Be warned: it quickly becomes gluey if over-cooked.

Buying and storing

Selecting fresh cassava is more important than how you store or cook it. The tuber should be covered in rough, patchy bark and never cracked, slimy or sour smelling – nowadays, however, it's usually given a wax jacket for export. Inside, the flesh should be perfectly white without bruising or dark patches. Store in

Recently harvested cassava

a cool place and slice off a chunk when you need it - the rubbery white juices will seal the wound. The shelf-life is short unless you cut it into chunks and boil it, when it will last for a week in the fridge. It freezes adequately: just peel it and cut it into chunks.

Medicinal and other uses

Nourishing, filling and an excellent source of carbohydrates, the cassava is gluten free, It also has a dark side: cyanide-laden varieties are used by South-American assassins. While lethal cassavas are not cultivated for consumption, it's wise to avoid any which taste bitter. The poison is removed through grating and squeezing, followed by heating and fermentation – a process familiar to the indigenous population, ignorance of which proved fatal to some of the early European colonisers.

Culinary uses

The cassava is a versatile vegetable, though starchy, bland and sorely in need of a dressing or sauce. Only the sweet variety can be eaten fresh. To prepare cassava for the pot, scrub, peel and cut it into sections, removing the central fibre, and bake, chip, fry, boil or steam. Cassava discolours quickly after peeling, so cover with cold water until needed. To make crisps, first boil until tender, slice thinly, dust with cornflour and deep fry. Additional uses: cassava juice is fermented to make a beer; and in season, the young leaves are boiled and eaten as a vegetable (see edible leaves p.46).

Yuca con mojo, cassava with a garlic
and coriander dressing

Yuca con mojo

(Cassava with garlic and lime)
Serves 4

**Plain-boiled cassava is a dull dish on its
own. In Cuba, it's given a lift with a sharp
little dressing. In season, bitter orange
juice – from Seville or 'marmalade'
oranges – takes the place of lime juice.**

*1.3k (3lb) cassava root, peeled and cut into
  chunks*
4 tablespoons olive oil
4 cloves of garlic, crushed
4 tablespoons lemon or lime juice
Salt

To finish:
Fresh coriander, chopped
Cassava chips

Boil the cassava chunks in salted water for
about 30 minutes until soft – don't worry if they
disintegrate at the edges. Drain thoroughly.

Meanwhile, in a small frying pan, heat the oil
and lightly fry the garlic to soften. Add the
citrus juice and bubble up. Pour the dressing
over the cassava chunks and finish with a
dusting of chopped coriander. Yuca con mojo
is traditionally served with fried plantains or
cassava chips (see below).

Yuca frita

(Cassava chips)
Serves 4

**A quick snack throughout the Caribbean,
cassava chips are particularly popular in
Cuba, where they are eaten with a fiery
green-papaya salsa. Cassava cannot be
made into chips without being boiled first
– without this preliminary, it tastes
unacceptably starchy. The idea is to cook
the peeled root in a shape which can be
sliced into rounds.**

*A piece of cassava about twice as long as
  your hand*
Vegetable oil for deep-frying
Salt

Peel the cassava – easiest under running water
– and cut into three pieces. Drop into boiling
water and cook until just tender – 15–20
minutes. Drain thoroughly and allow to cool.
Slice into rounds about 5mm (1/4in) thick.

Heat the oil in a heavy pan. When a faint haze
rises, slip in the chips in small batches.
Remove and drain on kitchen paper as soon
as they crisp and gild. Sprinkle with salt and
serve hot.

cassava flour

or manioc meal, harina de yuca, farhina

Prepared from the processed cassava root, cassava flour is used throughout the region in flatbreads and cakes, particularly the Yucatán's *cassabe* cakes and Colombia's rich little *pan de yuca*. As an everyday foodstuff, cassava flour takes the place of cornmeal in the diet of those whose terrain is not suitable for the cultivation of maize.

Manufacture

Bitter cassava root is boiled and then mashed and strained, or peeled and grated and then thoroughly squeezed. The juice is then boiled to a sticky black foodstuff called cassareep; at the same time it throws a starchy sediment, the raw material for both cassava flour and tapioca.

Appearance and taste

White to ivory-coloured, the flour comes in fine and coarse millings. The first is used for cakes and breads, the last is preferred for farofa, the Brazilian sprinkling-flour which is somewhere between a condiment and a foodstuff.

Making dough from cassava meal, Colombia

Cassava bread stall, Venezuela

Buying and storing

Cassava flour is available in West Indian and Latin American stores or in Indian supermarkets as *gari*. Find a brand which suits you and store it in an airtight tin.

Medicinal and other uses

Very bland and digestible, cassava flour is suitable for babies and invalids. It is not advisable as a single food-source, since it lacks protein and can lead to malnutrition.

Culinary uses

When used in baking, cassava flour is often combined with grated cheese for both substance and enrichment. As a pulp, it can be formed into cakes and baked slowly on a griddle, another way of increasing its shelf-life. When toasted to make farofa, it is added to soups and stews, or can be eaten straight from the bowl.

Farofa
(Brazilian toasted manioc meal)
Serves 6

In Amazonia, coarsely milled cassava-flour is used for farofa – toasted meal rather like fine breadcrumbs. Here the basic farofa is enriched by frying with a little palm-oil, an ingredient of African origin which adds a sunny golden tint. You can also stir in a handful of chopped onion, coriander leaves, dried shrimps, slivers of malagueta peppers – whatever comes to hand.

225g (8oz) cassava flour (manioc meal)
1 tablespoon dende or vegetable oil, plus a
little achiote or paprika

Sift through the flour. When your stew or soup is ready, heat the oil in a small pan and sprinkle in the flour. Fry gently, moving the mixture constantly with a wooden spoon so that it browns evenly. Serve as a finishing ingredient with a soup or stew, handing it round for people to add their own. The Amazonians like to sprinkle it over shredded, steamed manioc leaves, *maniva*. Indispensable with black beans in a feijoada, Brazil's national dish (see p.127).

Pan de yuca

(Colombian cassava breads)

Makes 24 small rolls

Little horseshoe-shaped cookies held together with cheese, these are very rich and crumbly. They are sold in Colombia's busy market-places as a quick breakfast for busy housewives.

110g (4oz) cassava flour
225g (8oz) grated cheese (cheddar or crumbled feta)
2 egg yolks
4 tablespoons softened butter

Preheat the oven to 200°C/400°F/gas mark 6.

Mix the ingredients together and knead until you have a softish dough – you may need a little water. Set aside for half an hour to allow the flour to swell. Wet your hands and divide the dough into walnut-sized pieces, then roll and shape each into a little horseshoe.

Transfer to a baking tray (no need to butter), and bake for about 20 minutes, until pale gold and crisp.

tapioca

(from the Tupi Indian word for cassava)

A manufactured grain, the product of processing the bitter-cassava root, this is the staple starch-food of the Amazonian nations in probably its most familiar form outside its home-territory. Once popular as a milk pudding, tapioca has fallen out of favour in recent years, maybe because so many milky desserts now come in instant form.

Manufacture

Tapioca is made by pushing detoxified, pre-cooked, mashed bitter-cassava through a mesh. The result is dictated by the size of the holes and the manner in which the root is prepared.

Appearance and taste

In dried form, tapioca resembles little white pellets. When reconstituted by cooking as a porridge, it is shiny and transparent with a nutty little heart. The taste is bland, the texture a little glutinous – you either love it or hate it.

Buying and storing

Look for large pearly grains of an even size and perfectly white appearance. Store it like rice, in an airtight tin, where it will keep for years.

Medicinal and other uses

Tapioca makes a digestible and fortifying porridge, perfect for invalids and babies.

Various grains – and avocados – on sale in a street market in Quito, Ecuador

Culinary uses

Tapioca is an alternative to rice in milk puddings and broths. By swelling to some four times its original volume, it takes on the characteristics of its cooking liquid, which means that the richer the broth or the creamier the milk the more delicious the dish.

Caldo al minuto

(Ready-in-a-minute soup)
Serves 1

This, a bowl of very hot chicken soup fortified with tapioca, was the comfort food of my childhood. When I lived in Montevideo – I remember a low white house with a flat roof and a view of the sea – my mother's cook would make this for me when I was poorly. Since this wasn't very often, it remained a treat.

A mugful of strong chicken broth
1 level tablespoon small-grain tapioca

To finish:
1 teaspoon finely chopped serrano or parma ham
1 teaspoon chopped hardboiled egg
1 teaspoon chopped parsley

Bring the soup to the boil, stir in the tapioca and simmer for about 20 minutes, stirring occasionally, until the grains are swollen, tender and transparent. Stir in the finishing ingredients and transfer to a bowl. Sit on the stoop and drink it while you watch the sunset.

Postre de tapioca con coco

(Tapioca and coconut-cream pudding)
Serves 4

**Could anything be more soothing than a
bowl of tapioca cooked gently like a rice-** pudding in coconut-cream, sweetened
with cane sugar and served cool?

4 tablespoons pearl tapioca
1.2 litres (2 pints) coconut milk
2 tablespoons sugar

Put the ingredients in a heavy pan and stir
them up. Simmer gently for an hour, until thick,
creamy and soft. Chill. Spoon into a glass bowl
or fresh coconut shells, if such should come
your way.

Peruvian
black

waxy yellow

fingerling

criolla

floury red

potato

or patata, papa (*Solanum tuberosum*)

The potato is a tuber-forming herbaceous plant related to the chilli, a member of the nightshade family. It is a plant of the Andean highlands, capable of surviving at high altitudes as well as in more amiable terrain. The potato was the staple foodstuff of the Andean nations, particularly valued by the Mapuche, an ancient people who have managed to retain many of their pre-Columbian customs and foodways and who cultivate it along the edges of the rivers and in the swamp-lands of southern Chile. A native of Peru and cultivated since the earliest times, the potato is resistant to cold and can be planted in poor soil – virtues which enabled the building of Machu Picchu, where the Inca kings took refuge from their enemies, surviving and thriving in impossible terrain. The potato is easy to cultivate and undemanding of labour. The planting of the potato in the Old World can be held responsible for the remarkable population increases of the 18th century which culminated in the two revolutions – social and economic – which altered the entire political life of western civilisation.

How it grows

The potato is a leafy annual whose stems swell underground – these are the edible tubers. It is more easily propagated by budding than by sowing seed, since the pretty, papery little cream-coloured flowers are frequently infertile. Nevertheless, the appearance of the flowers and the dying back of the leaves is an indication the crop is ready to be lifted. Certain Andean varieties are grown especially for freeze-drying, a natural process known to the Incas which reduces the tubers to what look like lumps of coal but can easily be reconstituted to palatability.

Sicuani market, Peru

Appearance and taste

Irregularly shaped brown, yellow or russet-skinned tubers, some potatoes have a distinctly pink tint, while a few varieties are a very deep violet, almost black and some even have dark purple flesh. The more common varieties have ivory to cream flesh beneath thin caramel to dark brown skin. The flesh is crisp and juicy when raw, but soft and floury when cooked. The tuber ranges in size from as small as a marble to as big as a football. There are now more than a thousand varieties known, with many more in its land of origin as yet unexploited. The flavour is bland and starchy but with a distinctive earthiness and nuttiness which is more pronounced in some varieties than others. A vegetable which, possibly more than any other, responds directly to the environment in which it's grown. Varieties grown in a stony field on the south side of a hill, say, will not taste the same as the identical variety grown in rich soil on a northern slope.

Buying and storing

Choose firm tubers which show no sign of rotting, spotting, sprouting or greening – a sign they have developed a potentially toxic chemical, solanine, which must be ruthlessly carved out before cooking. Store in a cool dark place, or the tubers will do what comes naturally and sprout.

Medicinal and other uses

The potato is a fine fuel-food, well-endowed with all the necessary vitamins, protein and, famously, carbohydrates. It is rich in potassium, good for the liver and as system-cleanser. Much of the vitamin and mineral content is concentrated immediately beneath the skin – you will get much less benefit if you skin it before you cook it. It is of far greater nutritional value if consumed raw (though this would certainly not be the gourmet's choice), particularly the juice, which is reputed to have antibiotic properties as well as a liberal endowment of vitamin C and minerals.

Culinary uses

Steaming rather than boiling is the recommended method of preserving as many of the vitamins as possible, although this is not a problem when the potatoes are cooked in the traditional Andean earth-oven. The Mapuche, who only go to the trouble of digging an earth-oven at tribal gatherings, will tell you that they cook their staple foodstuff in a closed pot not only to preserve the goodness, but as a reminder of the unity of all things. Modern recipes of the region either use a minimum of water – cooking the tubers down to complete dryness so that none of the juices are lost – or prepare the tubers as a soup, which allows the cooking water to be drunk as a broth.

Wide variety of potatoes in Cuenca, Ecuador

Papas a la huancaina
(Potatoes with cream and cheese)
Serves 4–6

This is Peru's national dish: nothing fancy, but when made with good ingredients, worth the attention of any gourmet. Plain-boiled potatoes are sauced with cheese melted with cream and flavoured with ají – chilli. Varieties of Peruvian bush-chilli, the upward-pointing triangular variety, range from the tolerable and mild to the screaming scarlet rocota, the chilli which put fire in the belly of the Incas.

1.8kg (4lb) small, round yellow-fleshed potatoes (criollas, for preference)
Sea-salt

The sauce:
350g (12oz) grated cheese
300ml (1/2 pint) cream
1 teaspoon arrowroot or cornflour mixed with a little water
1 teaspoon chilli flakes or 2–3 medium-hot ajies (chillies), toasted to blister and cut into ribbons

Wash the potatoes and put them in a heavy pan with just enough water to cover, add salt, bring to the boil, put the lid on tightly, turn down the heat and cook for about 15 minutes. Remove the lid and bubble up to evaporate excess liquid, cover with a cloth and cook over a very low heat for another 5 minutes or so, until the potatoes are perfectly tender and dry. Shake to crack the skins a little.

Meanwhile, melt the grated cheese into the cream, whisk in the arrowroot or cornflour and stir in the ají. Simmer until it thickens – 5 minutes or so. Pour over the potatoes.

Ecuador potato market

Chapale chileno
(Chilean potato bread)
Serves 4

A dense-textured potato bread, this is traditionally baked in an earth-oven, the chosen cooking-implement of the Mapuche, the indigenous inhabitants of the cold uplands of southern Chile, whose way of life depends on cultivation of the potato.

4 large potatoes, scrubbed
4 tablespoons chuchoca (polenta)
4 tablespoons grated cheese
1–2 links fresh chorizo, skinned and crumbled
1 teaspoon chilli powder
1 large egg, forked
Salt
Butter or oil for greasing the baking tin

Preheat the oven to 180°C/350°F/gas mark 4. In salted water, boil the potatoes in their jackets until tender – about 20 minutes, more if they're very large. Drain, saving the water. Peel as soon as they're cool enough to handle and mash roughly with a fork. Using your hands, but without crushing out all the lumps, work in the polenta, cheese, chorizo, chilli, egg and enough of the potato-water to make a soft dough.

Grease a roasting tin and spread in the dough, levelling off the top. Bake for 45–50 minutes, until brown and crisp. Cut into squares and eat with a modest shake of chilli sauce – southern *chilenos* like their food less fiery than the northerners.

Papas a la huancaina, bite-sized criolla potatoes, richly sauced and fiery with chilli.

amaranth

(Amaranthus caudatus, A. melancholicus, A. hypocondriacus, A. cruentus)

The amaranth is a broad-leaved plant, a member of the spinach family which grows wild throughout the region. In Europe, its usefulness as a food-plant was well known to the Ancient Greeks, who esteemed it both for the leaves and seeds. In the Americas, it was highly valued as a cereal crop by both the Inca and Aztec civilisations, second only to maize. Monteczuma, the Aztec Emperor at the time of the Spanish conquest, received enormous quantities in tribute – almost as much as was received in maize. His priests used the seeds, mixed with honey or sacrificial blood, to make effigies of their gods, which were then eaten by the priests and their victims. The Christian missionaries, horrified by what appeared to make mockery of the sacrament of the Eucharist, banned the crop, punishing those who continued to harvest or trade in it by cutting off the offending right hand. This, as might be expected, discouraged its use, and amaranth effectively vanished as a foodstuff, although not from the landscape.

Amaranth seeds

How it grows

The amaranth is a broad-leaf plant rather than a grass, a botanical distinction which makes the crop a seed rather than a grain. Indigenous to both India and the Americas, more than five hundred species are known world-wide, and it has adapted to the widest possible range of habitats, from lush tropical to arid dessert, from near-Arctic conditions to steaming jungle. A single plant produces dozens of seed-heads, each a droopy, bushy tassel yielding up to five thousand tiny seeds.

Appearance and taste

The grain is very small, almost sandy, ivory in colour but the seedheads vary from snowy white to a deep reddish brown to black; the taste is strong and nutty with a peppery aftertaste, rather like unskinned walnuts. As a porridge, it cooks to a texture rather like grain-mustard, a little gluey, never losing its shape. The greens – the best-known variety is Chinese spinach – are gloriously variable in colour. The wild varieties have rather tough and indigestible leaves, but those grown as greens are robust and chard-like, with a strong peppery flavour; the young stalks are also eaten (older stalks are tough and woody), tasting a little like artichoke.

Buying and storing

You'll find amaranth grains sold in packets in health-food stores; they're highly valued for their high protein content. Store the packet in a cool dry place or decant into a lidded jar. The greens, particularly those of a dark green, red-tinged, slightly fuzzy variety usually labelled Chinese spinach, can be also be found in season. Treat it as chard: cut off any dry ends and put the stems in water, or store them in a plastic bag in the fridge.

Medicinal and other uses

Gluten-free, rich in minerals and protein, higher in fibre than wheat, rice or soybeans, amaranth was rediscovered by US chemists in the 1970s and promoted as the ideal vegetarian foodstuff.

Paella de granos de paraíso, a delicate combination of amaranth grains and greens

First cook the amaranth. Bring the water to the boil, stir in the amaranth, put the lid on loosely, turn down the heat and simmer for 30–35 minutes,until soft, swollen and tender. Remove from the heat and allow to stand for 15 minutes, with the lid still on, to swell some more.

Meanwhile, in a large shallow pan, gently fry the garlic and diced peppers in the oil until the vegetables are soft – don't let them brown. Add the diced pumpkin and a splash of water, put the lid on and simmer for about 10 minutes, until the pumpkin is nearly tender but still holds its shape. Pop the shredded greens on top, season with salt and pepper, let it bubble up, put the lid on again and shake over the heat for another 5 minutes, just long enough to wilt the leaves. Fork in the amaranth grains, reheat and pile on a warm serving dish.

Pastel de los ángeles

(Angel cake)
Serves 6

Angel-food in every sense: light, nutty, digestible and delicious. The amaranth keeps the cake moist.

6 eggs
350g (12oz) caster sugar
175g (6oz) ground almonds
175g (6oz) pre-cooked amaranth grains
1 lemon, zest and juice

Preheat the oven to 180°C/350°F/gas mark 4.

Whisk the eggs with the sugar until frothy, light and white, a process which takes twice as long as you think. Fold in the almonds and amaranth grains, lemon zest and a tablespoonful of the juice, spoon into a 18cm (7in) round cake tin, buttered and lined with baking parchment, and bake for 40–50 minutes, until puffed and brown. It'll shrink back to a thick soft pancake when it comes out of the oven – no matter. Save the remaining juice to melt with honey to make a little soaking-sauce for the cake. Delicious with a scoop of coconut parfait (see p.225).

Culinary uses

It is a very versatile grain which can be used to add food-value to other grain-foods: use it in breads, biscuits, cakes and pancakes (remembering that it's gluten-free so will not rise or hold together unless heavily blended with wheat-flour). The grain can be quickly prepared as a porridge to be served savoury or sweet (delicious with cream and honey) or popped like popcorn with a drop of oil in a tightly lidded pan. Treat the leaves as cabbage or spinach: shred and cook in very little water.

Paella de granos de paraíso

(Amaranth paella with peppers and greens)
Serves 4

A paella, the Spanish risotto, takes its name from the container in which it's cooked, a wide, shallow double-handled iron pan of a design known to the Romans, who had it from the Ancient Greeks. If you can't find amaranth leaves, substitute any member of the spinach or cabbage family. Cook double quantities of the basic grains and use the leftovers to bake an almond cake (see below).

200g (7oz) amaranth grains
500ml (18fl oz) water
200g (7oz) piece pumpkin, diced
2 garlic cloves, finely chopped
4 poblano or 2 green salad peppers, de-
* seeded and diced*
2 tablespoons oil
A large handful amaranth or cabbage leaves,
* shredded*
Salt and pepper

chickpea

brown chickpeas

or garbanzo (*Cicer arietinum*)

A storecupboard legume cultivated for at least five thousand years, the chickpea was found in the middens of Mesopotamia, from where it spread throughout the temperate zones of Asia, Africa and Europe, finally colonising the Americas. Portable and easily reconstituted to make a nourishing soup, the chickpea is soldiers' fodder, the legume which fuelled the Muslim armies when they invaded Andalusia, provisioned Columbus' ships and, finally and most disastrously for the indigenous inhabitants, enabled Cortés' *conquistadores* to reach the court of Monteczuma. As a European import, it is now naturalised throughout the region.

green chickpeas

How it grows

The chickpea is a small bushy annual easily propagated from seed (the chickpeas themselves). The pods are short and hairy and contain no more than one or two seeds which, when fresh, are about the size of a small hazelnut.

Appearance and taste

As a stored pulse-vegetable, the chickpea is coffee-coloured with a patterned surface coming to a point at one end. The flavour is nutty and sweet: chestnuts with a scat of fresh hay. There's a short period in mid-summer when chickpeas can be eaten green and raw: while the flavour is much like fresh peas, the juices are so acid they stain your fingers black. In Andalusia where I lived with my young family, we grew a crop every year for the storecupboard; our neighbours, frugal housewives, taught me to add the pinched-out shoots to the beanpot.

Buying and storing

Buy from a source with a high turnover – dry-goods stores which serve ethnic communities – as chickpeas which have been stored longer than a single season take twice as long to soften. Freshly-dried chickpeas have a plump appearance, a slight give when squeezed, and an absence of any powdery deposit in the packet. Hispanic cooks choose the large, pale varieties, although Indian and Middle Eastern cooks appreciate black, red and dark brown varieties. Chickpeas are also available in cans – not the cheapest way to buy them, but convenient, particularly when they are being used as a secondary ingredient.

Medicinal and other uses

High in protein and gluten free, the chickpea is well-endowed with fibre and the necessary vitamins and minerals to sustain an army on the march.

Culinary uses

The chickpea is best appreciated whole in a stew, preferably in combination with pork-offal such as tripe and trotters, since both take the same amount of time to soften. Pounded and soaked, it makes a crisp little fritter. Chickpea flour, the milled version of the storecupboard legume, is used in breads and to thicken soups, giving a pleasantly nutty flavour as well as improving the food-value. It makes an excellent tamale dough, and mixed with water and allowed to stand and ferment a little, it makes a remarkably light, crisp frying-batter (particularly good as fritters made with small shrimps, *tortillitas de camarón*). Chickpea flour can also do duty as the Brazilian sprinkling-condiment farofa (see p.60), if manioc meal is unavailable.

Menudo colombiano

(Tripe and chickpeas)

Serves 6

The classic Colombian all-in stew – fortifying on a cold winter's day in the Andean uplands. The combination of pork and chickpeas is a happy one, particularly when enlivened with ají – the Andean form of the fiery chilli.

450g (1lb) chickpeas, soaked overnight
2 onions, skinned and quartered
450g (1lb) cleaned tripe
2 pigs trotters or a bacon knuckle
Short length cinnamon
2–3 cloves
1 teaspoon cumin
1–2 chopped, de-seeded chillies
600ml (1 pint) tomato pulp
1 teaspoon dried oregano
Salt

To finish:

450g (1lb) potatoes, cut into bite-sized chunks
600ml (1 pint) sweetcorn kernels
A handful macaroni or any tubular pasta
A handful fresh chickpeas or green beans, cut small
4–5 tablespoons olive oil
2 tablespoons drained capers

Drain the soaked chickpeas and transfer to a roomy cooking pot with the rest of the ingredients – don't add salt yet. Bring to the boil, turn down to simmer, put the lid on loosely and leave to bubble very gently for about 2 hours, until the chickpeas are perfectly tender and the meat is soft enough to eat with a spoon. Add more boiling water as necessary.

Add the potatoes and return to the boil. After 10 minutes add the sweetcorn and pasta, taste and add salt. Let bubble for another 10 minutes and add the fresh chickpeas or green beans. Return to the boil and cook for another 10–15 minutes, until the pasta is tender. The dish should be soupy but thick enough to support the weight of a wooden spoon. Finish with a swirl of olive oil and a sprinkle of capers.

Acarajé de garbanzos

(Chickpea fritters)

Serves 4

These are crisp Brazilian fritters made with pre-soaked but uncooked chickpeas, an alternative to the shrimp-enhanced black-eyed pea-fritters. The aim is a crisp shell enclosing a soft, floury interior. You can vary the flavourings – more or less chilli or cumin, no coriander – to suit your palate.

225g (8oz) pre-soaked chickpeas
2–3 garlic cloves, crushed
1 teaspoon chilli powder
1 teaspoon ground cumin
1 teaspoon salt
1/2 teaspoon baking powder
4 tablespoons finely chopped parsley and leaf coriander
Oil for frying

Drain the chickpeas and dry thoroughly. Pound in a mortar or the food-processor until you have a very smooth paste – the chickpeas must be absolutely dry before the pounding or the paste will fall apart in the frying. Add the remaining ingredients in the order given, processing between each addition, until well-blended. Leave to rest for an hour. Break off small pieces the size of a walnut and form into small patties about 4cm (1 1/2in) in diameter. Arrange on a plate ready to slip into the hot oil – they're too fragile to pick up in your fingers.

Heat the oil until lightly hazed with blue and use a spatula to push the patties into the hot oil, a few at a time. Fry until crisp and brown. If they splutter and split, the oil is too hot. Turn once and transfer to kitchen paper to drain. Serve with a shake of malagueta pepper sauce (see p. 51).

Menudo colombiano, a rich, spicy tripe and chickpea stew

rice

or arroz (*Oryza sativa*)

Although unknown in the Americas before the arrival of the Europeans (wild rice is unrelated), rice was enthusiastically naturalised in suitable estuary and swamplands, particularly those with populations of African origin such as the southern states of North America, the Caribbean and Brazil, where it features among the indispensable accompaniments to feijoada, the national dish (see p.127).

medium-grain rice

How it grows

The seeds of a water-dependent grass of Asian origin, rice is the staple grain of much of the world's most densely-populated areas. More than seven thousand varieties are grown, each with its own shape, colour, flavour and fragrance.

Appearance and taste

White rice – few Latin American cooks would thank you for brown or any other kind of rice – is prepared by stripping the grain of its outer layer or husk of bran, leaving a snow-white kernel with a delicate almost flowery fragrance which retains a seductively nutty flavour.

Buying and storing

A medium-grain rice – slender, absorbent, about twice as long as it's wide – is generally the most suitable for Latin-American recipes. Keep it in an airtight tin. Chilli-growing countries pop a chilli into the storage container to discourage creepy-crawlies.

Medicinal and other uses

White rice, extremely digestible and an excellent vehicle for other foods, is pure carbohydrate since most of the vitamins, minerals and fibre are lost in the husk-stripping process. When it was discovered that the exposed kernels are vulnerable to mould and insects, a practice developed of dusting the grains with talc – a product derived from the same source as asbestos. Talc-dusted rices are mostly sold in California, Puerto Rico and Hawaii, but only rarely appear elsewhere.

Culinary uses

Appreciated throughout the territory as a staple grain-food, rice is usually plainly cooked in water and served as a side-dish, or combined with one of the pulses of the indigenous bean family. Medium-grain rice takes up moisture

Rice thrives in swampy conditions

and retains it, remaining fluffy and absorbent – a virtue when served as an accompaniment. Long-grain rice never completely softens, and short-grain is inclined to stickiness, making both less suitable as a background-grain for the region's soupy stews and sauces.

Arroz brasileiro

(Brazilian rice)
Serves 6 as an accompaniment

In Brazil as in Portugal, rice is the obligatory accompaniment to all main dishes. Nothing to it, really. While Spain planted the Middle-Eastern medium-sized round-grain rice in its dependencies, Portugal preferred a long-grain, the rice popular in its Far Eastern dependencies.

3–4 tablespoons olive oil
450g (1lb) long-grain rice
Water (2¹/₂ times the volume of rice)
2 garlic cloves, skinned and very finely chopped
1–2 cloves
1 tablespoon rough sea-salt

Preheat the oven to 180°C/350°F/gas mark 4.

Heat the oil gently in a fire-proof casserole. Turn the rice in the hot (but not smoking) oil until the grains are transparent. Add the water, the chopped garlic, cloves and salt, bring to the boil and let it cook for 15 minutes. Transfer the dish to the oven and bake for 15–20 minutes, until the rice is tender and lightly crisped on top.

Jamaican rice'n'peas

Serves 6

Popular all over the Caribbean, this dish is best if made the day before. It varies throughout the territory since each community and household has its own special recipe. Some include meat – pork offal, usually; others a different pulse-vegetable such as black-eyed peas, lentils, chickpeas. Only the rice and the philosophical approach – nothing wasted, the pulse-broth used to cook the rice – never varies. In Jamaica, you can buy the combination ready-cooked, neatly sealed in a vacuum pack.

450g (1lb) ready-cooked red beans
1 ripe coconut
450g (1lb) medium-grain rice
2–3 sprigs thyme
2 cloves garlic, crushed
Salt and cracked black pepper
Pepperpot meats (optional)

Split the coconut by dropping it on a hard table-top or a concrete floor. Discard the water (unless you're thirsty). Ease the white flesh off the brown husk with a knife and break the flesh into small pieces. Pack the pieces in the blender and cover with cold water. Process until mushy, strain through a cloth, squeezing to extract all the liquid. Reserve the liquid and return the mush to the blender, repeating the process with more water. The first extraction is coconut cream; when the second is added to the first, it becomes coconut milk.

Put the rice in a roomy saucepan with enough coconut milk to cover. Bring to the boil, season with salt, tuck in the thyme, lower the heat, and simmer slowly until all the milk is absorbed.

Meanwhile, have ready the bean liquor diluted with a mugful of boiling water. Add this to the rice as it dries. When the rice is perfectly soft, stir in the drained beans and the garlic. You can if you wish also stir in slices of black pudding or precooked pig's tail, ears and trotters, suitably de-boned and shredded – easy if you have a pepperpot simmering slowly on the back of the stove. Taste and season. Reheat to serve.

quinoa

or quinua (*Chenopodium* spp.)

The quinoa is a member of the spinach family, whose leaves are eaten in much the same way. It is widespread throughout the world in various forms, happiest in the harshest conditions such as those of the Andean highland, and was known to the Incas as the mother-seed, the source of all life. As such it was one of the two grainfoods – the other the Aztecs' amaranth – targeted as unacceptable by the hispanic colonisers for religious as well as political reasons. It survived as a staple grain-food only among the people of Bolivia's Altiplano, particularly in the Cordillera mountains where it thrives at altitudes above three thousand metres. The quinoa has recently started to come back into favour thanks to its value in a vegetarian diet.

How it grows

The quinoa is a leafy member of the spinach family which comes in many colours – pink, red, orange, lavender, purple, black, yellow and white – and grows to a height of one to three metres, carrying its seed-heads in large clusters at the end of the stalk. Prolific and hardy, it thrives in extreme conditions. The quinoa is harvested mainly for its seed, though its leaves are indistinguishable from spinach.

Appearance and taste

The quinoa cooks and tastes like a nutty couscous – the grains swell up to four times their own volume – speckled with little crescent-shaped corkscrews, the debris of the outer coverings. It is sometimes known as the vegetarian caviar for the crunchiness and translucence of the small perfectly spherical grains which never lose their shine.

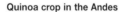

Quinoa crop in the Andes

Buying and storing

The quinoa has small, disk-shaped seeds which look like sesame in the packet. Seeds sold commercially will have been well-rinsed of their sticky coating of saponin, a bitter, soap-like resin which protects them from seed-eating birds and insects. Pay no attention to the few little black speckles, 'wild' quinoa, which neither soften nor burst but have a pleasantly peppery flavour. Buy from a shop with a high turnover – the grains are at their best when fresh – and store in an airtight container in a cool place. Bear in mind that in any recipe the flavour is enhanced by a light preliminary toasting. If milled into flour, this should be stored in the fridge since a high oil-content quickly turns it rancid.

Medicinal and other uses

Gluten-free, digestible, rich in proteins and minerals (particularly iron), quinoa is suitable for convalescents and muscle-building athletes alike. Volume for volume, it has more calcium than milk – useful in the prevention of osteoporosis – and more natural fat than any other grain.

Culinary uses

Quinoa is a versatile cereal, as useful to the pastry-chef looking for a way to lighten his cakes and biscuits as to the domestic cook feeding a family on a budget. As a cereal, treat it as bulgar-wheat: cook it in twice its own volume of water and serve either as a porridge, delicious sweetened with honey and cream, or as a pilaf, flavoured with fresh herbs. In Ecuador, quinoa is traditionally combined with lye-treated cornmeal when kneading tamales and tortillas. In cakes and pastries, use it either as a cooked grain or in the form of flour, bearing in mind that quinoa, although its lightness makes it suitable for the finest pastry-making, lacks the gluten necessary to hold a dough together. For best results, mix it with wheatflour in the proportions of 4 parts wheat to 3 parts quinoa, and grind in the food-processor to make a delicate, exquisitely hazelnut-flavoured flour.

Chaulafán de quinua y naranja

(Ecuadorian quinoa and orange salad)
Serves 4–6

A simple salad served as an accompaniment – condiment – in which the nutty sweetness of the quinoa is balanced by the acidity of the citrus.

450g (1lb) quinoa
1 chayote or a small cucumber, diced
6 spring onions, chopped with their green
Small handful flat-leaf parsley
Small handful mint
1–2 oranges, segments and finely-grated zest
2 green or red jalapeno chillies, de-seeded and chopped
6 tablespoons olive oil
2 tablespoons lemon or bitter orange juice
Salt

Rinse the quinoa under a tap until the water runs clear. In a large pan, cover the grains with double their own volume of water. Bring to the boil, reduce to a simmer, put the lid on loosely and cook for about 20 minutes or so, until the grains are translucent and the water has all been absorbed.

Combine with all the remaining ingredients. Taste and add whatever's needed: a little more salt, an extra squeeze of lemon, perhaps. Serve with thick slices of corn on the cob or (in winter) a fistful of arepas – thick tortillas made with the snowy white corn of the Andes – hot from the griddle.

Galletas de quinua

(Quinoa cookies)
Makes about 24 cookies

These crisp, nutty cookies made with quinoa flour are easy to make since the little seeds only take a moment or two to crush.

4 tablespoons quinoa grains
12 tablespoons self-raising wholemeal flour
4 tablespoons seed-oil

Chaulafán de quinua y naranja, a summer salad dressed with orange

4 tablespoons smooth peanut butter
4 tablespoons brown sugar or grated palm-sugar
4 tablespoons white sugar
1 large egg, lightly whisked
1/2 teaspoon vanilla seeds scraped from the pod
Milk or water
Butter for greasing

Butter a baking tray. Preheat the oven to 190°C/375°F/gas mark 5. Put the quinoa and the flour in the processor and whizz for a few minutes – it'll crush quickly and easily. Blend the oil with the butter, then beat in the two sugars until light and fluffy. Beat in the egg and vanilla seeds. Fold in the quinoa flour and enough water or milk to make a soft dough which drops easily from the spoon.

Drop spoonfuls of the mixture onto the tray, leaving plenty of room for expansion. Bake for 8–10 minutes, until well-gilded. Transfer to a baking rack to cool and crisp.

black-eyed pea

or cow-pea, fradinho (Brazil)
(*Vigna unguiculata* et spp.)

An annual legume, the black-eyed pea is a member of the pea family related to the Chinese mung-bean but of a strain long naturalised in Africa, popular in Brazil and among Afro-Caribbean cooks. It is one of the traditional seed-foods which, if eaten on the first day of the new year, will bring luck for the next twelve months.

How it grows

The black-eyed pea is a short erect or trailing plant with pods about as long a man's foot and no thicker than a pencil. It is fully mature and ready for shelling three months after planting.

Appearance and taste

The form popular in the region is a small, ivory-coloured kidney shape with a deep purple to ebony-black 'eye'. The flavour of the mature pea is robust and earthy, with an underlying sweetness and a smooth buttery texture.

Buying and storing

Check for freshness – the colour should be bright and the peas still have a little give when squeezed between the fingers – and the absence of a powdery deposit which indicates the presence of uninvited guests. Store in an airtight container in a cool corner.

Medicinal and other uses

The black-eyed pea is fuel-food for field-workers, high in carbohydrates and protein-rich, as are all the pulses.

Culinary uses

Fast food for busy people, black-eyed peas, unlike most store-cupboard pulses, need no preliminary soaking and cook to perfect tenderness in about 40 minutes. They can be eaten whole when tender and young, but are usually left to mature for store.

Soupe à Congo
(Black-eyed pea and pigeon-pea soup)
Serves 4–6

Martinique's contribution to the meal-in-a-bowl tradition is a mighty soup-stew in whose name can be traced its lineage. The pigeon peas – known as no-eye peas – are closely related to the black-eye, but soften to a mush, thickening the broth.

450g (1lb) black-eyed peas
225g (8oz) split pigeon peas (yellow dhal)
2 salted pigs' tails or 1 bacon knuckle
6 allspice berries, roughly crushed
1 sweet potato, peeled and diced
1–2 carrots, scraped and diced
2–3 garlic cloves, slivered
A generous handful okra, topped and tailed
Half a cabbage, shredded
Salt

To finish:
1 onion, finely sliced
1 aubergine, diced
3–4 tablespoons oil
1–2 fiery cayenne peppers, de-seeded and
chopped

Put the two kinds of peas in a large pan with the pigs' tails or bacon knuckle and add enough water to cover to a depth of the width of your hand. Bring to the boil, skim off any foam, and add the allspice berries. Turn down the heat, put the lid on loosely and cook for half an hour, until the vegetables begin to soften. Add the potato, carrots and garlic and more boiling water if necessary to maintain the volume. Remove the bacon knuckle, if using, strip the meat from the bone and return it to the pot (the tails can stay as they are). Bring back to the boil and cook for 10 minutes, then add the okra and the cabbage. Cook for another 10 minutes, until all is perfectly tender and the juices are thick and fragrant. Add more water as needed.

Meanwhile in a frying pan, fry the onion and the aubergine in the oil, adding the chilli and salting as the vegetables soften. Stir the contents of the frying pan into the pot. Serve with white rice and sliced avocado dressed with lime juice.

Acarajé

(Black-eyed pea fritters with shrimp)

Serves 4–6

Exotic little fritters made with black-eyes and dried shrimp, acaraje are fried crisp in dende oil. A Brazilian dish of African origin and a speciality of the Bahia, the fritters are cooked to order on the street by women in the traditional flounced white dresses, spotlessly clean and draped with coloured necklaces. You'll find the same fritters sold on the streets of Ghana and Nigeria. The same mixture formed into dumplings, wrapped in banana leaves and steamed, is called abara.

225g (8oz) black eyed peas, picked over,
* rinsed and soaked overnight*
1 small yellow onion, finely chopped
2 tablespoons dried shrimp (look for them in
* Chinese supermarkets)*
Salt
Dende oil for deep frying (or any vegetable oil)

Drain the beans and peel off the skins – a bit time-consuming, but pre-soaking makes it easier.

In the liquidiser or food-processor, process the skinned peas, onion, shrimp and a little salt – Brazilian dried shrimp are well-salted. Keep going until you have a smooth purée somewhere between a batter and a paste. If using Chinese dried shrimp, you'll need extra salt.

Heat the oil in a deep frying pan until a faint blue haze rises. To make small fritters, drop in walnut-sized spoonfuls of the batter a few at a time, so the temperature doesn't drop. They will be ready in 3–4 minutes. Transfer with a slotted spoon to kitchen paper to drain.

To make larger fitters, form the purée into saucer-sized patties and slide them gently into the hot oil. Flip them once, allowing 7–8 minutes in all. Serve with a shake of malagueta pepper sauce (see p.51).

fresh sweetcorn

or maíz tierno, choclo tierno, elote tierno, jojota tierno (*Zea mays*)

A maize co-operative in Nicaragua

Maize is the pre-eminent grain-crop of the Americas; pre-historic middens leave ethnobotanists in no doubt that it has been cultivated throughout the Americas for at least 7,000 years. Creation legends of both the Andean nations and the peoples of Central America present maize-corn as the raw material of life, much as Ancient Europeans attached mystical significance to wheat. The cob appears in depictions of elaborate ritual dishes; in Mexico, the Aztecs of Cortes' day planted the crop up and down their highways, so that no one might go hungry – generosity wasted on the *conquistadores*, who lost many of their number to starvation. Although of most practical use as a storecupboard grain, valued for both man and his domestic animals, the tender young cobs are eaten fresh (*tierno*) in season. In tropical lands, where summer and winter are largely irrelevant, this can be three or even four times a year.

How it grows

Maize is a tall – 4–5 metres high – bamboo-like grass whose fertile seed-heads, the cobs, grow at intervals up the stem, allowing the neat rows of seeds to mature inside a protective sheath of modified leaves, the husk. The stypes of the female flowers are the silky tassels which emerge from the tops of the cob-sheaths, ready for pollination by the male flowers which appear as a spray of tiny blooms at the top of the stem. It is often grown in association with pumpkin or squash, which acts as a mulch and weed-inhibitor between the rows, and beans, for which the stalks provide a climbing pole. Fittingly, the three can be combined in the pot.

Appearance and taste

Many different varieties are grown, though two main strains can be identified: the sunny yellow sweetcorn of Central America, and the larger, whiter, starchier corn of the Andean highlands. *Maíz morado*, a purple corn native to Peru, is the caviar of the crop, very sought after for its delicate lemon-blossomy flavour.

Buying and storing

Choose cobs still in their bright green jackets – there should be no sign of drying or yellowing – and resist the temptation to open them even a crack: exposure to air begins the hardening and drying process. The shorter the distance from field to pot the better. After only a few hours, the sugar in the kernels begins to turn to starch.

Medicinal and other uses

One of the best-balanced of the starch-foods, sweetcorn is very easy to digest when fresh and steamed or grilled – but it is less digestible as a stored grain. Sweetcorn is good for building muscle and bone, and excellent for the brain and central nervous system. Said to reduce the likelihood of cancer and heart disease, it is recommended in the treatment of some skin diseases – either eaten or applied topically.

Culinary uses

When the corn is perfectly fresh and tender at the beginning of the season, steam or grill and eat straight from the hand. Later, scrape off the kernels to make a creamy soup (see *Crema de elote*, p.197), or include the kernels in one of the myriad multicoloured stews, or cut it into thick slices and serve with a seviche or a soup instead of bread.

Maíz tierno a la brasa

(Barbecued sweetcorn)
Serves 4

This is the Mexican way with a fresh corncob. Allow 2 per person, 3 if the cobs are small or appetites are large.

8–12 fresh corncobs, unhusked

To serve:
Rough salt
3–4 large dried chillies, de-seeded and
  crumbled or 4 teaspoons chilli flakes
Quartered limes
Very cold tequila

Light the barbecue or heat the grill. Strip off the husks, leaving them attached as a handle, place the cobs on the barbecue and roast them over a high heat – the aim is to blister and blacken the tips for the shortest possible time. Don't salt yet and avoid prolonged roasting, or the tender kernels will dry out. Sprinkle with rough salt and chilli flakes, and serve with lime quarters and a little glass of ice-cold tequila on the side.

Humitas

(Fresh corn-dumplings)
Serves 4–6

These are little corn-dumplings steamed in the husk, as they like them in Chile and Ecuador, made with the large, milky Andean corn-kernels. Fresh sweetcorn is used in season, although humitas can be made with ground, lye-treated storecupboard corn, or a mixture of fresh and stored. The flavouring is albahaca, the fragrant Andean basil.

16 large, fresh corncobs still in the husk
A handful basil leaves, stripped from the stalks
1 small green serrano or jalapeno chilli,
  de-seeded and finely chopped
2 tablespoons soft pork-lard or oil
2 large onions, finely chopped
1/2 green pepper, finely chopped
1 egg (if necessary), mixed with a fork
Salt

Maíz tierno a la brasa, tender young corncobs grilled on the barbecue

Carefully strip the husks from the corn without tearing them. With a sharp knife, slice off the kernels, and reserve. Using the back of the knife, scrape the milky residue from the empty cobs, and add to the kernels. Add the basil leaves and the chilli. Either pound or use the food processor to reduce all to a soft, smooth mush.

Meanwhile heat the lard or oil in a small pan and gently fry the onions and green pepper, sprinkled with a little salt, until soft. Stir in the corn purée and simmer gently for another 10–15 minutes until the mixture has lost most of its moisture. Taste and adjust the seasoning. If the corn is not of the large-kernelled Andean variety, you'll need an egg to bind.

Assemble the humitas: lay two of the inner leaves of the husk side by side, overlapping the edges by a finger's width. Drop 2 tablespoons of the corn mush in the centre. Fold the bottom edge over the filling, then fold in the sides, finally folding over the top to make a neat little parcel - don't wrap it too tightly as the mixture expands. Secure with a fine strip of husk or strong thread. Repeat until all the mixture is wrapped.

Bring a big pan of salted water to the boil. Pack in all the little parcels – they should be completely covered with water. Bring back to the boil, turn down the heat and simmer for 40 minutes. Remove, drain and allow to cool a little before serving. A little dipping salsa would not come amiss, though this is not essential or even traditional. To reheat, allow 20 minutes in the oven at 190°C/375°F/gas mark 5. Or, for a delicious smoky flavour, roast them on the barbecue: Chile's rural housewives pop them straight on the coals.

masa harina

or tortilla flour, masarepa, arepa flour

masa harina

Masa harina and masarepa are prepared flours made from lye-treated, pre-cooked, milled corn, the raw material of tortillas and arepas, the daily bread of the southern Americas. Both are griddle-baked flatbreads of varying thickness which serve the same purpose as all other flatbreads, as food-wrapper, portable plate, spoon, fork and edible scoop. Table implements are kept to a minimum in the heat of the tropics for practical reasons of hygiene.

Manufacture

To prepare your own masa for both tortillas and arepas, you'll need dried corn-kernels stripped from the cob. Soak them in fresh water overnight with a pinch of lye, drain them, grind them to a soft mush by whatever means available, and knead with a little salt to make a smooth, soft dough.

Appearance and taste

Masa harina, tortilla flour, is yellow and a little speckled (variations in colour are admired in a maize-cob), while masarepa, arepa flour, is prepared from the whiter, starchier corn of the Andes. The flavour of the first is stronger and sweeter than the second, but both are satisfyingly nutty with a honeyed aftertaste.

Buying and storing

Buy it in the form of ready-prepared flour for the making of tortillas or arepas – pick a brand which suits you. Store in an airtight tin in a dry place, as for other flours. Masa harina is not to be confused with cornmeal or polenta, since ordinary milled corn has not been subjected to the necessary processing.

Medicinal and other uses

Cornmeal which has been treated with lye has far greater food-value than ordinary untreated milled corn. The method – originally a soaking with wood ash, replaced after the Spanish conquest with powdered lime (quicklime or whitewash) – was developed by both the Aztecs and Incas, who undoubtedly learnt it from earlier civilisations. The need for these preliminaries was not understood by the Europeans, who brought what was seen as a miracle foodstuff back to the Old World and planted it in their fields, replacing more ancient crops. Too great a dependence on untreated cornmeal as a staple leads to pellagra, a vitamin-deficiency disease which can prove fatal – still a problem in Africa, where mealies are sometimes the sole foodstuff.

Preparing tortilla dough in a Mexico City restaurant

masarepa

Tortillas

(Mexican cornbreads)
Makes about 24 tortillas

**The daily bread of Central America –
Guatemala and Nicaragua as well as
Mexico – is lightly milled, patted out by
hand and baked on a *comal*, an
earthenware griddle.**

450g (1lb) maize kernels
1.2 litres (2 pints) water
*About 30g (2 teaspoons) quicklime (from the
   chemist)*

Soak the maize overnight in the water, bring to
the boil and cook for an hour – the skins will
turn bright yellow and loosen. Rub off the skins,
rinse thoroughly and crush or grind the resultant
mush, *nixtamal*, in a corn grinder or *metate* –
the traditional stone mortar – until it forms a
dense mass. Knead until you have a soft,
smooth, flexible dough – not wet enough to be
sticky, and not so dry that it cracks or crumbles.
Divide into 16 walnut-sized balls.

Now you're ready to make the tortillas. Flatten
the doughballs lightly and cover with clingfilm to
keep them soft while you work. Pat or roll each
piece out into a thin pancake about 12cm (5in)
in diameter. To pat out by hand, dip your hands
in warm water before placing the flattened
dough ball on the palm of one and patting it out
with the other, reversing your hands between
each pat (difficult), or roll out between 2 sheets
of plastic (easy), or use a tortilla press (easiest).

Preheat a griddle or heavy frying pan and wipe
with a scrap of clean linen dipped in lard. Cook
each tortilla for 1 minute each side, until the
edges start to curl (half the time if using the
proper clay *comal*). Flip into a tea towel to keep
it warm and soft. Continue until all are done.

To soften by reheating in the oven, wrap in foil in
piles of no more than 6 and allow 20 minutes in
a medium oven. To reheat, place directly on the
electric hot-plate or on a very hot griddle and
heat until the edges char a little; place another
tortilla on top and flip the pair over to toast the
other side; repeat until all are heated. Eat them
while they're warm, spread with mashed
avocado, affectionately known as Aztec butter.

Culinary uses

When the basic prepared flour is mixed with a
little more than half its own volume of warm
water, with or without enriching fat, it can be
worked into a dough. This can be baked in the
form of a flatbread, or used as an enclosing
pastry for empanadillas, little pasties. Prepared
harina is also the raw material for tamales (see
p.82). In its most digestible form, it can be
taken as *atole*, either broth-based gruel, or
made with milk, sweetened and flavoured with
cinnamon – drunk hot or chilled.

Arepas

(Andean cornbreads)

**Andean corn, with its large starchy white
kernels, is used for the making of arepas.
These, being thicker and therefore easier
to make at home than the Mexican tortilla,
have a crisp crust, soft interior and a
remarkably short shelf-life.**

Arepas

450g (1lb) masarepa
About 300ml (¹/₂ pint) water

Dampen your hands and pat out the masarepa
to make small flat cakes 8cm (3in) in diameter
and ¹/₂cm (¹/₄in) thick.

Bake on a very lightly greased griddle, like a
pancake, flipping once to cook the other side.
Remove as soon as the surface blisters black.
Eat straight from the griddle. In Caracas, they
like to eat them with the doughy interior pulled
out and replaced with cream cheese or butter
and honey – high luxury. What can you expect
of city-dwellers?

When stale – a few hours old – treat as a
leftover. Soak in milk or broth to make a
porridge. Or make eggy-bread: tear in pieces,
dip in beaten egg, fry until crisp and eat with
chilli sauce.

tamales

or dumplings, humitas

The tamale is a maizemeal dumpling usually (though not always) filled with something piquant or delicious, then steamed or boiled until firm. Unlike any other dumpling, it is designed for portability and is always eaten straight from the hand. The tamale is traditionally treated as festive food since it takes many cooks to prepare and is open to as many variations as the imagination can devise. A feast of tamales – *tamalada* – is appropriate to a wedding, birthday or christening, but above all, to be taken to the churchyard to share with the ancestors on All Souls, the Day of the Dead. The indigenous inhabitants of the Americas, gathering together for a tribal occasion, feasted on tamales baked in the barbecue-pit along with any wild meat – peccary, turkey – the hunters brought home.

Another use for a tamale basket

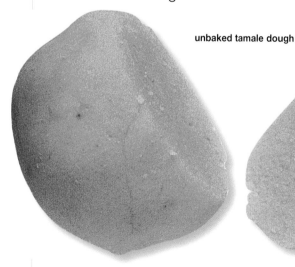

unbaked tamale dough

Manufacture

The basic material is farinaceous and the wrapper is any non-toxic foldable green leaf which will not disintegrate when heat is applied. The dough can be anything which can be mashed and will hold together, including fresh corn (the Andean *humita*, see p.79), yuca, potato, yam or plantain. A stuffing, sweet or savoury, is usual though not essential.

Appearance and taste

Variations in manufacture are many, as is only to be expected of so ancient a foodstuff. The mostly widely known is the Mexican tamale, a maize husk-wrapped dumpling made with masa harina – lye-treated precooked yellow cornmeal. Guatemala celebrates with sweet tamales coloured with chocolate. In the province of Oaxaca in southern Mexico, tamales stuffed with *mole negro* (see p.177) are wrapped in banana leaves; in Peru, where banana leaves are also used, fresh white corn dumplings are called *humitas* – wet ones. The southern Brazilians like their tamale dough moistened with coconut milk while the Amazonians make theirs with cassava meal. Each to his own – and it's as well not to argue.

Tamales rellenos

(Stuffed cornmeal dumplings)

Serves 4, allowing 3 per person

First choose your wrapper. Ready-prepared maize husks cut to size are available in packets, but these need soaking to soften. Fresh corn husks – outer leaves only, and you may need to overlap, must be trimmed at either end. Or use banana leaves cut into 30cm (12in) squares. Failing these, squares of foil will do.

The filling:

2 tablespoons oil
1 small onion, finely chopped
2 large tomatoes, skinned and chopped
About 225g (8oz) shredded turkey or chicken breast
1–2 squares black chocolate
1/2 teaspoon ground allspice
1–2 teaspoons chilli paste or flakes
Salt
Sugar (optional)

The dough:

450g (1 lb) masa harina, as above
1 teaspoon salt
3 tablespoons pork-lard or oil
Warm water or broth

The wrappers:

Lard or oil for greasing

Make the filling first. Warm the oil in a small frying pan and fry the onion gently until it softens. Bubble up and mash down to make a thick sauce. Season with salt and maybe a little sugar and stir in the remaining ingredients except the meat. Bubble up for 10 minutes to marry the flavours, and then stir in the shredded meat. Bubble up again and leave to cool.

Meanwhile, work the masa harina with the salt and lard or oil, and knead in enough warm water or broth to make a smooth, slightly sticky dough; the flour swells as you work it. Set the steamer on a low heat – enough to bring the water to a slow boil.

Now assemble the tamales. Lay the wrappers on a clean cloth, shiny-side up if using banana leaves; if using maize husks, brush lightly with oil. Dampen your hands and break off a piece of dough the size of a large walnut. Place it on a wrapper and spread with the heel of your hand as evenly as possible to make a rectangle the length and width of your hand. Drop a teaspoon of filling in the middle and bring the dough over to enclose, using a wet finger to seal the cracks. Continue until all are prepared. To wrap, fold one of the long sides of the wrapper over to enclose two thirds of the filling (the husk will bring the dough with it), fold over the other long side, then fold over the short sides to complete the enclosure. Secure with a strip of husk or string.

Bring the water in the lower deck of the steamer to the boil – a sieve set over a large saucepan will do. Line the steaming implement with leaves and pack in the tamales in neat layers, seam-side down. Cover with another layer of wrapper, lid tightly and steam for an hour, until the tamales are perfectly firm. Add more boiling water as necessary. As with any steamed pudding, the more even the cooking temperature, the lighter the dumplings.

Eat your tamales straight from the wrapper, without additional embellishment. They freeze well, if you have leftovers.

Tamales rellenos

empanadas

or empanadillas (diminutive), empada, empadhinas, pastel pies, pasties

Empanadas are street-food, hot from the frying-vat in the market or from a kiosk by the roadside and eaten from the hand. In Andean towns they are sold in every bar and gathering-place by empanadilla-ladies, the makers themselves, spotlessly aproned and wearing magnificent hand-woven wraps, making the rounds with their baskets.

empanada dough

Manufacture

A plain flour-and-water dough is rolled into a disk, stuffed with something delicious, folded over itself and deep-fried. Sometimes, though this is less usual, empanadas are baked, in which case the dough will have been enriched with lard or oil. It is the perfect way of making scarce or expensive ingredients work for a living.

Quiche Maya Indian market in Guatemala

Empada de picadinho

(Pork and chilli pie)
Serves 6–8

The Brazilian version of the meat pie: fragrant minced meat is enclosed in a hot-water crust enriched with oil. Shrimp, chicken, cheese or palm-hearts can replace the meat, and the same recipe can be used to make fist-sized pasties – *empadinha*s.

The filling:
2 tablespoons olive oil
2 garlic cloves, finely chopped
1 small onion, finely chopped
1–2 fresh chillis, de-seeded and chopped
2–3 tomatoes, finely chopped
1 tablespoon chopped oregano
350g (12oz) finely chopped or
*   minced pork*
2–3 tablespoons shredded greens or sliced
*   okra*
Salt and ground allspice

The pastry:
275g (10oz) self-raising flour
4 tablespoons olive oil
150ml (¼ pint) boiling water
½ teaspoon salt

Heat the oil in a frying pan, add all the filling ingredients and stir over a gentle heat until most of the liquid has evaporated and the meat is tender. Taste and add salt and a pinch of allpsice. Leave aside to cool while you make the pastry.

Preheat the oven to 350°F/180°C/gas mark 4.

Sieve the flour with the salt into a bowl. Make a dip in the middle and pour in the oil and boiling water. Using the hook of your hand, knead into a soft dough. Work it some more until it's smooth and elastic, then tip it onto a lightly floured board, form into a roll and cut the dough in half.

Work each piece into a ball, roll out thinly to make two rounds. Place the smaller one on an oiled and floured baking sheet and spoon the filling into the middle. Wet the edge and top with the other half. Cut a small cross in the middle for the steam to escape and mark the edges with a fork to seal.

Transfer to an oiled baking sheet and bake for 30-35 minutes, until golden and crisp. Then transfer to a baking-rack and allow to cool to room temperature. The hot-water crust won't absorb the juices and stays crisp for days.

Empanadillas de requesón

Empanadillas de requesón
(Fresh cheese pasties)
Makes about a dozen

These are little bite-sized turnovers, crisp and fragrant, made with tortilla dough and stuffed with green chillies and white cheese.

The dough:
450g (1lb) masa harina or masarepa
1 teaspoon salt
Generous 300ml (¹/2 pint) warm water

The filling:
3–4 fresh chillies, de-seeded and finely chopped
2 tablespoons chopped flat-leaf parsley
2 tablespoons chopped basil
4 tablespoons white cheese (crumbled feta, curd cheese)
A little milk or egg to bind

To cook:
Oil for deep-frying

To serve:
Pickled chillies, puréed with oil to make a dipping-sauce

Mix the flour with the salt and work in enough water to make a softish dough – err on the side of dampness. Wrap in clingfilm and leave aside for 30 minutes to swell. Meanwhile, mix the filling ingredients together.

When you're ready to fry, break off small pieces of arepa dough about the size of a walnut, roll into a little ball and flatten in the palm of your hand to make a small round disk – the thinner the better. Use your hands rather than a rolling pin or the dough will crack. Drop a little of the stuffing in the middle of the disk, paint the edge with water and fold one half over the other to enclose the filling. Continue until several are ready.

Heat enough oil to submerge the pasties completely. Slip the pasties into the hot oil one by one – the edges should acquire a fringe of small bubbles. Fry, turning once, until crisp and golden. This takes a little longer than you think. Drain on kitchen paper.

ready-made tortillas

The tortilla, a round flatbread made with yellow, white or blue cornmeal, is the daily bread of the Central Americas and – just as in wheat-growing lands bread and pasta is most often shop-bought – it is usually bought ready-prepared. Even Mexican housewives buy their tortillas from the tortilla-maker in the market: when I lived in Mexico City, ours came to the door twice a day with her basket. When no longer perfectly fresh – a few hours old – the tortilla is treated as a ready-made ingredient, taking the place of pasta or serving as the basis for many of Mexico's put-together dishes – *platos combinados* – for which half a dozen separately presented items is not considered excessive.

Manufacture

Although the tortilla is now a widely available prepared foodstuff, in its pre-commercial form, a disk of lye-treated cornmeal dough was patted out by hand and baked on a *comal*, an earthenware griddle which takes the heat of a charcoal fire evenly. Cornmeal tortillas are no larger than will comfortably sit on the spread fingers of one hand and are baked fresh every day.

Appearance and taste

Tortillas are not always round. In Colina, central Mexico, they're boat-shaped and have an edge; in the Yucatán they make double-thickness tortillas – *panuchos* – especially for splitting and filling with frijoles and hard-boiled egg. Nor are they always made of cornmeal. Wheatflour tortillas are increasingly popular, though undeniably a post-columbian preference: these are larger and paler, more pliable and fry faster than the traditional tortilla.

Buying and storing

Choose a brand you like, failing your own personal trusty tortilla-maker. Keep the tortillas in their sealed packet until required and store them in a plastic bag in a cool place once opened; they will keep for up to a week. For longer storage, freeze.

Tortilla seller in Guatemala. Note the blue-corn tortillas at the bottom of the pile

Culinary uses

The simplest way with a ready-made tortilla is to serve it as a *tostada*: left whole and fried crisp in oil or lard, topped with meat or fish or cheese, and served with beans, lettuce, chopped avocado and chilli salsa; or cut into any shape you please – ribbons (*chilaquiles*), squares (*totopos*), triangles (*nachos*) – and fried crisp before sauce is added. There is no need for deep oil – a finger's width will do. Leftover tortillas can also be layered like a lasagne – alternate layers of a creamy béchamel and chilli-spiked tomato sauce is delicious – and slipped under the grill until brown and bubbling. Then there's the *sopa seca* – 'dry soup' – a clear broth fortified with strips of tortilla in much the same way as the Chinese include noodles and the Italians add pasta.

Chilaquiles de requesón

(Chilaquiles with curd cheese)
Serves 4

This is Mexico's national breakfast. The easiest way with yesterday' s tortillas is to cut them in bite-sized pieces and reheat them in leftover sauce. Fresh tomato salsa and fresh curd cheese – the first stage in cheese-making – make this a particularly luscious version of the countryman's breakfast. Remember to snip up the tortillas the night before.

6–8 corn tortillas cut into small diamonds, dried overnight
Oil for shallow frying

The sauce:
2–3 fresh green serrano chillies, charred in a flame to blister and soften
3–4 ripe tomatoes, skinned and de-seeded
Sugar (optional)
Tomato paste (optional)
2 tablespoons finely-chopped onion
2 tablespoons chopped epasote (or dill)
Salt

To finish:
Ricotta or any fresh curd cheese
Soured cream

Reheat the tortilla diamonds in small batches in a few tablespoons of oil until they crisp a little – don't let them brown. Remove and drain.

Put the chillies and tomatoes in the processor and process to a purée. Taste and season – you may need a little sugar or a squeeze of tomato paste.

Heat a tablespoonful of the frying oil and add the sauce. Bubble up, stir in the fried tortilla pieces and bubble up again. Reduce the heat and sprinkle with the onion and optional epasote. Let it simmer gently for 8–10 minutes – shake the pan occasionally to avoid sticking.

Serve with a generous topping of ricotta and soured cream. Fortifying, particularly with refried beans (see p.94).

Totopos con huevos revueltos mexicanos

(Tortilla chips scrambled with eggs)
Serves 4

A fortifying snack enjoyed at any time, since in Mexico only one main meal is taken during the day, either at midday or at sunset, depending on the workday. Packet tortilla chips are a little on the salty side – it is best to prepare your own.

4 day-old tortillas
Oil for shallow frying
6 fresh eggs
4 tablespoons lard or oil
3 tablespoons chopped onion
4 tablespoons chopped, de-seeded ripe tomato
3–4 serrano chillies, deseeded and chopped
Salt

Totopos con huevos revueltos mexicanos, eggs scrambled with crisp tortilla chips

Cut the tortillas into small squares – the quickest way is to stack them one on top of the other and slice right through, discarding the edges for elegance. Heat a panful of shallow oil and drop in the squares, a handful at a time. Fry until lightly browned and crisp, which takes just a couple of minutes. Remove with a slotted spoon and drain on kitchen paper.

Use a fork to mix the eggs together gently with a little salt. Heat the lard or oil in a frying pan and gently cook the onion to soften – don't let it brown. Add the chopped tomato and chilli and bubble up for a few minutes to concentrate the juices – field-ripened tomatoes need less cooking to thicken. Stir the eggs and tortilla chips into the hot sauce, folding and stirring until the egg has set to soft curds.

maizemeal

or cornmeal, polenta, chuchoca (Chile)

Milled from maize-corn, this is a meal which has not been treated with lye. It is mainly found in the southern parts of South America, where the staple starch-vegetable is the potato, making the manufacturing process which produces bread or dumpling dough unnecessary.

Mayan tomb carving depicting an ancient maize god, Oaxaca, Mexico

Manufacture

To prepare your own maizemeal in the traditional way for breads and porridges, you'd need dried corn-kernels stripped from the cob and some means of grinding the corn. Modern roller-mills don't produce the right degree of roughness, so choose stone-ground if you can.

Appearance and taste

White, yellow, purple, brown, blue red and black corn is grown throughout the territory. Chuchoca can be any of these, each with its individual fragrance, or a mixture. The flavour is nutty, mild and clean, with the honeyed aftertaste common to all maize products.

Buying and storing

Maizemeal is readily available in packets, sold either as polenta or cornmeal. Polenta is usually a coarse milling, whereas cornmeal comes as fine, medium or coarse. Choose stone-ground whole-grain corn whenever you can – it has all its vitamins and minerals intact, cooks well and tastes exactly as it should. Store in an airtight tin, as other flours.

Medicinal and other uses

Maize is one of the most difficult of all grains to digest. When balanced with other foodstuffs, it's a good source of carbohydrate, minerals and vitamins. Related products include the oil extracted from the kernels, around half of whose volume is fat, much of it 'good' (i.e. polyunsaturated); cornoil is also high in linoleic acid, a substance useful in restoring the body's alkaline balance and recommended for the topical treatment of eczema.

Culinary uses

Maize-corn lacks sufficient gluten for bread-making, and is most useful in porridges and soups, or mixed with egg and milk, as a pancake. On its own, cornmeal will not make a raised dough – bread, cake or biscuit – unless blended with at least its own volume of wheat-flour. Cornbread is a bit of a misnomer: it is not a true bread at all but a baked porridge of variable density, needing to be ladled out with a spoon – hence, spoonbread. Related products: Cornflour (cornstarch), a powdery substance, is a by-product of the cornmeal industry; a thickening agent manufactured from the endosperm, it is used in desserts, particularly as an egg-substitute in custards. Corn-syrup, prepared by a process known to the Incas, is a popular replacement for maple-syrup and honey. Most nutritious in the form of *posole*, a digestible porridge and a speciality of Mexico's northern borderlands, which is made with white corn and has a delicately sweet flavour and can come as whole or cracked grains – grits.

Pan paraguayana

(Paraguayan spoonbread)

Serves 6

The festive food of Paraguay, this rich onion and cheese polenta-bake, quite soft and soupy, is served at weddings and home-comings – one of those nostalgic foodstuffs which remind expatriates of home.

225g (8oz) yellow cornmeal (fine-ground polenta)
425ml (15fl oz) hot water
110g (4oz) softened butter
4 eggs, separated
110g (4oz) fresh curd cheese (ricotta or cottage cheese)
110g (4oz) grated hard cheese (cheddar, gruyère)
1 small onion, finely chopped, lightly fried to soften
150ml (5fl oz) milk
1 teaspoon baking powder
1/2 teaspoon ground allspice
1/2 teaspoon ground cumin
1/2 teaspoon hot paprika or chilli powder
1/2 teaspoon salt

Preheat the oven to 200°C/400°F/gas mark 6. Put the cornmeal in a bowl, stir in the hot water and leave to soak and swell for 20 minutes or so.

Butter a roomy roasting tin. In a warmed bowl, beat the butter until fluffy, then beat in the egg-yolks and the curd cheese. Whisk the eggwhites until they hold soft peaks. Stir the soaked cornmeal and all the remaining ingredients into the butter-egg mixture and fold in the whisked whites. The batter will be soupy. Pour it into the tin and bake for 50–60 minutes, until firm and well-browned. Allow to cool and set for 15 minutes before cutting into squares.

Chupe de papas con chuchoca

(Polenta and potato porridge)

Serves 4 as a main dish

A *chupe* is a Chilean soup or savoury porridge – the word means to slurp – and can be as soupy or dry as you please.

Chupe de papas con chuchoca

Here chuchoca, cornmeal or coarse-milled polenta, is combined with potatoes to make a nourishing winter dish. Good with roast chicken.

2–3 large potatoes, peeled and chunked
1 thick slice pumpkin, skinned and cut into chunks
About 1.2 litres (2 pints) chicken or beef-bone stock or plain water
1 onion, finely chopped
2–3 garlic cloves, finely chopped
4 level tablespoons coarse-milled polenta
1 teaspoon chilli flakes or finely-chopped fresh chilli
A handful fresh basil, leaves stripped from the stalks
Salt
2 hardboiled eggs, peeled and quartered

Put the potatoes, pumpkin and stock or water in a roomy pan with the onions and garlic. Bring to the boil, stir in the polenta, add a little salt and bring back to the boil. Put the lid on loosely, turn down the heat and simmer for 30–40 minutes until the polenta is perfectly soft and the vegetables are tender. Finish with chilli flakes, basil and quartered hardboiled eggs.

Corn muffins

The Mexican equivalent of the scone – quick, easy and unbeatable for breakfast.

225g (8oz) fine-milled yellow cornmeal
225g (8oz) wheatflour
1 rounded teaspoon baking powder
1 egg
150ml (7 fl oz) milk
150ml (7 fl oz) vegetable oil

Preheat the oven to 190°C/375°F/gas mark 5.

Mix the dry ingredients together in one bowl. Mix the wet ingredients together in another. Blend thoroughly and drop into muffin tins, well-greased (or lined with butterpaper). Don't fill them more than two thirds full. Bake for 20–25 minutes, until well-puffed and beautifully brown.

These are best eaten straight from the tin, with a bowl of milky coffee or hot chocolate for dipping.

white bean

or haricot, white kidney, frijol blanco, frejol blanco, navy bean, poroto (Chile), habichuela, canellini, Great Northern bean (*Phaseolus vulgaris*)

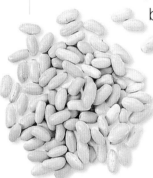

In all its shapes and sizes the bean is a remarkable foodstuff – the perfect diet in storable, portable form. Its transportability made it invaluable as ship's store: hence navy beans. A member of the pea-family native to the Americas, hundreds of different varieties had already been developed in pre-Columbian times, long before the arrival of the Europeans. Throughout its land of origin, taste in beans is astonishingly local; nevertheless, the white kidney-shaped is undeniably the universal bean: the bean which can take the place of all others, and does.

How it grows

The bean is easy to grow, undemanding of terrain and simple to harvest and store – in short, the ideal storecupboard legume. It is often grown in association with maize, which provides it with a convenient climbing-pole, and one of the squashes, which keeps the weeds down between the rows. Easy, when you've had a few thousand years to work it out.

Appearance and taste

Kidney-shaped, of varying size and multiple variations of colour, the most commonly appreciated variety outside its land of origin is the white haricot. Some five hundred bean varieties are now grown world-wide, each with its own distinctive shape, colour, degree of flouriness, creaminess, butteriness, firmness, tenderness and flavour. To generalise, the taste and texture is cooked-chestnut: floury, earthy and sweet.

Buying and storing

The fresher the bean, the better. This year's crop will feel a little springy under the pressure of your fingertips – so buy from a shop with a high turnover. Beans should not be stored from one year to another. Bury a few dried chillies or a garlic clove in the bean jar to keep the bugs at bay. To shorten preparation time, pre-soak and store in the freezer until needed.

Medicinal and other uses

This is the perfect body-and-brain food: cholesterol-free, high in vegetable-protein, rich in complex carbohydrates and liberally endowed with vitamins, minerals and fibre. The drawback? The bean-eaters well-known propensity to flatulence, a phenomenon which can be explained by the presence of oligosaccharides which make even the best-cooked bean hard to digest. Whatever they may say, neither cooks nor chemists have come up with an infallible method of counteracting the problem. Discretion is the better part of valour. Follow local custom and eat your beanpot at midday, avoid it in the evening, and leave it strictly alone when in love.

Culinary uses

The quality of the beans dictates the length of time they take to soften – really fresh beans take no more than an hour. Don't add salt until the end to avoid toughening the skins, and also wait until the end of the cooking to add acidic ingredients – tomato, vinegar, lemon juice – which, say those who know, can double the cooking time.

Bean market, Ecuador

Frijoles con morcilla, a creamy white-bean stew with crisply fried blood sausage

Meanwhile, fry the morcilla slices in a little oil (some morcillas are quite fatty enough to fry without assistance). Or you can, if you wish to keep it simple, stir the morcilla slices directly into the beanpot – morcillas are precooked, as are all blood-sausages, but frying gives a deliciously crisp texture and caramelised flavour.

Serve the beans in deep bowls, sprinkled with the fried morcilla, chilli, coriander and onion. Eat with a spoon.

Porotos con acelgas

(Beans and greens)
Serves 4 as a starter

A simple starter, useful when you have leftover beans. Tinned beans are fine. Although I suggest hardboiled egg, the topping can be anything which excites the taste-buds: crumbled chorizo crisped in a little oil, pinekernels or flaked almonds instead of peanuts – whatever you have in the cupboard.

Frijoles con morcilla

(Haricot beans with black pudding)
Serves 6–8

These are pre-Columbian beans given a hispanic enrichment: there were no meat-animals in the Americas before the arrival of the Spaniards, who brought in pigs as well as cows and chickens to remedy what they saw as a serious lack. Spanish black puddings – *morcilla* – are deliciously spicy, garlicky, and flavoured with oregano.

450g (1lb) white beans, soaked overnight and drained
A whole head of garlic, singed to blacken the covering
2 mild dried chillies (pasilla or pimenton), de-seeded and torn
A short length cinnamon-stick
2–3 cloves
1 tablespoon crumbled oregano
2 carrots or parsnips, scraped and cut into chunks
1 tablespoon salt

To finish:
450g (1lb) small potatoes, rinsed and scrubbed
A handful spinach, rinsed and shredded
1 ring (about 225g/8oz) morcilla (black pudding), sliced
A little olive oil
1 fresh red chilli, de-seeded and finely chopped
3 tablespoons chopped coriander
3 tablespoons chopped onion

Drain the beans and transfer them to a roomy pot with the garlic, chilli, cinnamon, cloves, oregano, carrot or parsnip. Add enough water to cover generously, bring to the boil, turn down the heat and simmer, with the lid on loosely, for 1–2 hours, until the beans are perfectly tender.

Remove the garlic head (squeeze the soft interior back into the pot) and add the potatoes and the salt. Bubble up again (you may need some boiling water), and simmer for another 20 minutes or so, until the potatoes are tender. Stir in the spinach and bubble up for another 5 minutes, until the leaves wilt.

600ml (1 pint) ready-cooked white haricot beans
Generous handful chard or spinach, shredded
Juice of 1 lemon
4 tablespoons olive oil
1 dried chilli (pasilla or ancho), de-seeded and cut into matchsticks
2 tablespoons toasted peanuts, roughly crushed
1 tablespoon chopped spring onion
2 hardboiled eggs, peeled and chopped
Salt and pepper

Bring the beans and a little of their cooking liquor to the boil in a small pan, drain and toss with the shredded greens – the heat will be just enough to wilt the leaves. Dress with the lemon juice and 3 tablespoons of the olive oil, as well as salt and pepper.

Heat the remaining oil and fry the chilli strips – a moment, no more, just until they change colour and become crisp. Tip the contents of the pan on the beans. Finish with crushed peanuts, spring onion and chopped hardboiled eggs.

black bean

or turtle bean, frijol negro (Mexican and other Spanish-speaking countries), feijao nero (Brazil) (*Phaseolus vulgaris*)

The black bean is a smallish, ebony-coloured kidney-bean. A staple of the store cupboard throughout the territory, particularly in Mexico, the Caribbean, Venezuela and northern Brazil, including Rio – where it's the star of the feijoada, Brazil's national dish (see p.127) – it's relegated to cattle fodder in Colombia.

How it grows

A very pretty plant, the flowers of the black bean are blush-pink, the pods a sunny yellow, and the seeds as black and shiny as onyx, the sacred stone of the Aztec priesthood – perhaps accounting for its esteem in the land of Monteczuma.

Appearance and taste

The black bean is the gourmet bean. The flavour is subtly earthy with more than a hint of mushroom and an underlying chestnut sweetness. The flesh cooks to a creamy softness, while the skins, though long cooking makes them tender, never lose their shine. In Mexican cooking the black bean often appears in mashed form, as *frijoles refritos* (see p.94), a bean-hash which also serves as a stuffing for tacos and tamales.

Buying and storing

Look for even-sized beans with a clean, shiny skin and no powderiness; check for dryness – a sign the beans are a little long in the tooth. They should still feel a little springy when pressed between the fingertips.

Medicinal and other uses

Look no further for the perfect diet in a pod, complete with protein, carbohydrate, vitamins and all necessary minerals.

Culinary uses

Usually cooked on its own and only combined with other foodstuffs at the moment of serving, the black bean takes longer than most to soften, so a little forward planning is advisable. For convenience, cook in advance and freeze supplies for later.

Plato combinado mexicano

(Mexican mixed platter)
Serves 1

The combination-platter is a way of eating rather than a specific recipe, since the composition is no more or less than exactly what pleases you within the limitations of your purse, with beans and tortillas the only immutable. Each additional element is presented separately and as appetisingly as possible, with attention paid to nutritional balance, digestibility and visual drama. Colours are mingled for contrast or compatibility: white

on black, green with green, red for drama, and so on. The care invariably taken in putting these simple basic foodstuffs together – some needing lengthy preparation, others virtually none, but making the most of each – says much about the Latino attitude to life.

Choose from:
Frijoles de olla (see opposite)
Tomato, coriander and chilli salsa
Rajas poblanos (ribbons of roasted green pepper dressed with oil and garlic)
Soured cream
Crumbled fresh white cheese (ricotta is a good approximation)
Sliced or mashed avocado dressed with lime-juice
Rough salt
Fried eggs
Quartered hard-boiled eggs
Shredded chicken or pork
Shredded lettuce
Onion slices soaked in salted water to soften, dressed with sugar
Pickled chillies (jalapenos, naturally)

Arrange your choices on an oval platter. You will need tortillas for scooping. Eat with your fingers and be thankful.

Frijoles de olla
(Mexican black beanpot)
Serves 6–8

This is best prepared a day ahead to give time for the flavour to develop. In Mexico, plain-cooked pot-beans are served on their own after the main course, with a soft tortilla for mopping, or during the main course, in a little bowl on the side, to be dipped into at will.

900g (2lb) black beans
1 onion
2 tablespoons oil (the Mexicans use fresh pork lard)
About 2.4 litres (4 pints) hot water
Salt

Run the beans through your hands – it is therapeutic, like worry-beads – and discard any tiny stones which sneak through even in the best brands. Rinse twice: black beans are vulnerable to unwanted visitors. You can pre-soak them overnight to speed up the cooking process, but this is not essential.

Put the beans in an earthenware or enamel casserole with the onion and oil or lard. Pour in enough hot water to cover the beans to a depth of at least 8cm (3in). Bring to simmering point, then turn down the heat, put the lid on tightly and leave to simmer (if you prefer in a moderate oven, set it at 170°C/325°F/gas mark 3). Keep an eye on them, add hot water if necessary, and leave to cook for as long as it takes for the skins to soften completely – about two hours, sometimes three. Then add salt. (Never salt beans until the skins have softened, or they will be tough.)

Continue to cook until perfectly tender. If you need to add water – check regularly – it should always be hot; and never drain the beans after cooking and throw away the liquid: evaporate the liquor by removing the lid from the pot if you want your beans dry rather than soupy. Those who use a pressure cooker should allow 40 minutes.

Serve with soft tortillas. For a Venezuelan version, add extra boiling water and finish with finely-chopped chilli, a sprinkle of cumin and a swirl of oil coloured bright red with achiote. For the Cuban version, stir in a dash of rum.

pinto bean

or speckled bean, frijol refrito, brown bean (*Phaseolus vulgaris*)

This is the everyday bean of the Mexican beanpot, the commonest of the tribe. The peasant's reliable field-crop, it is to be found simmering on every stove throughout the region.

Appearance and taste

A highly hybridised medium-sized bean, the brown bean is squarish in shape and caramel to chestnut in colour. The flavour is earthy and robust, the texture mealy, softening to a mush.

Buying and storing

Look for the fresh pods in the autumn and buy from a reliable source with a high turnover. Test for freshness by squeezing gently between your finger and thumb – you' re looking for a slight give.

Medicinal and other uses

Like other beans, it is high in protein, with the full complement of carbohydrate, vitamins and minerals. The skin softens satisfactorily in the pot, allowing for easy digestion.

Culinary uses

The brown bean is best eaten fresh in season, when it benefits from the inclusion of something sweet: a seasoning of corn-syrup or a handful of fresh corn-kernels. Beans from store are good for soups and for making baked beans, probably best known as the everyday refrito bean, when they are first tenderised by boiling, then fried in lard or oil to form a soft, homogeneous mass which can be scooped up with a tortilla.

Sacks of beans on sale in Sicuani, Peru

Frijoles refritos

(Refried brown beans)
Serves 4

A second cooking – *un refrito* – reduces the soupy contents of the bean pot to a thick deliciously roasted paste. When once prepared it can be frozen almost indefinitely. In Mexico, a plain refrito is eaten for breakfast with fried eggs, at midday after the meat, with tortilla chips for supper – in fact at any time a person might feel hungry.

950g (2lb) ready-cooked beans (with their
*   liquor, if home-cooked)*
6 tablespoons good lard, dripping or oil
2 garlic cloves or 1 small onion, finely chopped
Tortilla chips

Heat the lard or oil in a large heavy frying pan. Add the garlic or onion and fry for a minute or two, until it softens – don't let it brown. Add a ladleful of the beans and their liquor and mash down over the heat until all the liquid has evaporated, scraping and turning to avoid sticking. Add the rest of the beans a ladleful at a time, until all is reduced to a thick aromatic paste which sits like a soft pancake in the pan. That's all. The same technique can be applied to any left-over bean dish. However soupy, sooner or later, it will dry and thicken.

Frijoles pintos con masa mora

(Brown beans with mushy corn)
Serves 4–6

Robust and satisfying, this is the traditional summer Sunday lunch, made when the beans are still tender and the corn is young and sweet.

450g (1lb) fresh, shelled beans
450g (1lb) piece pumpkin, skinned and chunked
1 tablespoon soft pork-lard or oil
1 link soft chorizo, crumbled (or 4 slices bacon, diced)
2 large mild onions, finely chopped
1 red pepper, de-seeded and diced
1 carrot, scraped and coarsely grated
Salt
600ml (1 pint) fresh corn kernels
A handful epasote or fresh basil leaves, chopped

To finish:
2 garlic cloves, skinned and roughly chopped
1 tablespoon pimentón picante (or paprika with a pinch of powdered chilli)
1–2 tablespoons oil
Salt

Put the shelled beans and the pumpkin in a roomy pot, add enough hot water to cover to a depth of two fingers, bring to the boil, reduce the heat, put the lid on and simmer until the pumpkin has melted to a soupy sauce and the beans are perfectly tender: 40–60 minutes.

Meanwhile, heat the lard or oil gently in a small frying pan and fry the chorizo or diced bacon until it takes a little colour. Add the onion, red pepper and carrot, salt lightly and fry until soft and a little caramelised. Stir into the beans and simmer for another 10 minutes.

Meanwhile, put the corn-kernels in the liquidiser with a ladleful of the bean-liquor and the epasote or basil leaves (reserve a few of the best). Process to a purée, stir into the beans and simmer for another 15 minutes – dilute with a little boiling water if it looks too thick.

To make the finishing oil, crush the garlic cloves with a little salt and work in the oil and pimentón. Serve in deep earthenware bowls, with a swirl of scarlet oil and an epasote or basil leaf to finish.

red bean

or poroto pinto, cranberry bean, borlotti, bolita
(*Phaseolus vulgaris*)

A medium-sized kidney-shaped bean, the colour varies from the deep crimson of the poroto pinto (*pinto* means 'coloured') to the coffee-and-cream cranberry bean to the prettily speckled borlotti. The bolitas (little balls) are multi-coloured, small and irregularly shaped beans – as unalike one another as pebbles on the beach. Red beans keep their carmine colour when cooked and remain glossy when cooled, making them pretty in a bean salad. On those Caribbean islands which came under Spain's influence, they're combined with rice cooked in coconut milk in a dish called *moros y cristianos* – Moors and Christians.

Culinary uses

A word of warning; red beans, if pre-soaked, accumulate toxins in the skin which must be neutralised. Rinse after soaking, bring to the boil in fresh water, boil for 10 minutes, then drain and add fresh boiling water before continuing cooking. This preliminary boiling is essential. To avoid toughening the skin, use soft water for the soaking and cooking-broth – rainwater or bottled water with a low calcium content. This is because calcium slows down the cooking time to such an extent that the beans can fall apart without ever achieving tenderness.

Appearance and taste

The cranberry or red bean is a mealy bean with a deep red skin, pale creamy flesh and a markedly robust, earthy flavour. Red beans are particularly popular in Chile, the Caribbean and southern Brazil. They are eaten in the Caribbean in combination with rice and coconut (see Jamaican rice'n'peas, p.73).

Buying and storing

Choose beans with a clear bright colour which feel a little springy when pressed between the finger and thumb. To sidestep the problems outlined in Culinary uses, below, buy them ready-prepared in cans.

Medicinal and other uses

Red beans – particularly the *bolita* – are higher in calcium and sodium than other beans.

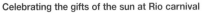

Celebrating the gifts of the sun at Rio carnival

Ensalada de porotos pintos con pencas

(Red bean salad with wild artichokes)

Serves 4 as a starter

Red beans are here combined in a simple salad with *pencas*, the rosettes of a wild artichoke, a member of the thistle family and one of the first wild vegetables of spring – a successful combination of flavours. The wild thistle can be replaced by the cultivated: cardoons or artichokes.

450g (1lb) ready-cooked red beans (canned is fine)
4 pencas or 2 cardoon sticks or 6 artichoke hearts, sliced
Lemon juice
1–2 fresh chorizos, sliced
2–3 tablespoons olive oil
1 red onion, finely sliced into half-moons
1 tablespoon crumbled or chopped oregano
Salt

Scrape the thorny edges off the pencas and trim off any brown or stringy bits. If using cardoon or artichokes, trim, scrape and slice. Cook in a little water for 10–15 minutes until the vegetables soften. Stir in the beans, reheat and leave to cool.

When you're ready to serve, fry the chorizo slices in the oil until caramelised and crisp – don't let them burn. Pour the contents of the frying pan onto the beans, salt lightly and finish with lemon juice, onion and oregano.

Bolitas con jamón

(Chilean red beans with bacon)

Serves 4–6

This is the classic Chilean beanpot, fortified by a bacon knuckle and finished with *color chileno* – pork lard flavoured with garlic and coloured a rosy red with achiote or pimentón (see p.186).

450g (1lb) bolita (or any other red bean), soaked overnight
A bacon knuckle
1/2 whole head of garlic
1–2 onions, peeled and roughly chopped

3–4 cloves
1 large carrot, scraped and diced
1 short stick cinnamon
Scraping of nutmeg
1–2 dried chillies, de-seeded and torn

To finish:
450g (1lb) small yellow potatoes, scraped
450g (1lb) mild paprika peppers, roasted and cut into strips
1–2 tablespoons color chileno (see p.186)
Salt

Drain the beans and rinse them in two changes of fresh water. Put them in a roomy saucepan with water to cover generously, bring to the boil, cook for 10 minutes, and drain. Tuck in the bacon knuckle and enough fresh water to cover to a depth of two fingers.

Ensalada de porotos pintos con pencas, a sophisticated combination of red beans, red onion and artichokes

Bring the pot to the boil and skim off the grey foam which rises. Add the remaining ingredients (stick the cloves in an onion for ease of retrieval). Bring back to the boil, turn down the heat, put the lid on and cook for 2–3 hours, until the beans are quite soft. Keep the broth at a gentle boil – don't let the temperature drop or add salt or the skins won't soften. If you need to add more water, make sure it's boiling.

When the beans are floury and tender, add the finishing ingredients: first the potatoes, and then, after 15 minutes, the pepper strips. Bubble up each time. Allow another 10 minutes and stir in the color chileno. Serve with plantain fritters, *patacones* (see p.207).

lima bean

or habas grandes, limenos, butter beans
(*Phaseolus limensis*)

Peru's native bean is a large, ivory-white bean, flattish and kidney-shaped, first cultivated by the Incas on the Altiplano. It is the largest of all the store-cupboard legumes.

Preparing lima beans by a Peruvian roadside

How it grows

The lima bean is a vigorous climber, prolific, cropping over several months and capable of yielding two crops a year.

Appearance and taste

These are tender, creamy-fleshed beans which hold their shape in the pot and have a delicate flavour of freshly skinned walnuts: the aristocrat of the bean family.

Buying and storing

They are worth seeking out fresh in the pod – bright green – when they appear on the market in the early winter. The variety known as the Christmas lima (*limeno de navidad*) is particularly large and plump, ivory-white with a distinctive maroon streaking. It is sometimes sold vacuum-packed, when it can be surprisingly expensive. When fresh and young, the skin should be soft enough to pierce with a fingernail. Lima beans are also available in jars and cans – useful for salads and as a side-dish, less so for a slow-simmered stew.

Medicinal and other uses

When fresh, limas are easily digestible, high in protein and heavily alkaline: good for building muscle. Store-beans are harder to digest and the skins can irritate delicate internal organs.

Culinary uses

The lima contains toxins, potentially deadly cyanide compounds, which must be removed in the cooking process (not necessary if buying ready-cooked). Boil the beans in an uncovered pot so that the gases can escape with the steam. This precaution is necessary for all lima-bean foodstuffs – fresh, dried or sprouted.

Ensalada navideño

(Christmas salad)
Serves 4 as a starter or side-dish

A simple salad, good with roast meats or on its own as a starter. While Peruvian lemons are mild and sweet, the bitter orange (Seville or 'marmalade') gives the dish its own special aroma.

450g (1lb) cooked lima beans
1 mild onion, finely sliced
Juice and zest 1 bitter orange or 1/2 lemon
*   and 1/2 orange*
4 tablespoons olive oil
1 green or yellow chilli, de-seeded and finely
*   chopped*
2 tablespoons chopped parsley
Salt

To serve (optional):
Fresh sweetcorn, plain boiled

Combine all the ingredients, leave in a cool place for a couple of hours to soften the onion and marry the flavours, and serve at room temperature, with slices of lightly cooked fresh sweetcorn.

Cocido limeño

(Butter beans with pumpkin)

Serves 4–6

Peru' s favourite Christmas dish, made with the year's new crop: country-woman's beanpot. When cooked on the doorstep over an open fire, the pots fill the narrow streets of the mountain villages with fragrant steam.

*225 g (8oz) butterbeans (limas), soaked
  overnight*
*450g (1lb) yellow-fleshed potatoes, peeled and
  cubed in bite-sized pieces*
*450g (1lb) pumpkin or any winter squash,
  cubed in bite-size pieces*

600ml (1 pint) fresh or frozen corn-kernels
Salt

Flavouring salsa:
3 yellow aji (chilli), de-seeded and chopped
1 small yellow onion, finely chopped
*2 scallions or 6 spring onions, finely chopped
  with their green*
3 garlic cloves, finely chopped
2 tablespoons olive oil

To finish:
Chopped parsley
Crumbled white cheese such as feta

Cocido limeño, a cheerful winter beanpot

Cook the beans in a roomy pot with enough water to cover. Don't put the lid on. The water should tremble but never come off the boil. Allow 2 hours (1 hour if the beans are fresh) and cook until soft but not mushy. Add boiling water as and when necessary, but no salt.

Meanwhile, bubble up the salsa ingredients in a small pan, and set aside to combine the flavours.

When the beans are tender, add the vegetables and extra boiling water, salt and the prepared salsa, and cook for another half hour, until the vegetables are perfectly soft. The dish should be moist but not soupy. Finish with a handful of chopped parsley and crumbled white cheese – feta is the right texture.

eggs, dairy and cheese

Eggs and dairy-foods are relative newcomers to the New World kitchen. Since there were no barnyard animals in the pre-Columbian Americas, Europe's domesticated egg-layers and milk-producers – along with the sty-pig, who cleans up the by-products of the dairy-industry – were absorbed straight into an existing culinary habit. The welcome was enthusiastic, since both added not only variety and protein, but a touch of the exotic to everyday dishes, making them special. The appearance of a quartered hardboiled egg poised elegantly on its bed of vegetables, or a handful of crumbled white cheese sprinkled over a dish of black beans, is greeted with pleasure and a festive sense of enjoyment, even today when eggs and dairy products are common culinary currency.

eggs

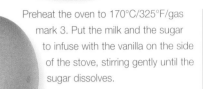

or *huevos, oves*

The eggs of wild birds, reptiles and some insects were eaten by the indigenous peoples of the regions, but it was not until the arrival of the Europeans that the hen's egg became available.

Buying and storing

To tell if an egg is past its best, put it in water: if it lies flat on the bottom, it's fresh; if it tips up at the broad end and sits vertically, it's stale; if – heaven forbid – it bobs up to the surface and floats horizontally, you've been had for a chicken.

Medicinal and other uses

The egg is incomparably useful as a foodstuff. A quarter of the egg's volume delivers equal quantities of protein and fat along with all the vitamins and minerals necessary to nourish a chick. Its admittedly high content of artery-clogging cholesterol is balanced by a pair of unclogging substances, lecithin and amino acids.

Culinary uses

Eggs are included in both sweet and savoury recipes, though their functions are rather different. Hardboiled eggs, quartered or sliced, are often popped on top of vegetarian dishes – particularly the traditional beans/maize/squash combinations – as a luxurious finishing touch. When used in desserts, it is in the form of sensationally sweet custards and cakes: Latin ladies have a great fondness for sugary treats.

Flan
(Caramel custard)
Serves 4

Flan – a baked egg custard – is Latin America's most popular pudding, as it is in Spain. You can buy it as a packet mix, but it's easy and much more delicious if you make your own.

600ml (1 pint) full cream milk
3 tablespoons castor sugar
1 inch vanilla pod
1 whole egg plus 4 egg yolks

For the caramel:
3 heaped tablespoons castor sugar
3 tablespoons water

El Alto market, La Paz, Bolivia

Preheat the oven to 170°C/325°F/gas mark 3. Put the milk and the sugar to infuse with the vanilla on the side of the stove, stirring gently until the sugar dissolves.

Make the caramel by melting the sugar and water together in a small pan and heating it until the sugar caramelises. Take it off the heat as soon as it turns a rich beech-leaf bronze: once the colour turns it will be black in no time. Pour the caramel into the base of 1 large or several small moulds and roll the caramel round the sides to coat.

Remove the vanilla pod from the infusion, split it and scrape all the sticky little black seeds back into the milk. Use a fork to mix in the eggs, taking care not to incorporate air, and pour the mixture into the caramel-coated moulds.

Set the moulds in a roasting tin. Pour in enough boiling water to come halfway up the sides. Bake for 40–50 minutes, by which time the custard should be firm. If the temperature is too high, it'll bubble and acquire watery little air holes; if it's too low, it'll take longer to set. This keeps well in the fridge. Don't unmould it until you're ready to serve, then reverse it onto a plate. The caramel provides its own sticky little pool of sauce.

Huevos rancheros

(Ranch-hand's eggs)

Serves 4

The best breakfast in the world, as served in every Mexican trucker's pull-in from the cactus-country of upstate Tijuana to the forests of the River Uxumazintla.

4 tablespoons oil
4 corn tortillas
8 free-range eggs

The sauce:
1/2 mild onion, chopped small
1 garlic clove

1 green chilli, de-seeded and diced
450g (1lb) ripe tomatoes, diced
Salt

To finish:
2 tablespoons grated cheese
1/2 ripe avocado, roughly mashed with a little lime or lemon juice, salt and chopped coriander leaves

Heat the oil in a frying pan and slip in the tortillas one by one to heat up – they should soften but not brown. Remove to warm plates. In the same pan, fry the eggs so that the edges of the whites are frilly and the yolks are just set, and pop each onto its tortilla.

Now make the sauce. Fry the onion and garlic in what's left of the oil (you may need a little more) – letting it sizzle and soften for a few minutes but not letting it brown. Add the chilli and turn up the heat. Add the chopped tomato and let everything bubble up and reduce fiercely for a few minutes until you have a fragrant little sauce. Taste and season – a little sugar, perhaps?

Spoon the sauce over the eggs, finishing each plate with a little pile of grated cheese and a spoonful of the chopped, dressed avocado. Beats a Sunday morning hangover any day of the week.

Huevos rancheros, fried eggs with all the trimmings

milk and cream

Fresh, condensed and evaporated goat's and cow's milk are available throughout the region. Although Andean herdsmen sometimes milked their cameloids in the suckling season for local consumption, milk and cream were not known elsewhere until the arrival of the Hispanic colonisers.

Manufacture

Condensed and evaporated milk is often preferred to fresh, a taste acquired in the days when refrigeration was either unavailable or impractical. Condensed is the term applied to sweetened whole or skimmed milk reduced by two-thirds. Evaporated is whole milk reduced by two-thirds but unsweetened.

Buying and storing

Fresh milk is susceptible to adulteration and contamination, so care should always be taken when buying from unknown sources in a hot climate. If in doubt, boil to sterilise. Homogenised, pasturised and all forms of treated milk sold in sealed containers are a sensible alternative.

Medicinal and other uses

Milk is just about the perfect foodstuff for babies and grannies alike, equipped with protein, calcium, phosphorus, vitamins A and D, sugar in the form of lactose, and riboflavin. On the minus side, it's a bit high on sodium. Milk in all its forms is digestible and nourishing, although lactose intolerance – leading to digestive upsets – is a reaction not confined to non-dairy nations. Goat's milk does not normally cause the same problems. Condensed and evaporated milk, when diluted according to instructions, is more easily digested than fresh.

Culinary uses

Fresh milk and cream, luxury items before fridges were available, are used in Latin America as in the European kitchen – combined with fruits as a refreshing drink, included in fruit desserts, and used as an enrichment or cooking-liquid in soups, sauces, milk-puddings and custards both sweet and savoury. Tinned milk – condensed or evaporated – is stirred into infusions such as coffee and chocolate instead of cream. Peruvian fruit syrups are often topped with condensed milk.

Dulce de leche
(Caramelised milk)
Serves 4–6

This is unquestionably the best-loved of all Latin American desserts. As a child, however, I hated it. I first tasted it as a schoolgirl in Montevideo, when it was the inevitable conclusion to school dinners.

Llamas can provide milk for Andean herders

Dulce de leche with whipped cream

Perhaps my dislike was because as a war-baby, I had little experience of sweet things – a peculiarity which made me popular at meal times, since my school-mates were only too happy to mop up my helping. Nowadays I love it with whipped cream.

1 large can (14oz) sweetened condensed milk
1 large can (12oz) evaporated milk

Combine the two milks in a heavy saucepan and cook gently, stirring steadily, over a medium heat for 20–30 minutes, until thick and lightly caramelised. The longer you cook it, the thicker and darker it becomes. It keeps for months in or out of the fridge, though after a few days, it goes grainier.

In Peru, it is used as a stuffing for churros – deep fried tubes of pastry-dough – a street food much enjoyed by both adults and children. It is also used as a layering for cakes, to stuff cream-puffs, and as a basis for ice creams.

Coajada con nuez moscada, soft milky curds dusted with grated nutmeg

Coajada con nuez moscada

(Junket with nutmeg)

Serves 4

Junket is the soft curds which form when fresh milk is 'turned' with rennet.

600ml (1 pint) fresh whole milk
1 teaspoon rennet
1 tablespoon sugar
Freshly grated nutmeg

Warm the milk to blood temperature, reproducing the natural heat of the milk when fresh from the cow. Add the sugar, then stir in the rennet, pour into glasses or earthenware jars and leave to set at room temperature – it'll take a couple of hours. Dust with nutmeg and serve with a crisp biscuit.

butter and lard

or manteca, mantequilla

Butter – fresh or clarified – is used for cakes and biscuits among the cooks of those Caribbean islands which came under the influence of the Celtic nations of Europe: Britain and France. Elsewhere, pork-lard is the natural choice for shortening – although this is being replaced by margarine.

Manufacture

Butter is the fatty element in milk separated from the liquid by churning. Simply put fresh milk in a container and shake it: sooner or later you'll have butter. In this form it can either be heated and the fat further separated from the whey – a process called clarifying, which increases shelf-life without refrigeration; or it can be salted (heavily or lightly) and kept cool. Pork lard – the enriching fat of choice throughout the hispanic world – is used for shallow-frying as well as in baking to shorten the dough for pies and pastries. Pure white lard, mild and sweet, is made by melting pork fat very very slowly in the lowest possible oven with a little water to keep it from any possibility of browning – commercially-prepared stuff won't do.

Buying and storing

The purer the product, the more delicious it is. Store it in the fridge; if kept cool and in the dark, it will last for months.

Medicinal and other uses

According to new research, both butter and lard soften the effects of too much red wine. Our ancestors knew they kept you warm in winter and made other foods more palatable and digestible. And anyway, a little of what you fancy does you good.

Culinary uses

In recipes for biscuits and cakes, lard gives the lightest results, butter the most delicious flavour. Take your pick. As a frying medium, clarified butter and pure lard have a burn-point only a little lower than oil, allowing you to cook at high temperatures. Cakes and biscuits made with clarified butter or lard stay fresh for longer.

Beijos de cafezinho

(Coffee kisses)
Makes about 2 dozen little biscuits

Brazilian coffee cookies made with a beaten-biscuit mix, delicious with *doce*

de banana **(see p.205) and vanilla ice cream. Clarified butter, though not essential, gives a crisper result. To clarify butter, warm till it liquefies, then pour off the oil, leaving the milky residue behind.**

350g (12oz) plain flour
125g (4 oz) clarified butter, softened
125g (4 oz) brown sugar
1 medium egg
2 tablespoons very strong black coffee
Coffee beans to decorate

Sieve the flour with a pinch of salt. Beat the butter and sugar until light and fluffy, then beat in the egg forked up with the coffee. Work in the flour to make a ball of soft dough – you may need a little more flour. Cover with clingfilm and leave to rest in the fridge for an hour to firm up.

Heat the oven to 220°C/425°F/gas mark 7. On a lightly floured board, roll out the dough. Cut out rounds and arrange on a buttered baking sheet, allowing plenty of space for them to spread. Dampen the coffee beans and pop one on each biscuit. Bake for 20-25 minutes until golden. Transfer to a baking rack while still soft and warm – they crisp as they cool.

Cattle grazing in front of Osomo volcano in the Chilean lake district

Mantecados navideños
(Christmas biscuits)

Makes about 2 dozen biscuits

Literally translated, lardy-biscuits. Very soft and delicate, wrapped up in scraps of tissue paper for storage, this is the treat all good children hope to find in their shoes when the Three Kings bring them their presents on January 6th. This is a beaten dough – rather easier and quicker than the more familiar rubbing-in method.

225g (8oz) flour
4 tablespoons roughly-ground blanched
  almonds
1 tablespoon ground cinnamon
1 teaspoon ground cardamom
225g (8 oz) fresh white lard, softened
4 tablespoons icing sugar
1–2 tablespoons cold water

Sieve the flour into the ground almonds and mix in the spices. Beat the lard with the sugar until light and fluffy – easiest in a food processor. Work in the flour and nut mixture until you have a soft ball of dough. Cover with a clean cloth, and leave to rest for an hour in a cool place to firm up.

Heat the oven to 350°F/180°C/gas mark 4. Roll the dough out to twice the thickness of a pound coin. Cut out neat little rounds with a biscuit cutter and transfer to a well-buttered baking sheet. Press together the scraps with the tips of your fingers and cut out as many more rounds as you can.

Bake for 15–20 minutes, until pale gold. Transfer gently to a baking rack and leave to cool. The result is like very soft, crumbly shortbread. Wrap in scraps of tissue paper before storing in an airtight tin.

Beijos de cafezinho, crisp coffee biscuits from Brazil

cheese

soft curd cheese

mature cheese

fresh cheese

pressed curd cheese

or queso fresco, queso maduro

In Latin America – which in cheese-related matters takes its lead from Spain and Portugal – store-cupboard cheeses are mostly nothing fancy, belonging to the familiar Mediterranean tradition of one-type-fits-all, cut-curd, basket-drained cheeses which take their flavour from the milk – cow's, goat's or sheep's – from which they're made. Mexico has a heat-treated mozzarella-type cheese, *queso asadero*, which melts in long strings, and a cheddar-type, *queso chihuahua*, much liked for quesadillas.

Manufacture

All cheese begins with a curd – the soft lumps which form when milk turns sour or when a curdling agent such as rennet is added. Rennet is a substance found in the stomach-lining of all lactating mammals (ourselves included). Milk can also be 'turned' – in essence, a process of digestion – with curdling agents found in a wide variety of plants, particularly the young buds of several members of the thistle family (including artichokes), fig-tree sap and an infusion of any member of the flytrap family (insectivorous little plants with glaucous leaves).

Appearance and taste

Traditionally, farm cheeses are small enough to be transportable, and round, since this is the most convenient shape both for cutting and storing. They are often rubbed with chilli-powder and popped on a beam to dry and mature.

Buying and storing

Hard cheese should be stored in a state which excludes air. It should not need refrigeration unless the climate is warm and damp – as in, say, a centrally heated kitchen.

Cheese stall in the Mercado de la Abundancia, Montevideo

Medicinal and other uses

Cheese, a form of milk-food which has been subjected to souring (the initial process of fermentation) or renneting (a form of pre-digestion), retains most of the virtues of the raw material but is more digestible

Culinary uses

In many Latin American recipes, grated mature cheese is mixed with fresh cheese – hard cheese in its immature, soft, crumbly state – both in the form of *requesón* (naturally soured curds, drained) and *queso fresco*, the first stage of the matured cheese, for which feta is a convenient substitute. The Andean nations use grated cheese as a binder for farinaceous foods such as manioc (see Pan de yuca, p.61 and Cassava coconut cake, p.173). White sauces are often made without a thickening of flour and fat, simply by melting cheese into cream or milk – a surprisingly successful method of both enriching and thickening.

Bolinhos de queijo

(Brazilian cheese balls)

Serves 6–8 as an appetiser

The classic Brazilian appetiser – *salgadinho* **– which makes a gathering of friends into a party. Every cook has her own recipe for what everyone's mother cooks to perfection: some include potatoes, some are rolled into little torpedo-shaped croquettes instead of balls, some fried, some baked. And every household has its own preferences in the way of dipping-sauces. In Brazil the cheese of choice would be the hard, salty white cheese made in Minas Gerais.**

225g (8oz) grated parmesan or pecorino or dry cheddar
225g (8oz) fresh mozzarella, grated or finely chopped
3 egg whites, whisked until stiff
2 heaped tablespoons flour
Oil for frying

Mix the two cheeses and fold into the egg whites. Form into little balls or bolsters, roll in flour and deep-fry in shallow oil – no more than will submerge the fritters.

Bolinhos de queijo al horno

(Oven-baked cheese croquettes)

Serves 6–8 as an appetiser

Another version of Brazil's favourite finger-food. The mixture can be fried, but baking is considered more modern.

175g (6oz) self-raising flour
175g (6oz) grated parmesan
175g (6oz) unsalted butter
1 large egg, separated
About 4 tablespoons fine, dry breadcrumbs

Preheat the oven to 180°C/350°F/gas mark 4. In a roomy bowl, mix the flour with the cheese and butter and work to a paste with the egg-yolk. Form into balls or bolsters, dip into the forked-up egg white and roll in the breadcrumbs. Arrange the balls on a lightly buttered or non-stick baking sheet and bake for 25–30 minutes, until puffed up and brown.

Quesadillas, crisp tortilla turnovers filled with melted cheese

Quesadillas

(Mexican cheese turnovers)

Serves 4, lightly

Wheatflour tortillas make the best and lightest quesadillas. Use a combination of cheeses – one crumbly, one melting.

225g (8oz) mature cheese – gruyère or cheddar, grated
175g (6oz) fresh white requeson or feta-type cheese, crumbled
8 wheat-flour tortillas
1 large red pepper, roasted, skinned and cut into ribbons
1 teaspoon chilli flakes or powder
1 tablespoon chopped coriander
Oil for frying

Mix the cheeses together, lay out the tortillas and top each with a spoonful of cheese – drop it off-centre, leaving a wide margin round the edge. Top each dab of cheese with a pepper ribbon, a pinch of chilli and a few scraps of coriander. Dampen the edges and fold in half to enclose the filling.

Heat a finger's depth of oil in a large frying pan. Fry the quesadillas for a few minutes each side, until the filling melts and the tortilla crisps and browns. Or brush with oil, sprinkle with chilli flakes and bake at 350°F/180°C/gas mark 4 for 6–7 minutes.

poultry and meat

All barnyard birds – chicken, goose, duck and guinea fowl – are post-Columbian except the turkey, which is indigenous to Mexico and the southern parts of the northern American landmass. Recipes for barnyard birds are also suitable for feathered game; a pheasant or guinea fowl will give you a better idea of the flavour of the region's semi-wild barnyard bird than the fat and flabby chickens of modern breeding.

Very little meat was available to the indigenous inhabitants of Central and Southern America until the arrival of the Europeans. Although the Andean nations herded cameloids – llama, alpaca, vicuña – which they kept mainly for wool but also for meat and milk in the breeding months, they had no knowledge of the domestic animals of the Old World: cattle, pigs, sheep and goats. Once established, the herds had a dramatic effect on the landscape as well as the diet of the region.

chicken

Rural housewives of the region – and many a town-dweller, given a back-yard – keep poultry for their productive life as egg-layers. A young cockerel might be fattened up to be roasted for a festive meal or to fetch a price in the market-place, but traditional recipes reflect the expectation that any table bird will be tough.

Buying and storing

In Hispanic cultures, killing poultry for the pot was always reckoned women's business; in outlying districts, the bird is still sold live and on the hoof. This, it goes without saying, makes refrigeration unnecessary. Otherwise, keep the chicken in the fridge and don't waste the little unborn eggs you'll find in the cavity – gather them up and add them whole to the broth at the very end of the cooking.

Medicinal and other uses

Chicken soup, the housewives' cure-all – calmative, restorative, fortifying – has lately been confirmed by medical scientists as doing what granny always said it did.

Culinary uses

The thrifty housewife turns an old hen into two meals: a nourishing broth with vegetables, and a filling for tortillas, empanadas or tamales.

Pollo a la cubana

(Cuban chicken)
Serves 4–6

A fine way with a small, tender, free-range bird – chop it into small pieces and don't waste any of it, including the neck and gizzard. Four elements make the dish:

Grilling chicken over an open fire in an Argentinian estancia

crisply fried chicken, caramelised bananas, a fiery chilli sauce and a background of plain-cooked rice.

1 small free-range chicken, jointed into bite-
   sized pieces
2–3 tablespoons seasoned flour
Oil for shallow frying
8 baby or 4 large bananas, peeled, halved
   lengthwise

Chilli sauce:
450g (1lb) ripe tomatoes, chopped
1–2 garlic cloves, skinned and chopped
1–2 habanero chillies (Scotch-bonnet), de-
   seeded and chopped
1 tablespoon olive oil
1 teaspoon sugar

To serve:
White or saffron rice

Dredge the chicken pieces through the seasoned flour, shaking to remove any excess. Heat 3–4 tablespoons of oil in a roomy frying pan, lay the chicken pieces in it and fry gently until perfectly cooked through and deliciously brown. Add more oil if you need it. Remove the chicken pieces and reserve.

Fry the bananas, turning them once and removing them carefully as soon as the surfaces are lightly caramelised. Meanwhile, attend to the chilli sauce: put all the ingredients in the liquidiser and process to a purée, then transfer to a small pan, bubble up fiercely for a few minutes to concentrate the juices, then reduce the heat and leave to simmer for 10 minutes to marry the flavours. Arrange the chicken, bananas and rice on serving dish and hand around the chilli-sauce separately.

Ajiaco santafereno

(Chicken hot-pot)
Serves 6–8

Chicken-in-the-pot, as they like it in Colombia, is made with a sinewy old hen past her laying days, the best material for any broth. The three varieties of potato stipulated by the ladies of Santa Fe – *patuso*, *sabanero* and *criollo* – each bring their own characteristics. *Patuso* are firm and waxy, providing body; *sabanero* are floury and crumbly, dissolving to thicken the broth, and *criollo* are little round yellow potatoes which hold their shape and add sweetness. The main flavouring-herbs, huasca leaves, are occasionally available dried; failing these, use basil – much liked in Colombia in combination with sweetcorn.

The broth:
1 boiling-fowl or free-range chicken or guinea
   fowl
2 onions, roughly chopped
2–3 bay leaves
2 tablespoon huascas or 2–3 sprigs fresh basil
Salt and peppercorns

Ajioco santafereno, Colombia's favourite Sunday lunch

The vegetables:

1 cassava root, sliced lengthwise, hard core
 removed, peeled and cut into chunks

1kg (generous 2lb) patuso potatoes, peeled
 and cut into chunks (firm-fleshed reds)

750g (1¹/₂ lb) sabanero potatoes (floury
 whites)

450g (1 lb) criollo potatoes (small, yellow,
 waxy)

4 fresh corn-cobs, chunked

Salt and pepper

To serve:

Ají (salsa) of finely chopped yellow chillies,
 coriander, spring onion and lemon juice

Sliced avocado

Soured cream

Capers

Simmer the bird until perfectly tender in a
roomy pot with the onions, herbs, salt and
peppercorns in enough water to cover
generously. The surface of the broth should
tremble, no more. An old bird will need 2–3
hours, a young one will be ready in half the
time.

Leave to cool, strain the broth, lifting off the fat
and return to the heat. As soon as the first
bubbles rise, add the cassava chunks and the
first potatoes, peeled and cut into chunks.
After 10 minutes, add the second batch of
potatoes, also peeled and cut into chunks,
and return to the boil. After another 10
minutes, add the little potatoes, scrubbed but
not peeled, and the chunks of fresh corn.
Return to the boil and allow another 20
minutes, until the small potatoes are perfectly
tender. Finish with an extra sprinkling of
huascas or basil.

Serve in deep bowls with its accompaniments,
for people to help themselves.

turkey

or guajalote (Mexico), peru (Brazil)

The only barnyard bird indigenous to the region, the turkey was domesticated by the Aztecs. Spanish colonisers first encountered it in Venezuela (four live birds were brought to Seville in 1500) and for two centuries after its arrival, the Jesuits held a profitable monopoly on what was soon to become the Christmas roasting bird.

shredded turkey meat

Appearance and taste

In the wild, the tom – male – is a handsome bronze-feathered bird with magnificent blue and scarlet wattles used in courtship rituals; the hen – female – is smaller and usually lacks the beard-like tassel on the breast. In its semi-domesticated state, the turkey is relatively small-breasted, with robust flesh. It is chewy rather than flabby, and has a markedly gamey flavour.

Buying and storing

The turkey is not a bird whose gastronomic qualities are improved by intensive husbandry. For texture and flavour, choose free-range every time. Allow a pound per person dressed weight: the bones weigh heavy.

Medicinal and other uses

Lean – virtually fat-free – turkey is an excellent choice for slimmers.

Culinary uses

Interchangeable with chicken in all recipes for barnyard birds, the turkey is at its most interesting in the traditional dishes of the region: tacos, tamales and the kind of slow gentle closed-pot cooking which mimics the traditional earth-oven.

Peru a la brasiliera

(Turkey roasted in banana leaves)
Serves 8–10

Closed-pot cooking, a refinement of the earth-oven method, produces tender, succulent meat bathed in plenty of fragrant juice.

A 4.5–5.5kg (10–12lb) turkey
900g (2lb) salt (don't worry)
3 banana leaves or husks from 12 corn-ears

Chilli-baste:
3 malagueta chillies, de-seeded and chopped
3 tablespoons wine vinegar
2 onions, finely chopped
6 garlic cloves, finely chopped
6 tablespoons oil
3 mild red salad-peppers, de-seeded and chopped
1 teaspoon powdered cinnamon
$1/2$ teaspoon powdered cloves
$1/2$ teaspoon grated nutmeg
1 wine-glass cachaca or white rum

A fine turkey specimen, Mexico

Wipe the bird inside and out and singe off any little whiskery feathers. Check the wings for feather stumps and remove if necessary with tweezers. Douse the bird inside and out with the salt. Place in a large basin, cover with cold water and set in a cold place overnight.

Next day, rinse the bird under running water, making sure all the salt is washed away, and pat it dry. Make the chilli-baste. Put the chillies to soak in the vinegar. Fry the onion and garlic gently in 3 tablespoons of the oil until soft and golden. Push aside, add the remaining oil and fry the chopped pepper until it caramelises a little. Sprinkle in the spices and add the cachaca or rum. Bubble up to evaporate the alcohol. Tip the contents of the pan into the processor and liquidise with the chillies and their soaking-vinegar.

Place the bird on the table with the neck cavity facing you. Using your fingers, work the breast skin free of the flesh. Start gently and be careful not to tear the skin – it's easier once you get started. Loosen the skin all the way down the bird almost as far as the tail, going through the membrane which covers the drumsticks. Reserving a couple of tablespoons of the chilli-baste, carefully work the rest down both sides, until the entire breast and the drumsticks are covered. Secure the neckflap underneath with a skewer. Preheat the oven to its maximum, 240°C/475°F/gas mark 9.

Line the bottom of a deep, earthenware casserole (large enough to accommodate the bird) with half the maize-husks or banana leaves, first cut into 46cm (18in) squares and softened by being held over a flame. Place the turkey on the leaves breast-side up, and brush with the reserved chilli-baste. Roast at the high heat for 10 minutes. Cover with the remaining leaves, reduce the oven to 170°C/325°F/gas mark 3 and roast for 2 –2¹/₂ hours (depending on the size of the turkey), until the juices of the thigh run clear when it is pierced with a knife. Leave the bird to re-absorb its juices and settle for 10 minutes before carving into bite-sized pieces. Serve on fresh banana leaves if available, moistened with its own juices (hand more around separately), accompanied by soft cornmeal (polenta), white rice, black beans and okra sautéed with garlic and lemon juice.

Tacos de guajalote

(Turkey tacos)
Serves 4, allowing 3 per person as a light lunch

This is the original Mexican taco, made with the meat of the muscular semi-wild woodland-bred turkeys which provided both the Mayas and the Aztecs as well as the Pilgrim Fathers with good reason for thanksgiving.

The filling:
1 poached turkey breast, cooled in its own
  broth
A ladleful of cooking broth
3 tablespoons oil
1 small mild onion, chopped
2–3 green jalapeno chillies, de-seeded and cut
  into matchsticks
4 tomatoes, skinned de-seeded and diced

The wraps:
12 tortillas
Oil for shallow frying

To serve, choose from:
Roughly mashed or sliced avocado
Soured cream
Shredded lettuce or other greens
Mashed beans
Grated cheese
Pickled or fresh green chillies
Chilli-tomato salsa

Prepare the filling first. Shred the turkey-meat by pulling the fibres apart with 2 forks. In a small frying pan, heat the oil and fry the onion and chilli – a minute, no more. Add the tomato and bubble up for 5 minutes or so to make a smooth sauce, mashing to break down the lumps. Stir in the shredded turkey and its broth, and simmer until shiny and almost dry – about 10 minutes. Divide the mixture between the tortillas, roll up, secure with cocktail sticks and fry in shallow oil until golden. Drain on kitchen paper and serve immediately, with sliced avocados or whatever accompaniments you please.

Tacos de guajalote, shredded and sauced turkey breast on a crisply fried tortilla

feathered game

Duck, pigeon, quail and curassow (an indigenous species of pheasant), along with birds of the seed-eating kind – including several members of the parrot family – are traditionally hunted for the pot. Raptors, as elsewhere, are eaten only in times of famine.

Appearance and taste

It is by no means easy to tell the difference between one game-bird and another once it has been subjected to long cooking. When young enough to roast, the flesh of wild creatures reflects their diet: grain-eaters taste like chicken, water birds can taste noticeably fishy. The flavour of wild meat is stronger than that of a domestic table-bird.

Choosing and storing

Game birds are tender if plucked and eaten on the day of gathering; otherwise they should be left to mature for 4–7 days, depending on size, the stage at which they once again become tender. Water birds should be gutted and eaten as soon as possible.

Medicinal and other uses

Wild meat is very lean – good for those with cholesterol problems – and dense, delivering all that is necessary to sustain life. Combined with grains and legumes in the Latin American manner, a little goes a long way.

Culinary uses

The larger game-birds are tough and chewy, needing gentle stewing or fine-chopping if they are to be palatable. The traditional method of tenderising wild game was by what was effectively a form of pressure cooking: the food is wrapped in leaves, packed into an earth-oven – the *curanto* – and left to develop tenderness and succulence over several hours underground.

Pozole casero

(Hominy with wild meat)
Serves 6–8

The hunter's version of Mexico's famous all-in stew – nobody knows what's in there once it's in the pot. In its land of origin, vinagretta – the sharply acidic leaves of the Bermuda buttercup – is used instead of sorrel, and anis-flavoured epasote rather than dill is the flavouring herb.

450g (1lb) hominy: lye-treated maize kernels
1.8kg (about 4lb) game birds, whole, halved
*   or quartered (size dictates)*
2–3 bay leaves
1–2 sprigs oregano
6 allspice berries
Salt

The finishing sauce:
6 tomates verdes (or 450g/1lb green
*   gooseberries), chopped*
A handful shredded sorrel or spinach with a
*   squeeze of lemon*
2–3 green serrano chillies, de-seeded and
*   chopped*
1–2 stalks epasote or dill-fronds, chopped
1 small onion, finely chopped
2 tablespoons lard or oil
4 tablespoons toasted pumpkin or sunflower
*   seeds, powdered*

To serve, choose from:
Soured cream, avocado slices, shredded
*   lettuce, chopped onion, lime quarters,*
*   chicharrones (pork cracklings), grated or*
*   curd cheese*

Put the hominy in a roomy pan with plenty of fresh water, put the lid on loosely and cook until tender: from 1½ to 2 hours, depending on age and toughness. If you need to add water, make sure it's boiling. You'll know the hominy's ready when the kernels 'flower': the grains burst open like little blossoms. There should still be at least half a litre or just under a pint of broth.

At the same time, cook the birds until tender in a separate pan with the aromatics, a little salt and enough water just to submerge. Strain the broth and strip the meat from the bones. Return the meat to the broth and reserve.

Meanwhile, make the sauce. Cook the chopped tomato with a little water until mushy, bubbling it up for a minute or two to concentrate the juices; transfer to a processor with the sorrel or spinach, the chillies, the garlic and the epasote or dill and blend to a purée.

Heat the oil, fry the onion until soft but not browned, add the chopped green tomatoes or gooseberries and simmer until thick – 5 minutes or so. Stir in the ground pumpkin seeds, season with salt and cook for another 10 minutes, until the sauce is really thick. Add the flowered hominy and half a litre of its cooking water, and cook for 10 minutes more to blend the flavours. The finished dish should be moist rather than soupy.

Serve ladled into deep bowls, topped with a heap of bird-meat well-moistened with its own broth, and a dollop of soured cream. Hand the rest of the accompaniments around separately.

Pato en pepitoria
(Duck with pumpkin seeds)
Serves 4–6

**The jointed bird – include all the bits – is
simmered gently in a nut-thickened sauce.
Succulent and delicious.**

2 wild ducks, jointed (1 barnyard bird)
50g (2oz) lard or 4 tablespoons olive oil
2 garlic cloves, peeled and chopped
1 tortilla or slice day-old bread, crumbled
50g (2oz) pumpkin seeds
Few sprigs oregano, chopped or crumbled

$^1/_2$ teaspoon powdered cloves
1 teaspoon powdered cinnamon
1 tablespoon pimenton dulce (mild paprika)
1 teaspoon chilli powder
2 onions, finely sliced in half-moons

To serve:
2 sweet red peppers, roasted and cut into strips
Soft cornmeal tortillas

Wipe the joints, which should be small enough
to pick up and eat with the fingers. Fry the
garlic, breadcrumbs and pumpkin seeds in 2
tablespoons of the oil or lard until they gild –
don't let them brown. Sprinkle in the oregano
and the spices, and reserve.

Gently fry the duck joints with the onion in the
remaining oil. When the duck is well browned
and the onions are soft, stir in the pumpkin
seed mixture, and add enough water to just
submerge the duck pieces. Bubble up, put the
lid on loosely and turn down the heat. Simmer
gently until the duck is tender – about 30
minutes. Add a little more water if necessary.

Serve with the pepper-strips and soft tortillas.

pork

Of all the Old World's meat-animals, none received so enthusiastic a welcome as the pig – perhaps because its identity was recognisable through the indigenous peccary, the hunter's most valuable prize. It was imported by the Hispanic homesteaders who, unaware of the processes necessary to render the native foodstuffs palatable, imported those things they understood. The pig quickly became, and remains, the most important of the region's domestic meat-animals – not least because its consumption was actively encouraged by Roman Catholic missionaries, since it proved that the pork-eater was neither a Muslim nor a Jew, a matter of considerable concern to the Hispanic colonisers, who had just reclaimed their southern lands from the Moorish caliphs.

Appearance and taste

Pigs reared in the Hispanic – southern Mediterranean – tradition are not expected to be as fat and soft-fleshed as northern pigs. Their meat, relatively lean, goes to make store-cupboard sausages (chorizos) while the blood is transformed into black pudding (morcilla), variously spiced, and sometimes blended with meat and fat or bulked out with grains.

Buying and storing

Pork deteriorates quickly in a hot climate. Buy only fresh meat, salt it lightly and store it briefly in a refrigerator if you must. Wash it thoroughly before cooking.

Medicinal and other uses

Pork-meat pleases because it tastes good. It tastes good because it's threaded through with delicious little globules of fat. Although pork-lard is considered a 'bad' fat in these health-conscious times, the reputation is not entirely deserved. According to the US Department of Agriculture, unhydrogenated (pure) pork fat is low in saturated fat and contains less than half the cholesterol found in butter.

Fattening pigs for the market, Paraguay

Culinary uses

Meat and fat are equally valued in the Hispanic kitchen. While pork, although eaten fresh for a celebration, is the great store-cupboard meat, the lard, melted and refined and stored as a pure-white fat, is used for frying and preserving as well as baking (see p.107).

Carne de cerdo en manteca
(Preserved pork)
Serves 4–6

One of those delicious little preparations which never seem to appear in recipe books: lean, diced pork (fillet or leg or shoulder, it doesn't really matter) is cooked very slowly in pure lard, and coloured and flavoured with garlic, herbs and paprika. You will need to start a day ahead.

900g (about 2 lb) lean pork, cut into bite-size cubes
900g (about 2lb) pork kidney-fat (or very fatty belly-pork)
1 tablespoon crushed dried oregano
6 garlic cloves, crushed with 1 tablespoon salt
2 tablespoons vinegar
2 tablespoons mild pimentón
1 teaspoon chilli powder

Mix the meat cubes with the oregano, crushed garlic and vinegar. Work thoroughly and leave overnight in a cool place to take the flavours. Meanwhile, prepare the lard: cook the kidney fat very slowly with a glassful of water in a low oven or in a heavy pan on a very gentle flame. When the oil has separated from the fibre and is floating on the water, pour it off, strain and reheat to evaporate all remaining moisture – gently, it shouldn't gild.

Drain the pork-cubes and brush off excess marinade. Heat the lard in a roomy pan and add the meat. Cook very gently for 30–40 minutes: the lard should bubble gently, a sign that the meat is losing its juices. When the meat is cooked right through and the lard no longer bubbles, remove from the heat and stir in the pimenton and chilli powder. Pour everything into an earthernware jar, making sure all the meat is submerged, and set it in the fridge to firm up. Meat preserved in this way keeps for a long time in a cool larder, provided each time you take some out, you melt the potful down to ensure the remaining meat remains submerged. The trick is to ensure that no air can get at anything perishable.

The lard can be eaten like butter, or stirred into bean dishes to add flavour, richness and colour; the meat – very rich and fragrant – is delicious with black beans and soft tortillas, as part of a Mexican *plato combinado* (see p.92). To prepare, remove the required number of cubes – 4 per person is ample – and heat gently in a pan until the fat runs. As a quick snack, wrap in a tortilla or slip into a split arepa with a squeeze of lime, a lettuce leaf and a fiery pickled chilli. Very delicious.

Tatemado

(Mexican pork pot-roast)
Serves 8–10

A succulent pork pot-roast jacketed with spices and chillies, a dish served at weddings and christenings in northern Mexico, which takes its name from the Nauatl word for pit-barbecue: food-for-the-fire.

Tatemado, pot-roast pork with a fragrant chilli crust

1 pork shoulder on the bone – about 2.25k (5lb)
2 pig's trotters, scrubbed and split
600ml (1 pint) white wine vinegar
6 garlic cloves, crushed with a little salt
1 teaspoon peppercorns
110g (4oz) dried chili ancho (mild and fruity)
110g (4oz) dried chili guajillo (sharp and hot)
1 teaspoon powdered ginger
2–3 sprigs thyme
¹/₂ teaspoon coriander seeds

To serve:
2–3 red onions, finely sliced, dressed with lime
  juice and salt
Shredded lettuce
Sliced radishes
Tortillas

Put the meat and trotters in a roomy bowl. Pierce the skin in several places with a knife. In a blender, process the vinegar with the garlic, a little more salt and the peppercorns. Pour this aromatic bath over the meat and set aside in a

cool place for a couple of hours. Slit the chillies open and scrape out the seeds and pale veins. Keep 1 teaspoon of the seeds. Tear up the chillies and soak in a bowl of boiling water for 20 minutes or so.

Preheat the oven to 300°F/150°C/gas mark 2. Drain the meat, reserving the vinegary juices, and transfer to a casserole. Put the vinegar in the blender, add the chilli a little at a time and process between each addition until smooth. Strain and discard the bits. Return the liquid to the blender along with the ginger, thyme, chilli seeds and coriander; blend to a smooth paste. Spread the paste over the meat and add enough water to come halfway up the joint. Cover tightly, transfer to the oven and cook for 2–3 hours, until the meat is tender but not yet falling apart. Remove the lid, raise the heat and cook for another 20 minutes or so, to brown the skin and reduce the sauce. Serve with sliced onion, shredded lettuce and radishes – all ready to wrap in a tortilla fresh from the comal.

beef

Beef-cattle, a post-Columbian introduction to the grasslands of the New World, provided a new crop – beef, preserved first by salting and barrelling, and later by freezing – for shipping back across the Atlantic to the cities of Europe to feed the newly affluent workers of the Industrial Revolution. Vast cattle ranches were established throughout the temperate zones of the territory – the borderlands of northern Mexico, the pampas of Argentina, Uruguay, Paraguay, Chile and Peru, and the southern grassplains of Brazil. Recipes reflect this profitable trade. The *asado*, the Argentian gaucho's barbecue, is a whole carcass of young beef, killed on the spot, skinned, split and roasted on a spit set over a couple of forked branches, or on a pole hammered into the hard red earth at an angle to the fire. In the great cities of Brazil – Rio and São Paolo – *churrascarías*, restaurants which mimic the gaucho's daily dinner, serve nothing but roast meats, big slabs of it turning on the spit to be carved to the customer's order.

Medicinal and other uses

The cowboys and herdsmen who roamed the range lived exclusively on meat for months at a time, for practical reasons as well as preference, without suffering ill effects: the very reverse. Whether meat-eating brings toughness, resilience and resourcefulness is arguable – Hollywood says it does, and the rest of us believe.

Culinary uses

Traditional recipes in the meat-packing lands make good use of offal and variety meats – the butcher's cast-offs and the food of the urban poor – readily available only where there's a market for the rest. In Peru, *anticuchos*, grilled beef-hearts, are the most popular street-food. In the cities and ports where the meat is processed, tongue, tripe and cow-heel are combined with beans to produce nourishing stews, while the bones are prized for broth.

Tostadas de carne apache
(Tostadas topped with marinated steak)
Serves 4–6

Carne apache – Indian steak – is a popular street snack in the cattle-herding borderlands of Mexico's northern states. The principle is the same as steak tartar, though nowadays the tenderising agent is lime juice rather than the cowpoke's saddle. Start a day ahead.

12 corn tortillas

The topping:
450g (1lb) twice-chopped or fine-ground steak
Juice of 4–5 limes
1 onion, finely chopped
1 mild red pepper, de-seeded and diced small
2–3 fresh serrano chillies, de-seeded and finely chopped
2–3 tablespoons chopped leaf-coriander
(Optional) 1–2 tablespoons chopped green olives
Salt

Spread the tortillas on the table to dry. In a large, clean bowl, mix the chopped steak with the lime juice, cover and set in the fridge overnight. Turn it from time to time so it takes the lime-juice evenly – a venerable cooking-process. Drain, bring back to room temperature, and blend with the remaining ingredients.

Toast or fry the tortillas until crisp and brown, and pile with the prepared steak. Tomatoes, shredded lettuce or cabbage, radishes, olives, pickled chillies and Tabasco sauce are all appropriate accompaniments.

Herding cattle in the dry season on the slopes of Mount Concepción, Nicaragua

Estofado argentino, lean beef braised with aromatics, red wine and root vegetables

Estofado argentino

(Argentinian pot-roast)

Serves 6–8

More sophisticated than the cowboy's barbecued carcass, this is a homestead dish cooked in a closed-pot, earth-oven style, with vegetables and aromatics and the rough red wine of the countryside. If convenient, leave it overnight in the lowest possible oven – in the morning you will be rewarded with the most succulent beef you've ever tasted.

2kg (about 4lb) round roast – the tip of the leg-fillet
900g (about 2lb) mature carrots
110g (4oz) parsley, finely chopped
4 garlic cloves, finely chopped
4 tablespoons oil
450g (about 1lb) small onions, peeled

A few sprigs thyme and oregano, a bay leaf
1 bottle rough red wine
Pinch sugar
Salt and pepper

To finish:
3–4 red and yellow peppers, de-seeded and chunked
900g (about 2lb) scrubbed new potatoes (or mature, peeled and cut into chunks)

To serve:
Chimichurri salsa (see p.199)

Shove a sharp knife right through the heart of the joint to make a deep incision from end to end – starting at the blunt end, the knife-point should appear at the tip. Grate a quarter of the carrots, mix with parsley and garlic, and stuff this fragrant paste into the incision. If necessary, tie the joint with string.

Heat the oil in a roomy casserole and brown the meat on all sides. Remove and reserve. Fry the onions and the remaining carrots, cut into chunks the same size as the onions. Return the meat to the pot, tuck in the aromatics, add the wine and the sugar and season with salt and pepper.

Bring to the boil, cover tightly – use foil as well as a lid – and transfer to a very low oven. Leave to steam gently in its own juices – overnight is not too long. When perfectly tender, remove and leave to rest. Add the finishing vegetables to the pot-juices and cook until tender. Slice the meat and arrange it on its bed of fragrant vegetables.

Serve with a chimichurri salsa: finely chopped thyme, parsley, garlic and onion, marinated with olive oil and a little wine vinegar.

exotic and wild meats

air-dried charqui meat

In the absence of reliable refrigeration, it is in the form of *charqui* or jerky – meat preserved by natural dehydration – that most wild meat comes to market. This, the most ancient method of conserving the hunter's booty, is simply fresh meat, trimmed of sinew and fat, cut into thin strips and hung to dry in the ice-cold mountain breezes from the Andes without salt or preservatives or flavourings. Once perfectly dehydrated, it can be stored almost indefinitely and rehydrated at will.

The process, well-known to all primitive peoples, was (and is) chiefly used for conserving and transporting valuable protein gathered by hunting as well as that of the Andean herd-animals such as llama and vicuna whose diet is free from human intervention.

Exotics – meat-animals reared for the table as well as wild-gathered – include rodents such as the guinea pig or *cuy* (pronounced kwee), a prolific breeder first domesticated by the Incas and still valued. The traveller new to Peru will be startled to see the little creatures running around under the table in rural households, much as chickens or rabbits – whose meat is very similar. Argentina and Chile have the agouti, a small rodent bred for the table, as are the rather larger paca, viscacha and the world's biggest water-rat, the capybara, which earned the distinction of being classified as a fish by the early missionaries in order that it could be eaten on Catholic fast-days. Elsewhere, particularly among the Amazonian peoples, turtle and tortoise are both considered good eating when roasted in the shell or baked in an earth-oven.

Both meat and eggs of iguanas and snakes are still eaten in country districts, offered for sale by children at the roadside – though these days the hope is that the tourists will ransom the unfortunate creature, which can then be recaptured and recycled.

Appearance and taste

Rodent meat is much like wild rabbit: tender and mild-flavoured when young, tough and chewy in its maturity. Reptile meat has a stringy consistency close to the texture and flavour of chicken's neck – actually, it's indistinguishable from chicken as a filling for tacos or empanadas, the form in which it usually appears.

Medicinal and other uses

Wild meat is lean, low in cholesterol and full of all necessary nutrients. It is not usually fed to small children or the elderly, since it's considered over-fortifying and indigestible.

Guinea pig is part of the feast in this portrayal of the Last Supper in Cuzco Cathedral, Peru

Culinary uses

Dried meat is best used sparingly: quality wins over quantity. If you get the chance to cook rodent, think rabbit; South American rodents are herbivores, delicately flavoured and as tender as chicken.

Conejitos ajímaní

(Little rabbits with garlic and peanuts)
Serves 4

The Peruvian way with any edible rodent – but particularly good with guinea pig, the rabbit of the New World. You will need to start up to a day ahead to allow time for the meat to marinate.

900g (2lb) jointed rabbit or any mid-size rodent such as cuy

For the marinade:
1 teaspoon crumbled chilli
2 tablespoons oil
2 tablespoons white wine vinegar
1 teaspoon achiote, crushed
2 garlic cloves, skinned and finely chopped
150ml (¹/4 pint) cream
2 tablespoons crushed toasted peanuts
Salt and pepper

Joint the meat into bite-sized pieces. Turn the joints in the marinade ingredients, cover and leave overnight. Drain and pat dry. Strain and reserve the marinade.

Grill or barbecue the joints over a medium heat for 5 minutes per side if you like it rare – more if you like your meat well done. Or roast in the oven: allow 15–20 minutes at 200°C/400°F/gas mark 6. Leave for 20 minutes by the side of the fire or in the lowest possible oven to relax.

Bubble up the reserved marinade with the cream to make a little sauce, taste and season, and pour over the joints. Finish with a sprinkling of toasted peanuts.

Charquicán

(Jerky hot-pot)
Serves 4

A sophisticated version of a classic Chilean vegetable stew finished with a flavouring fry-up of *charqui*, strips of wind-dried hunter's meat prepared in the old way. If you can't find jerky, steak roasted on the barbecue will have to do.

1 thick slice pumpkin, cut into bite-sized pieces
1–2 carrots, cut into chunks
4–5 small potatoes
300ml (1/2 pint) fresh corn-kernels
300 ml (1/2 pint) fresh peas
600ml (1 pint) broth or plain water
Salt

To finish:
225g (8 oz) charqui (jerky, biltong, or any wind-dried meat)
2–3 tablespoons oil
2–3 onions, finely slivered
1 teaspoon crumbled oregano
1 teaspoon paprika or dried mild red chilli, finely chopped
1 teaspoon cumin
Salt and pepper

To serve:
Pickled pearl onions
Pebre chileno (see below)

Put all the vegetables in a roomy pot with the broth or water, season, bring to the boil, turn down the heat to simmer, put the lid on tightly and cook for 15 minutes, until nearly tender.

Meanwhile, pick over the jerky, remove any sinewy bits and chop. Heat the oil in a small frying pan and gently fry the onions until they soften and take a little colour. Add the jerky and flavourings, season and cook for 5 minutes or so, until well blended. Stir the contents of the frying pan into the vegetables, remove the lid and bubble up to evaporate the juices. The stew should be deliciously moist but not soupy.

Serve in bowls, with pickled pearl onions and *pebre chileno* – Chilean pepper salsa. To prepare: pound 3 fresh hot chillies to a paste with 2 tablespoons coriander leaves, 1 tablespoon oil, 1 tablespoon chopped onion and 1 chopped garlic clove.

variety & salted meats

offal, morcilla, chorizo

The salt-drawer, the draining-hook and the brine-pot are where the pig ends up when the weather is too warm and damp to permit the conservation of meat in any other way. There was a time when all households with access to a backyard kept a household pig to eat up the scraps and provide the family with its annual supply of cured meats: sausages, morcilla (blood puddings), bacon and ham. In the outlying districts, many still do. The brine-pot, too, is where the bits-and-bobs of the butcher's shop end up – and these have become the food of the urban poor. In lands where the indigenous peoples, judged unco-operative or simply slaughtered, were replaced by the slave-traders with people of African origin – Brazil, the Caribbean – dishes were made with offal, the bits of the pig considered unfit for the master. The stupendous Brazilian *feijoada* and the fiery Caribbean pepperpot – creations which not only delight the palate but have come to define an entire culinary habit – emerged from these sorry beginnings.

chorizo

black pudding

smoke-cured bacon

Buying and storing

When choosing chorizo, pick the right man for the job. Fresh chorizo – soft, brightly-coloured, juicy – is good for frying or grilling. Mature chorizo – firm, with a soft white bloom on the skin – is good for slicing to eat raw, or for including in a slow-simmered stew. When choosing meat from the brine-pot, ask the butcher for instructions: he'll know how long it's been taking the salt and how long you need to soak it. Store chorizo out of its plastic or any other wrapping on a hook in a dry corner, never in the fridge. Once the meat is out of the brine-pot, use it as soon as possible.

Medicinal and other uses

Salt-cured meats are as high in sodium as they are in protein – use sparingly. You have been warned.

Culinary uses

Cured meats and sausages are the mainstay of the rural kitchen, added in small quantities to improve the flavour and boost the food-value of roots, gourds, beans and grains. As for offal, variety is what makes it festive. It's the thrill of discovery: a bit of this and a bit of that allows everyone to choose exactly what they like.

Anticuchos peruvianos

(Peruvian beef-heart kebabs)
Serves 6–8

Spicy, chilli-spiked and deliciously succulent scraps of meat threaded on skewers and grilled to order on every street corner in Peru. The name comes from the Quechua meaning 'Andean foodstuff cooked on a stick'. The correct chilli for marinade is the fiery *ají mirasol* (the sunseeker), the dried version of the fruity yellow *ají amarillo*, a long pointed torpedo-shaped chilli, thin fleshed and hot as Hades – but jalapeños or serranos will do.

1 beef heart, about 1.8kg (4lb), trimmed of fat and fibre

The marinade:
4 tablespoons wine vinegar
4 tablespoons oil
2–3 fresh chillies, de-seeded and finely chopped
2 tablespoons chopped coriander
2 garlic cloves, finely chopped
1 small onion, finely chopped
1 tablespoon powdered cumin
1 tablespoon dried oregano
Salt and pepper

To cook:
6–8 long skewers (bamboo or fine metal knitting needles)

Rinse the beef heart and pat dry. Cut into bite-sized cubes and mix in a bowl with all the marinade ingredients, then cover with clingfilm and leave to take the flavours in a cool place for several hours – overnight in the fridge is best.

Light the barbecue or heat the grill. If using bamboo skewers, they should be soaked for an hour or two.

Remove the meat from the marinade and drain thoroughly. Strain the marinade and reserve the liquid. Thread the meat on the skewers and grill fiercely until the outside caramelises – about 2 minutes a side – basting with the marinade as they cook. Serve with hot arepas or freshly baked bolillos: crisp-crusted, dense-crumbed rolls just right for holding in the hand.

Spoiled for choice in a Montevideo market

Feijoada

(Brazilian cured meats with black beans)
Serves 12

A stupendous dish for a party, Brazil's national treasure. The meats are variable – don't worry if you can't get them all. Fresh oxtail can be substituted for *carne seca*, the Brazilian beef-jerky, available in Portuguese or Latin American delis. Start on Friday to serve for lunch on Saturday.

900g (2 lb) black beans
2 bay leaves, a quartered onion, 2–3 garlic
*   cloves*

The meats:
1 salted, smoked beef-tongue
450g (1lb) carne seca (strips of air-dried beef)
900g (2lb) salt pork (sparerib for choice)
450g (1lb) slab (fatty) bacon
2 pig's ears (singed and scrubbed)
2 pig's trotters (scrubbed and split)
2–3 pig's tails
1 bacon knuckle
4–6 links linguica or chorizo (paprika sausage)
4–6 links morcilla (black pudding)

To finish:
2 tablespoons olive oil
2 onions, finely chopped
2 cloves garlic, finely chopped
2-3 large tomatoes, grated
1–2 malagueta peppers, chopped

To accompany:
Finely shredded greens (kale or chard), wilted
*   in a little olive oil*
Plain-cooked white rice
Toasted manoic meal (farofa, p.60) for
*   sprinkling*
Pickled malageta peppers
Quartered oranges

Put the beans to soak overnight in a large pot with enough water to cover generously. Soak the tongue at the same time, if not ready soaked by the butcher.

Next day, bring the dried beef and the tongue to the boil in a roomy pot with the pig bits, turn down the heat, lid loosely and simmer until all is tender – 2–3 hours. Add the pickled pork for

Feijoada, Brazil's ultimate beanfeast, strictly for Saturday lunchtime only

the last hour of the cooking. Remove the meats to a large platter. As soon it's cool enough to handle, skin the tongue and remove the little bones and gristle.

Meanwhile, drain the beans and bring them to the boil in plenty of fresh water with their aromatics, turn down the heat and simmer for 30 minutes. Add the bacon-joint to the beans and simmer for another 1½hours.

Slice and fry the sausages and black pudding in the oil until well-browned (you can boil them in a separate pot, but they taste even more delicious when crisped). Remove and reserve while you prepare the flavouring sauce.

Gently fry the onion and garlic in the oily sausage drippings until soft and golden, then stir in the tomatoes and chilli and squash down to break up the fibres. Bubble up to make a rich little sauce, then stir in a couple of ladlesful of the cooked beans, mashing to blend. Stir

this mixture into the beanpot, along with the fried sausage and the reserved meats. Simmer for another hour, adding boiling water when necessary to make sure the water level never drops below a handspan. Remove the meats from the beans and leave in separate dishes in a cool place overnight.

Next day, reheat with more boiling water for an hour. Arrange the cooked meats, suitably sliced – de-rind and cube the bacon, slip the meat off the ear-gristle, slice the tails and bone-out the trotters – on a single large platter or several smaller ones, and moisten with a little bean-liquor. Serve the beans in their sauce in a large warm bowl. Arrange the accompaniments around the bean-bowl, for everyone to make their own combinations. A jugful of Caipirinhas – fresh lime juice, white rum or cachaça sweetened with sugar-cane juice (see p.183) – makes the party go with a swing.

lamb and kid

Sheep are mainly confined to the southern tip of the landmass – Patagonia and the Andean highlands – while goats, the universal forager, are pastured on marginal land throughout the territory. Recipes are inherited from the repetoire appropriate to their predecessors on the high plateaux, the Andean cameloids – llama, alpaca, vicuña, guanaco – all of which have been domesticated since the earliest times.

Appearance and taste

The meat from animals pastured on the Andean uplands is lean and sweet. If it smells a little strong, wash it thoroughly before cooking.

Buying and storing

Meat does not have a long shelf-life down on the plain – particularly that from young animals – any more than it does on the butcher's shelf. It is best to buy it as fresh as possible and consume without delay. In the Andean mountains in winter, storage is not a problem since the meat will remain frozen and safe so long as it's hung out of the reach of predators.

Culinary uses

Mountain lamb is sinewy and tough compared to the soft-living valley-reared. Chop the meat thoroughly unless you intend to subject it to long cooking. Kid, the meat of young goats, has a gluey texture particularly good in a slow-simmered stew; when roasting, a gentle heat is better than fierce.

La señalanda – marking sheep for purposes of identification – Argentina

Ropa vieja
(Old clothes)
Serves 4–6

A hash by another name – one of those leftover-dishes into which anything goes – just as they like it in Venezuela. The principal is the transformation of something soft and bland into something crisp and tasty. Patience, expressed as long gentle frying, is the key.

450g (1lb) cooked meat – lamb, kid, whatever
4–5 tablespoons olive oil
1–2 onions, finely sliced into half-moons
2 garlic cloves, skinned and cut into slivers
1 tablespoon chopped fresh marjoram or oregano
2–3 fresh chillies, de-seeded and chopped
Salt and pepper

Shred the meat, fat and all. Fry in the oil with the onion, garlic and other flavourings. Season and continue frying, turning over the mixture as it browns. Eventually it will acquire the most exquisite crust and a wonderful fragrance. Eat with plain-boiled potatoes, arepas or whatever takes your fancy.

Pastel de choclo

(Chilean shepherd's pie)
Serves 4–6

A savoury base of *pino* **– a variable mixture
of meats topped with puréed sweetcorn –
is given a crisp crust under the grill. The
traditional cooking pot is a dish of
unbaked red clay from the village of
Pomaire, in the mountains to the east of
Santiago, the capital.**

Pino:
700g (1¹/₂ lb) finely chopped lamb or kid
900g (2 lb) onions, finely sliced
3 garlic cloves, finely chopped
4 tablespoons oil or butter
2 rounded tablespoons mild paprika (pimentón)
1 teaspoon powdered cumin

1 teaspoon dried oregano
600ml (1 pint) diced pumpkin
3 tablespoons raisins
A dozen pitted green olives, roughly chopped
Salt and pepper

The topping:
2.4 litres (4 pints) fresh sweetcorn
600ml (1 pint) creamy milk
1 egg, mixed with a fork

To finish:
3 hardboiled eggs, quartered lengthways
Icing sugar and chilli flakes

First prepare the pino. Put the lamb or kid,
onions, garlic and oil in a heavy pan, add a
ladleful of water and cook gently, the lid on
loosely, for about an hour, until the meat is

tender. Add the remaining pino ingredients and
cook for another 30 minutes (add water if it
looks like drying out). Bubble up to reduce the
juices to a rich gravy. Stir in the raisins and
olives and season with salt and pepper.

Meanwhile, purée the corn with the milk,
transfer to a pan and cook until the mixture has
thickened a little – 5 minutes. Remove from the
heat and let it cool a little. Stir in the egg and
salt lightly.

Preheat the oven to 180°C/350°F/gas mark 4.
Spread the pino in an earthenware gratin dish,
top with the hardboiled eggs and finish with the
sweetcorn purée and a powdering of icing
sugar and chilli-flakes. Bake for half an hour,
until brown and bubbling. For an even more
caramelised topping, slip it under the grill.

fish and shellfish

The fishermen of the region – as a glance at the map will confirm – have access to one or other of three great waters: Pacific, Atlantic and Caribbean. A fortunate few, mainly those who inhabit the lands of the Maya and Aztecs, have access to all three. But the richest of these fishing grounds is where the chilly waters of the Antarctic meet the warmth of the Pacific when the cold Humbolt current curves round the shores of Chile. Here, great drifting clouds of plankton feed the rainbow shoals which spawn on Chile's narrow continental shelf and provide molluscs and other rock-dependent sea-creatures with a reliable foodsource. The shelf, a shallow pasture out of reach of ocean predators, serves as a nursery for vulnerable offspring. Names are confusing: a gilt-head bream, for instance, is known as dorado among Spanish-speakers, whereas in Caribbean markets, dorado is the local name for dolphin-fish, known on the west coast as mahi-mahi, which is not a warm-blooded sea-mammal but a blunt-nosed seafish with brilliant golden flanks – hence its name. For this reason, I have not given exact species, but have chosen ingredient-groups for culinary purposes – round-bodied whole fish, steak fish and so on – remembering there are many more fish in the sea than I have room to list.

bivalves

Clams, razor-shells and related shellfish

Clams and all manner of assorted bivalves are to be found all along the coastlines. Since none of the bivalves are mobile – with the exception of the scallop – they are concentrated wherever there is a ready foodsource. All are edible and most are appreciated locally, while a few have commercial value and are exported.

Habitat
They are found all along the shoreline from the chilly Straits of Magellan to the Sea of Cortez by way of the tropical sands of Brazil.

Appearance and taste
Size, colour and flavour are very variable: there are literally thousands of hinged-shell molluscs, some more delicious than others. Since the bivalves get their nourishment by pulling water through their shells, any danger normally comes from what the creatures have ingested. As for culinary virtues, price in the market is the best indication of quality. The taste is usually a little of iodine, although the more delicately flavoured are as close to an oyster as anyone might wish.

Buying and storing
When buying fresh, check that fish are still alive in their shells: a quick shake will encourage them to close. Too many open shells – or worse, dried-out and gaping ones– indicates they're not perfectly fresh. Discard any which are cracked or dirty. Local names are usually derived from the local language.

Medicinal and other uses
Shellfish, though of general value as a supplementary food-source since prehistoric times, supplied all the dietary needs of the coastal dwellers of Chile who subsisted comfortably on a harvest of razor-shells, a seemingly inexhaustible shore-crop, judiciously supplemented by sea-vegetables.

Culinary uses
Bivalves can be eaten raw or cooked. If the former, bear in mind that raw clams are even harder to prize open than oysters: use a short, strong, double-bladed knife either inserted between the shells or in the hinge, whatever works. If the latter, they are best cooked until they open in a closed pot in a minimum amount of liquid for the shortest possible time: longer cooking or reheating makes them rubbery. If gathering your own bivalves, to clean them, put them in a bucket with plenty of cold water and enough salt to produce the same salinity as seawater – 100g (4oz) salt to 4 litres (7 pints) water – and leave them for a couple of days to spit out their sand. For inclusion in stews, large clams should be chopped; small ones can be left whole.

Cazuela del pescador

Cazuela del pescador

(Fisherman's clams)
Serves 4

A fisherman's dish, nothing fancy. Simple but good. Leave the clams to soak overnight in cold water and discard any with cracked or gaping shells and those which feel too heavy – a sign they're full of something other than live fish. Shellfish can stay fresh for as long as they can hold water in their shells.

1.8kg (4lb) clams or any fresh shellfish
2 tablespoons olive oil
2 garlic cloves, finely chopped
1 green frying chilli, de-seeded and chopped
1 fresh red chilli, de-seeded and finely chopped
1 tablespoon chopped parsley

Pick over the clams and rinse thoroughly. Heat the oil in a roomy pan and fry the garlic and chillies for 2–3 minutes, just enough to perfume the oil. Tip in the shellfish, turn up the heat and bubble for 3–4 minutes, until all the shells gape open in the steam – turn them with a spoon so that the ones on top can get to the heat. When all are open, they're done. Remove the pan from the heat immediately – shellfish toughens if it's overcooked. Finish with freshly-chopped parsley.

Empanadas de mariscos al horno

(Oven-baked seafood pasties)
Serves 6–8

Little pasties stuffed with seafood, a reminder of pre-Columbian feasts, these are baked in the wood-fired baking oven which in modern Chile takes the place of the old earth-oven, the *curanto*.

The filling:
900g (2lb) shellfish – razor-shells, clams, mussels
1 glass white wine
450g (1lb) prawn or shrimp
2 tablespoons olive oil
2 onions, finely chopped
2 garlic cloves, finely chopped
1 red pepper, de-seeded and diced small
1 teaspoon crumbled thyme
1 chilli, de-seeded and chopped
Salt and pepper

The pastry:
275g (10 oz) self-raising flour
1/2 teaspoon salt
4 tablespoons olive oil
2 tablespoons white wine
150ml (1/4 pint) warm water

Cook the shellfish in a pan with a tablespoonful of the wine: bubble up, put the lid on tightly and shake over the heat until they open. Remove and leave to cool. Cook the prawns in the remaining juices with the rest of the wine, removing them as soon as they blush scarlet. Shuck the shellfish and chop the meat if necessary (small clams can be left whole). Peel the prawns or shrimp and chop roughly. In another pan fry the onion, garlic and pepper in the oil until soft. Sprinkle with the thyme and chilli, season with salt and pepper, add the winey juices and bubble up to reduce to a fragrant little sauce. Stir in the prepared shellfish and prawns and leave to cool while you make the pastry.

Preheat the oven to 200°C/400°F/gas mark 6.

Make the pastry. Sieve the flour with the salt. In a small pan, heat the oil, wine and water until just bearable to a finger. Pour the warm liquid into the flour, and knead to a soft, elastic dough ball. Form the dough into a thin roll and divide into 20 pieces. Roll out each piece on a well-floured board into a thin round the size of a coffee-saucer. Dot with a teaspoon of the filling, wet the edges and fold one half over the other to enclose the filling, pressing down with a fork to seal. Continue until you have 20 little pasties. Transfer to an oiled baking sheet.

Bake for 15–20 minutes, until crisp and brown.

oysters

Oysters are shore-dependent bivalves with rough shells and delicately-flavoured, soft, succulent flesh: the cream of the shellfish crop.

Fishing boats in Valparaiso, Chile

perfectly good from the freezer – a process, which, if you freeze your own, has the advantage of opening the shells.

Medicinal and other uses

Oysters are a well-known aphrodisiac. It's something to do with appearance and scent – but I'm sure you can work it out for yourself.

Habitat

The oyster is a tidal creature, at home in the alternately salt and sweet waters of estuaries and river-mouths.

Appearance and taste

The oyster-family divides into two main species: the long narrow-shelled *Crassostrea* (varieties of which include the Portuguese *angulata* and the giant Pacific *gigas*) and *Ostrea* spp., the smaller, smoother, rounder natives – also known as *belón* or plate-oyster – which are considered the more delicate in flavour. A fresh oyster tastes of sea-spray, without a hint of fishiness.

Buying and storing

A reliable supplier is the best guarantee of freshness and wholesomeness. Kept cool and damp, oysters can remain alive for as long as they can keep water in their shells: ten days is not unreasonable. Oysters for cooking are

Culinary uses

To open, hold the oyster firmly in a clean cloth, and slip the point of a short strong knife in round the side of the hinge. It will open with a gentle pop. It's better if you own one of those purpose-designed knives with a fist-guard – but no matter if you don't. Slide the blade across parallel with the top shell and sever the connector muscle, taking care not to lose any of the delicious juices. Then slip the knife underneath and sever the bottom muscle. To serve raw, leave the oyster on the deeper of the two shells and on no account rinse away all the delicious sea-juices. When cooking, save the juices and use them to flavour the sauce.

Chupe de ostras con elote

(Chilean oyster and sweetcorn chowder)
Serves 4

A delicate soup in which the sweetness of the corn complements the fresh flavour of the oysters. To make a stock, beg a kilo

(2lb) of white-fish bones and heads from your fishmonger and simmer in a litre (2 pints) water with a quartered onion, a stick or two of celery, a bay leaf, peppercorns and salt. After 20 minutes, strain and boil rapidly to reduce to 850ml (1¹/₂ pints) of well-flavoured stock.

850ml (1¹/₂) pints fish stock
24 oysters

To finish:
2 egg yolks
2 tablespoons double cream
300ml (¹/₂ pint) fresh sweetcorn kernels
Salt and pepper
A few basil leaves, torn

If using fresh oysters (frozen are perfectly acceptable) open them carefully and save all the liquor. Bring the fish stock to the boil with the wine and bubble up for 5 minutes or so, until the steam no longer smells alcoholic. Add the oyster liquor and the sweetcorn and simmer for 5 minutes, until the corn is tender.

Slip the oysters with all their juices into the hot soup. Simmer for 3–4 minutes, then take off the heat.

To finish, whisk the egg yolks with the cream, and then whisk in a ladleful of the hot broth. Stir into the soup and reheat gently. Taste and season with salt and pepper and serve sprinkled with a few torn leaves of basil. Do not re-boil, or the egg will scramble and the oysters harden.

Seviche de ostras

(Guatemalan oyster seviche)

Serves 4

Guatemala's favourite seviche. In neighbouring Mexico, prawns are often included, while expense dictates an increase in the vegetable quota – avocado, mild green peppers and tomato often come in a halved avocado. In Ecuador, a conch seviche dressed with bitter orange juice is the morning-after pick-me-up.

2 dozen oysters, shucked and roughly
  chopped
2 yellow or green chillies, de-seeded and finely
  chopped
2–3 spring onions, trimmed and roughly
  chopped
4 tablespoons lime or lemon juice or
  white wine vinegar
Salt

To serve:
Chopped coriander
Pickled chillies
Quartered limes or lemons

Combine all the ingredients, leave to marinate for 3–4 hours, drain, spoon back into the shells or glass bowls, dress with freshly chopped coriander and serve well-chilled, with pickled chillies and quartered limes.

Seviche de ostras, a cool salad of marinated oysters

mussels

You can tell the difference between shore- and rope-grown mussels by the clusters of tiny barnacles on the shore-grown ones, the colour of the shell which is blue-black in shore-grown mussels rather than browny-gold, and the shape, which in the shore-grown is shorter and broader than the relatively easy-living rope-mussel.

Browny-gold rope-grown mussels

Culinary uses

Mussels are visually dramatic in their blue-black shells with pearly-white linings which cradle plump little orange cushions – particularly when served with a snowy pile of rice. Don't scrub or scrape the mussels until you're ready to cook them: once bearded, they die.

Habitat

The mussel is a prolific breeder whose tiny spat cling to any available sea-washed surface, reaching full maturity in 3–4 years, colonising estuaries, rocky promontories and anywhere a mollusc can find something to cling to while it feeds on passing debris. For this reason, when gathering, make sure you pick a clean shoreline well away from any effluent.

Appearance and taste

Shells are blue-black to honey-gold and the meat is ivory to a deep orange, depending on diet and time of year. Small mussels are more tender than large ones: anything over 8cm (3in) long is inclined to be tough. The taste is sweet, sea-breezy and only mildly fishy.

Buying and storing

Bivalves can remain alive for as long as they can hold water in their shells. Store them under seaweed in a cool damp place – no longer than a week in a tropical climate, a fortnight if the weather is cool and damp.

Medicinal and other uses

There is an official quarantine in North America on all wild bivalves from May 1st to October 1st – the summer months, the breeding season – which, if applied in the Americas of the southern hemisphere, would run roughly from December to March. The quarantine is imposed because mussels, clams and oysters are filter-feeders which can concentrate quantities of a toxic one-celled organism which 'blooms' in warm waters in summer. The toxin, which is not destroyed by freezing or cooking, can be fatal. Aqua-cultured shellfish such as rope-grown mussels are regularly monitored and tested for toxic build-up, so can be considered safe throughout the year.

Mejillones gratinados

(Grilled mussels)
Serves 4

Big fat bay-mussels given a fragrant little hat of parsley and cheese.

900g (2lb) live mussels in the shell
2 cloves garlic, finely chopped
2 tablespoons finely chopped parsley
4 tablespoons fresh white breadcrumbs
4 tablespoons olive oil
Tabasco or any hot chilli sauce
*2 tablespoons slivered parmesan or any hard
   cheese*

Scrub and beard the mussels. Rinse and transfer to a roomy pot with a splash of water. Put the lid on tightly and shake over the heat until the shells open.

Open the mussels completely, leaving the meat on one half of the shells and discarding the other. Arrange neatly on a grill pan. Sprinkle each mussel with a little garlic, parsley and breadcrumbs, trickle with oil and a shake of chilli sauce, and finish with a sliver of cheese. Grill under a high heat until the breadcrumbs are brown and crisp and the cheese melted.

Mariscada do Baiana

(Mussels with rice and coconut milk)
Serves 6–8

Big fat mussels which thrive on the rocky headlands of the Bay of Bahia are served in a deliciously soupy rice enriched with coconut cream.

*2.5 litres (4 pints) mussels, bearded and
  scrubbed*
2 glasses white wine
1 bay leaf
3 tablespoons extra-virgin olive oil
1 large onion, skinned and chopped
2 garlic cloves, finely chopped
350g (12oz) long-grain white rice

*450g (1lb) skinned, chopped, fresh tomatoes
  or canned plum tomatoes*
Finely grated zest of an orange
1 tablespoon chopped parsley
1 tablespoon chopped basil
1 teaspoon chopped coriander
150ml ($^1/_4$ pint) unsweetened coconut milk
Salt and pepper

To serve:
Malagueta pepper sauce (see p.51)

In a large, heavy soup kettle or steamer bring the wine to the boil with the bay leaf. Tip in the cleaned shellfish, cover and steam over a high heat for long enough to open the shells: 5–6 minutes should do the trick. Remove the mussels, discarding any which haven't opened.

Strain and reserve the liquor. Heat the oil in a heavy pan over a medium heat and sauté the onion and garlic until translucent. Add the rice and turn it in the hot oil. Add the tomatoes and let it all bubble up for a couple of minutes. Finally, add the orange zest, mussel liquor and a mugful of boiling water, bring to the boil, and cover. Simmer for 10 minutes, stirring from time to time.

Stir in the herbs and season with salt and pepper. Simmer for another 5 minutes and stir in the coconut milk. Bring back to the boil, add the mussels and carry on cooking until the rice is tender but still soupy – a few more minutes. Hand pepper sauce separately.

shrimp, prawn, crayfish and lobster

All the usual crustaceans, including shrimp, prawn, crayfish and lobster – both common and spiny – are prolific on the eastern and western shores of the region. Brazil is particularly blessed, as are those parts of the Caribbean where stocks have not been fished to extinction. Lobster, though in short supply on the Atlantic coast, provides a livelihood for the creel-fishermen of Juan Fernández, a volcanic archipelago 500 miles off the coast of Chile, the islands which gave shelter to the shipwrecked Alexander Selkirk, Robinson Crusoe's alter ego.

Appearance and taste

When raw, shrimp and prawns are generally grey-green to almost transparent, though some deep-sea species can be a beautiful carmine. All turn browny-pink to a deep red when cooked. The flesh is sweet, fragrant and, when perfectly fresh, a little chewy. Deep-sea lobsters, when uncooked, are a darker blue than those which live in shallower waters. Crawfish – variously called langouste, langoustine and crayfish – are mottled orange-red when caught and don't noticeably change colour in the pot.

Buying and storing

Buy fresh from the creel whenever you can. If in the market, buy your lobster live (the tail should snap back when flattened). With shrimp and prawn, check for firmness and bright, black button-eyes, and use your nose. If ready-cooked, lobster should have a curl to the tail – a sign it was still lively when popped in the boiling pot; prawn and shrimp should look plump and bright rather than dull and shrunken.

Culinary uses

To cook shrimp or prawn, bring to the boil in plenty of salted water, re-boil, wait for a minute or two until the carapaces turn red, and drain under the cold tap. To prepare live lobster, shove a sharp instrument into the space between the back of the head and the carapace, then plunge it into boiling water, holding it under until the shell reddens and the water re-boils. Allow 15 minutes for a 450g (1lb) lobster, 20 minutes for a two-pounder and so on, adding 10 minutes per pound or 20 minutes per kilo. Allow it to cool in the cooking water and then split it straight down the middle with a sharp knife. Carefully lift out the dark intestinal sack which runs round down the back, and remove the feathery little dead men's fingers (gills) from the head.

Croquetas de gambas

(Prawn croquettes)
Serves 6–8

Time-consuming, to be sure – but patience is well rewarded by the pleasure of these crisply jacketed little morsels with their melting, creamy hearts. It is best if you make your own stock – simmer the shrimp debris with plenty of onion, carrot and green celery – though ready-made will do.

450g (1lb) shelled, cooked shrimp or prawn, chopped
1/2 mild onion, grated, or 4–5 spring onions, finely chopped
1 heaped tablespoon parsley

The sauce:
4 tablespoons butter
4 tablespoons flour (more, if you're not confident of your skill)
600ml (1 pint) hot fish stock
Salt and cayenne pepper

To finish:
A plateful of seasoned flour
1–2 eggs, lightly forked with a little milk
A plateful of fresh breadcrumbs
Oil for frying

Mix the chopped shrimp or prawn with the onion and parsley.

Melt the butter in a heavy-bottomed pan. As soon as it froths, stir in the flour. Lower the heat and stir for a moment or two until it looks sandy (don't let it brown). Whisk in the hot stock in a steady stream, until you have a smooth thick sauce. Season with salt and cayenne pepper. Continue simmering for 5 minutes to cook the flour. Stir in the prawn mixture, spread in a dish, leave to cool, cover with clingfilm and set in the fridge to firm for an hour or two or overnight. Form the mixture into neat little bite-sized bolsters – work as quickly and lightly as you can and have a bowl of warm water ready for dipping your hands. Dust through the flour, dip in the egg whisked with its own volume of milk, and then roll delicately in the breadcrumbs. If there are any bald patches, repeat the egg-and-breadcrumbing. Leave in a cool place for 30 minutes to set the coating.

Heat enough oil to submerge the croquetas. Wait until the oil is faintly hazed with blue, then slip one in. If the coating splits open, the oil's too hot. If it stays soft, the oil's too cool. The first croqueta is simply experimental.

Once you have adjusted the heat, fry in batches, a few at a time. Remove and drain as soon as they crisp and gild. Serve with chilli sauce for dipping, or a dish of pickled chillies.

Moqueca de camarão, a spicy shrimp stew enriched with coconut cream

Moqueca de camarão
(Bahian shrimp stew)
Serves 6

The sauce in which the fish is cooked – *moqueca* – takes its name and approach, steam-cooking, from the *pokekas*, the Guarani earth-oven. Following the earth-oven principle, the ingredients are simply what comes to hand, in any combination. The shrimp can be replaced with chicken and a grander version can be made with lobster; it can even be made with vegetables alone. The two constants are the rice and the finishing with dende oil or oil coloured with paprika or anatto.

700g (1¹/₂lb) fresh raw shrimp or prawns
2 tablespoons vegetable oil
225g (8 oz) chorizo, sliced
1 large onion, finely chopped
2 garlic cloves, skinned and finely chopped
1 red pepper, de-seeded and chopped
1–2 red chillies

450g (1lb) tomatoes, skinned and chopped
150 ml (¹/₄ pint) coconut milk
Salt

To finish:
1 tablespoon dende oil or vegetable oil coloured with anatto or a pinch of paprika
White rice, ready-cooked

Pick over the shrimp and rinse. Peel them or not, as you please. Heat the oil in a heavy frying pan. Fry the chorizo slices until the fat runs and it browns a little, then remove and reserve.

Add the remaining oil to the hot juices in the pan and fry the onion, garlic, red pepper and chillies gently until soft – don't let them burn. Add the tomatoes and bubble up, mashing with a wooden spoon to soften the fibres. Add the coconut milk and simmer for 10 minutes till rich and thick. Taste and add salt. Lay the shrimp on top to cook in the steam – a minute or two. Pile on white rice and finish with a trickle of dende or paprika oil.

crab

centolla (spider crab), cangrejo (common crab), caranguejo (Brazilian mangrove-crab), siri (common crab)

A round-bodied crustacean with or without claws, the crab varies when alive from pale, almost translucent green to brick red, but it is always red when cooked. In common with all crustaceans, the crab is a scavenger.

Habitat

Opportunist and voracious feeders, crabs are found wherever there's a ready source of edible debris – human or piscine – on beaches, rocks and in shallow waters, with some species – Brazil's mangrove crabs – living their lives on shore. Lobstermen hate them because they devour everything in the creel. Inshore fishermen use them for bait and take home the claws which get caught in their nets. Deep-water crabs take refuge in wrecks during storms.

Appearance and taste

Of all the many species of crab, the most interesting gastronomically are the common crab, Cancer sp, including the small-clawed Dungeness native to the Pacific coast as far as Alaska; the blue crab, an Atlantic species found in the Caribbean – also known as the soft-shell for its annual shedding of its carapace; and the spider-crab, more troublesome to pick over but with the sweetest flavour, which is popular in Chile. In Brazil, mangrove crabs, *caranguejo*, are held in high esteem – they are more often found on restaurant menus than sea-crabs. All crabs, when cooked, have delicate, slightly sweet, snowy-to-cream flesh which flakes easily.

Buying and storing

Crabs are available alive (and they must be truly lively – don't pay money for dead meat); ready-cooked and in the shell; as dressed crab – the meat ready-picked and packed back into the shell; or ready-picked, meat only, sold by weight (best for freezing).

Culinary uses

To cook live crabs, allow 12 minutes for a 1kg (2lb) crab, brought gently to the boil in unsalted water (add salt as soon as it boils), timed after the water returns to boil; in a steamer, allow 15 minutes. Once it is cooked, pull the body from the carapace and leave it to drain, cool and set. Separate the body from the shell, crack off the mouthpiece and remove the feathery grey gills which fringe the carapace. Now you're ready to pick your crab with whatever you can; use one of the legs as a prodder to get into the corners. As well as the white meat which has to be carefully picked from the body, all crabs have darker, smoother meat just inside the shell: the crab-butter or dark meat. Don't discard this, but incorporate it in your dish. Ready-picked crab-meat is perfect for soups and sauce-based dishes such as croquettes. Soft-shells – moulted crab – are best fried whole: there is no need to pick. Mangrove-crabs have the most delicate meat and need no sauce: boil and eat with a squeeze of lemon and a shake of malagueta pepper.

Crabs for sale by the roadside, São Francisco do Sul, Brazil

Pil-pil de cangrejo
(Chilli crab)

Serves 4

Chileans like their seafood – including baby eels and frog's legs – cooked in a little sauce of oil, chilli and garlic, and served so hot you need a little wooden fork to eat it with.

I large crab weighing 1kg (2^1/$_2$lb), yielding 450g (1lb) meat
4 cloves garlic, slivered
1 teaspoon small dried chillies or 2 fresh chillies, de-seeded and chopped
150ml (^{1}/$_4$ pint) olive oil
1 small glass brandy
Salt

If your crab is alive, bring it gently to the boil in plenty of salted water. Allow 15 minutes for the first pound and 10 minutes for each subsequent pound. Pick all the meat out of the shell and claws: the only non-edible bits are the mouth-piece and the feathery grey gills, the 'dead man's fingers'. Heat the oil in a shallow pan until a faint blue haze rises. Add the garlic and chillies and fry for a moment. Stir in the crabmeat and the brandy. Allow all to bubble up fiercely to evaporate the alcohol. That's all.

Jamaican crab patties
Serves 6

Delicious little appetisers, hand-held – these should be served with a rum punch.

The meat from 1 large crab or 2 smaller ones
2–3 tablespoons oil
4 spring onions, rinsed and chopped
1 teaspoon peppercorns, roughly crushed
1 teaspoon turmeric
^{1}/$_2$ teaspoon salt
1 tomato, roughly chopped
450g (1lb) puff-pastry
1 egg, beaten

Pick over the crab, discarding any bits of shell. Warm the oil in a frying pan and add the onion and the spices and salt. Stir for a moment. Add the tomato and bubble up, crushing down to make a sauce. Add the crabmeat. Fry gently for a few minutes and put aside to cool.

Pre-heat the oven to 190°C/375°F/gas mark 5.

Roll out the puff pastry and cut into hand-sized rounds with a 8cm (3in) pastry-cutter or a wine-glass. Put a dab of the crab-mixture on each round, wet the edge and fold it over to make a semi-circular patty. Paint the tops with beaten egg. Bake for 15–20 minutes, until well-risen and golden.

Pil-pil de cangrejo, sizzling crabmeat with chilli

dried shrimp

or camarão or camarón seco

These sun-dried shrimp are spread out to dry in the warm sea-breezes of the coast and sent inland to be enjoyed by those who don't have ready access to the shore. Dried shrimp are important in Brazil and Mexico, both of which have large Catholic populations for whom it is a useful resource for fast-days when meat cannot be eaten: the forty days of Lent, Fridays and the eves of all the saints' days.

Manufacture

In Brazil, dried shrimp are prepared by the shrimp fishermen themselves who rub the catch with a little dende oil and spread it in the sun to dry. To prepare your own, toss fresh shrimp in dende oil (or any oil infused with anatto) and dry in the highest possible oven for 12–20 minutes. Finish under the grill to crisp the shell (don't allow it to blacken), then toss with salt. They keep for a week in the fridge.

Appearance and taste

Bright red, crunchy, salty but sweet, with a flavour of parmesan and honey, sun-dried shrimp are the ingredient which defines the cooking of Bahia, Brazil's most populous province. In all the fishing villages along the coast, you'll see the fishermen tossing glistening hills of tiny crustaceans dyed bright red with dende oil, raking them over and over again in the scorching sun. At night the heaps are covered with a tarpaulin to protect them from the ocean-breeze. The process is repeated for two days until the shells are crisp and crunchy and the flesh tender but still a little chewy. Sometimes they're smoked as well, to add a little extra shelf-life.

Buying and storing

Dried shrimp are to be found in West African grocery-stores and are readily available in oriental foodshops in plastic packets. The oriental shrimp may be a little chewier than the Bahian version, and will lack the remarkable colour of the dende oil, but are perfectly acceptable. Stored in a jar in a cool dry place, they keep almost indefinitely.

Medicinal and other uses

Storability is dried shrimp's great virtue, delivering protein, minerals and vitamins which may be in short supply.

Culinary uses

Particularly good as a finishing sprinkle for a bean salad or a soupy dish of rice, dried shrimp add texture as well as flavour. To prepare for any recipe which calls for fresh shrimp, soak in warm water for half an hour to rehydrate.

Casting a fishing net over Lake Vittoria Espíritu Santo, Brazil

Camarón seco con frijole blanco

(Mexican dried shrimp and white beans)
Serves 4

Dried and semi-dried shrimp – moist and orangey in colour – form an important part of fast-day food throughout Latin America. This is a Lenten dish from the beautiful valley of Oaxaca in Central Mexico, where fresh fish was hard to come by.

175g (6oz) dried shrimp
2 large tomatoes, skinned (or 1 can plum tomatoes)
1 small onion, roughly chopped
4–5 garlic cloves, chopped
3 tablespoons seed oil
450g (1lb) cooked, drained white haricot beans
2–3 epasote leaves or dill fronds

Put the dried shrimp to soak in a little warm water for 10 minutes, then drain. Process the tomatoes to a thick pulp with the onion, garlic and a little water until smooth. Heat the oil in a frying pan, add the liquidised tomato and simmer until thick – about 15 minutes.

Stir the tomato mixture into the soft beans along with the epasote or dill. Stir in the shrimp, add a cupful of boiling water and simmer until the shrimp are tender – 10 minutes, no more.

Serve with soft tortillas for scooping, Mexican style. A ripe avocado roughly mashed with a little salt and lime juice would be an appropriate accompaniment.

Vatapá

(Bahian dried shrimp relish)
Serves 4–6

A relish or dipping-sauce, vatapá is made with crushed nuts, coconut milk and sun-dried shrimp, thickened with bread and served with seafood in much the same way as mayonnaise. It is eaten as street-food with acarajé, black-eyed pea fritters (see p.77), or – for more formal dining – a skewerful of barbecued prawns, a fish stew or a grilled lobster. Vatapá is also used to thicken the juices of Bahia's surf-n-turf

Camarón seco con frijole blanco, a white bean salad topped with crunchy shrimps

dishes – pork and shrimp, poultry and prawns, and is indispensable with a shrimp moqueca (see p.139) or to thicken the juices of a chicken-and-prawn xinxim (see p.173).

225g (¹/₂lb) yesterday's dried-out country bread
300ml (¹/₂ pint) coconut milk
110g (4oz) dried shrimp
110g (4oz) roasted cashews and roasted peanuts
1 walnut-sized piece fresh ginger, grated
Salt and malagueta pepper sauce (see p.51)

To finish:
Juice of half a lime
1 tablespoon dende oil or any oil coloured with achiote

Crumble the bread and soak thoroughly with the coconut milk and leave to swell for at least 1 hour.

Put the shrimp and the nuts in a mortar or a food-processor and pound to a powder. Mix with the soaked bread in a heavy porridge pot, and transfer to the top of the stove. Add the ginger, season with salt and malagueta pepper, dilute with a glass of water, bubble up, turn down the heat and cook gently for about 10 minutes, until thick and smooth. Beat in the juice of half a lime and a trickle of oil. The consistency should be light and soft rather than dense and porridge-like – a little more coconut cream will lighten it if necessary. Serve with quartered limes, plain-boiled rice and farofa (see p.60) for sprinkling.

large steak-fish

Swordfish, tuna, shark, dolphin-fish: these are the predators, the lords of the ocean, using all the world's waters as both thoroughfare and foodsource.

tuna steak

Habitat

These migratory fish are to be found wherever a foodsource can be assured, particularly near the large coastal cities, where smaller fish find nourishment among the effluent.

Appearance and taste

The firm, steak-like flesh ranges from the pure-white flesh of the swordfish to the deep ruby red of the tuna.

Buying and storing

The larger the fish the longer its shelf-life – a fact which is both a blessing and a curse. On the one hand, steak-fish comes fresher to market than its smaller cousins, on the other hand, it's more difficult to tell the good from the almost-bad. Use your nose and finger. Steak-fish should smell sweet – never ammoniacal – and be firm to the touch.

Medicinal and other uses

Tuna and dolphin-fish – mahi-mahi – contain measurable quantities of histidine, an amino acid which turns to histamine when the fish is caught in tropical waters and not properly cooled and stored. Histamine poisoning – the main symptoms are flushing, dizziness and a headache – can be treated with antihistamines, which make the effects quickly disappear.

Culinary uses

Throughout the territory, but particularly on the Pacific coast, fresh fish – filleted and diced or beaten to tenderise – is eaten raw in the form of seviche: small pieces of fish marinated in an acid bath, a remarkably rapid process. In pre-columbian times, before the Europeans planted citrus groves, the marinade was the juice of the indigenous passionfruit.

Reed fishing boats drying on a Peruvian beach

Seviche de atún peruviana

(Lime-marinated tuna)

Serves 6

In Peru, a seviche is served as a full meal with a variety of accompaniments.

450g (1lb) fresh tuna, skinned and diced
1 level teaspoon sea-salt

To dress:
6 tablespoons lime or bitter orange juice
1 mild onion, chopped
3 tablespoons peanut oil
2 tablespoons roughly crushed toasted
* peanuts*
1 fresh red chilli, de-seeded and finely chopped

Dice the fish and turn it with the salt in a bowl. Mix the dressing ingredients together and toss them with the fish in a bowl. Cover and leave in a cool place for at least an hour to take the flavours. Taste, adjust the seasoning, and finish with a little more oil. Serve with slices of cooked sweet potatoes and sweetcorn, shredded lettuce, fresh or pickled chillies and onion rings soaked to soften in a little salted water.

Budín de cazón

(Baked fish pudding)

Serves 6–8

Shark meat – *cazón*, dogfish – straight from the blue waters of the bay of Mexico, is a favourite of the housewives of Campeche who prepare it as a *sopa seca* or dry soup. Here it's given a quick oven-gilding, much like a lasagne. Any other firm white fish can be substituted.

450g (1lb) shark meat (dogfish) or any firm-
* fleshed white fish*
1 onion, thickly sliced
1 bay leaf
1 stalk epasote or dill (optional)
1 tablespoon white wine vinegar
Salt

To finish:
6–8 wheatflour tortillas, cut into squares
6 tablespoons unsalted butter

Seviche de atún peruviana

6 chiles poblanos, charred, de-seeded and cut
* into ribbons*
600ml (1 pint) fresh tomato sauce
300ml (1/2 pint) soured cream
4 tablespoons grated white cheese (cheddar
* is fine)*

Preheat the oven to 200°C/400°F/gas mark 6.

Poach the fish in the aromatics, vinegar, salt and enough water to cover in a lidded pan. When the fish is firm and opaque – 8–10 minutes – remove and bubble up the poaching liquid until it is reduced to a couple of tablespoons. Skin, bone and flake the fish and moisten it with the poaching liquor.

Meanwhile, fry the tortilla pieces in a little of the butter in batches, until golden and crisp, and reserve. Heat the tomato sauce in the remaining butter and bubble up, mashing down to thicken, and reserve.

Assemble the budín. Cover the base of a gratin dish with half the tortilla pieces and top with a layer of shredded fish, chilli ribbons and half the tomato sauce. Follow with a layer of the remaining tortilla pieces, then the rest of the sauce and finish with the soured cream and the cheese. Bake in the oven for 20–25 minutes, until deliciously brown and bubbling.

medium-sized round-bodied whole fish

Sea bass, congrio, scrod, mullet and grouper are all white-fleshed fish which can be cooked whole.

Appearance and taste

Sea bass and related fish of the drummer family – *Sciaenidae* – whose means of communication is a loud drumming sound produced by snapping their air bladders, are slender, round-bodied silver-scaled fish with easily visible bones and flesh which cooks to large creamy flakes. Congrio is not, as it would be in Spain, an eel but a big-headed, narrow-bodied member of the grouper family which looks and cooks like monkfish: firm, white and dense.

Buying and storing

An open mouth and gaping gills are a sign a fish is very fresh. The most sought-after members of this group are close to being

Fishing boats, Ciudad de Carmen, Mexico

fished beyond receovery. Among these, the corvina or Chilean sea bass, *Dissostichus eleginoides*, also known as the Patagonian toothfish and Australian sea bass, has been fished to the edge of its sustainable level – in other words, we shouldn't be eating it at all. A great many very fine fish are sold under the general name of sea bass – go for the farmed varieties.

Medicinal and other uses

Fish is the ideal food. Without going into detail, this is practically fat-free, unadulterated protein in easily digestible form: in other words, all a person needs to sustain life in one easy package. The only part of a fish which can be toxic is the liver, although it is a delicacy in some, such as skate and members of the cod family; it is best avoided unless you're sure of your species.

Culinary uses

All fish share the same anatomy, a basic knowledge of which will help you deal with unfamiliar species. The spine – a jointed, highly flexible central bone from which grow finer lateral bones which support the flesh and provide an anchor for the dorsal fins – runs from head to tail. When the fish is raw, pressing along the spine loosens the flesh ready for filleting. When cooked whole, the flesh can be lifted off the bone without disturbing the central spine or the lateral bones (which also form the rib cavity). Gently does it. The cheeks are a delicacy, as is the sweet meat just behind the head – one reason for cooking the fish with its head on.

Causa a la chiclayana

(Fisherman's seafood platter)
Serves 6

A Peruvian assembly of fish, potatoes, cheese, eggs and vegetables – a fisherman's dish, made with whatever swam into the net too late or too early to market. All are welcome, none indispensable.

700g (1¹/₂lb) congrio or monkfish fillets
1 tablespoon seasoned flour
4 tablespoons olive oil
900g (2lb) yellow-fleshed potatoes, peeled and cut into chunks
2 tablespoons finely chopped parsley
1 garlic clove, finely chopped
Salt

Vegetable accompaniments:
2 fresh sweetcorn, each sliced into 3 pieces
450g (1lb) sweet potato, peeled and thickly sliced
450g (1lb) cassava root, peeled and thickly sliced
3 ripe plantains, peeled and sliced lengthwise, then crosswise

Dressing:
3 onions, finely sliced
2 hot red chillies, de-seeded and cut into strips
1 wine-glass white wine vinegar
1 wine-glass olive oil

To serve:
Crisp lettuce leaves
3 hardboiled eggs, quartered
6 slices fresh white cheese
A handful black olives

Lightly salt the fish fillets, dredge through the seasoned flour and fry quickly in 2 tablespoons of oil for a minute or two, turning once, until firm and a little golden. Remove to kitchen paper and reserve. Boil the potatoes in plenty of salted water until tender – about 20 minutes. Drain, mash with the parsley, garlic and remaining oil, and heap in the middle of a serving dish.

Meanwhile, attend to the vegetable accompaniments: boil the sweetcorn without salt for 5 minutes; boil the sweet potato and cassava until tender – about 30 minutes; and fry the plantains in a little oil until they brown. Arrange all the accompaniments on a serving dish around the mashed potato.

Now make the dressing. In a small pan, bring the onions and chilli strips to the boil in enough salted water to cover. Drain, return to the pan and add the vinegar and oil. Bring back to the boil and pour the hot dressing over the mashed potato. Arrange the lettuce leaves round the edge of the platter and top with the fish fillets, hardboiled eggs, cheese slices and olives.

Corvina colombiana

Corvina colombiana

(Sea bass baked in coconut milk)

Serves 4–6

Simple but delicious: the coconut milk keeps the fish moist and makes its own creamy sauce. Any medium-sized, round-bodied, white-fleshed fish will do – bream and congrio are also excellent candidates – so long as your choice is beautifully fresh and bright-eyed.

1 whole fish, 1.3–1.8kg (3–4lb) in weight
Salt
1 yellow or red chilli, de-seeded and finely
  chopped
1 sprig thyme
2–3 whole heads fresh fennel (or 6 baby
  fennel), sliced lengthways
1 large onion, finely sliced
600ml (1 pint) coconut milk

sea bass

Wipe the fish inside and out, season the cavity with salt and a few scraps of chopped chilli, and tuck in the sprig of thyme.

Preheat the oven to 180°C/350°F/gas mark 4. Lay the fish on a bed of fennel in an oval heat-proof casserole with a lid (or use a roasting tin and lid with foil). Cover with sliced onion, season with salt and the remaining chilli, and pour the coconut milk around it. Bake for 45–55 minutes, until the flesh is firm to the finger when pressed. The time it takes is dictated by thickness rather than weight.

medium-sized flat-bodied whole fish

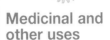

bream

Species in this category include bream, porgy, snapper (sometimes known as red-fish) and dorado (a name applied to bream on the west coast but to dolphin-fish, otherwise known as mahi-mahi, in the Caribbean).

Habitat
These fish are found in harbours, estuaries and tidal waters as well as deep sea. As a child in Uruguay, I used to fish half-pound dorado – young gilt-head bream – off the harbour wall at Punta del Este, now a fashionable seaside resort but at the time, in the 1950s, a small fishing village at the mouth of the River Plate.

Appearance and taste
These flat-bodied fish of medium size share one important culinary characteristic: their bodies are compressed – flattened – allowing them to be quickly cooked without needing to be filleted or cut into steaks. Although they don't fetch high prices in the market, they're excellent everyday eating, succulent and sweet-fleshed.

Buying and storing
Look for a bright eye, flesh which is firm to the finger, and a clean, sweet sea-scent.

Red snapper for sale on the pier in La Libertad, El Salvador

Medicinal and other uses
While all sea-creatures are edible, a few store up toxins in their livers or ovaries – a protective measure against predators. Two of the Pacific's coastal fish have poisonous roes, the cabezón and the alligator gar.

Culinary uses
The most valuable characteristic of these flat-bodied fish is their shape – even the largest can be poached, steamed, baked or fried in no more than 10 minutes.

Patacones del pescador
(Fisherman's fishcakes)
Serves 4–6

Easy, convenient, delicious and cheap: make these spicy fishcakes with leftovers or frozen fish if you can't find fresh.

The fritters:
225g (8oz) flaked, cooked fish
700g (1¹/₂lb) potatoes, cut into chunks
1 mild onion, grated
2 tablespoons grated cheese
3 eggs
1 tablespoon pimentón (mild paprika)
1 teaspoon chilli flakes
Olive oil for frying

The salsa:
1 green chilli, de-seeded and finely chopped
1 mild onion, finely chopped
2 garlic cloves, finely chopped
6 tablespoons finely chopped parsley
2 lemons, juice and zest
1 teaspoon sugar

Boil the potatoes in enough salted water to cover. Drain and mash thoroughly with the grated onion and cheese. Beat in the eggs and mix in the flaked fish, and season with pimentón, chilli and a little salt. Refrigerate for half an hour.

Meanwhile, combine the salsa ingredients and set aside in a cool place to marinate – the flavours need a little time to blend.

Heat a panful of olive oil for shallow-frying. When it is lightly hazed with blue, drop in teaspoonfuls of the fish mixture – not too many at a time. Wait until they puff and gild, turn them over once, then remove with a slotted spoon and drain on kitchen towel. Serve straight from the pan with the salsa handed around separately.

Brotola al horno

(Oven-baked bream with root vegetables)

Serves 4

This is the way Esperanza, my mother's cook in Uruguay, liked to prepare the morning's catch. As a diplomatic family, we were the proud owners of the first electric oven in Montevideo, and Esperanza made the most of it. Any of the medium-sized estuary fish can be given the same treatment, accompanied by any root vegetables, though an element of sweetness is essential.

1 sea bream, weighing about 1kg (2lb) cleaned weight, head left on

450g (1lb) sweet potatoes, peeled and cut into chunks

450g (1lb) potatoes, peeled and cut into chunks

450g (1lb) smallish yellow onions, skinned and quartered

450g (1lb) ripe firm tomatoes, cut into chunks

1 glass dry white wine

4 tablespoons olive oil

Rough salt and chilli flakes

Wipe over the fish, salt the cavity and set aside to come to room temperature.

Preheat the oven to 180°C/350°F/Gas4.

Arrange the vegetables in a roasting tin, pour in the wine, trickle with the oil and finish with liberal dusting of salt and chilli flakes. Cover with foil, shiny-side down. Bake for 20 minutes, until the vegetables are nearly tender. Carefully remove the foil. Place the fish on the bed of vegetables, sprinkle with salt and chilli flakes, replace the foil and bake for another 10 minutes, until the fish is cooked right through. It's ready when it feels firm to your finger. Remove and leave on one side for another 10 minutes, so that the heat can penetrate right through to the bone. The cheek is the cook's perk.

small fish and fry

fresh anchovies

Sardines, anchovies, herring, pejerreyes (the Chilean smelt) and the small fry of larger fish are the bread-and-butter of the inshore fishing fleets. A short shelf-life – the result of natural oiliness and relatively small size – means that the catch, unless salted or preserved in some other way, stays close to home.

Habitat

Small fish – shoal-fish whose survival strategy depends on numbers – provide larger fish with a foodsource. Find one, and you'll find the other. Perhaps because of this, the movements of small fish shoals are notoriously unpredictable, but when you catch one, you catch plenty. While fritter-fish are usually a sea-harvest, the small, silver Chilean smelt, very delicate and delicious, is found in rivers and lakes as well as the ocean.

Appearance and taste

Sardines are silver all over, with large, visible scales which loosen and flake off as the fish deteriorates; they have short blunt heads and shiny dark eyes, and the heads take on a bloody look the longer they've been out of the water. In size, they vary from small as your thumb to twice as long as your hand. Anchovies and smelts are noticeably more slender, with small pointed heads and no visible scales. The anchovy has a dark stripe down the flanks and a distinctly emerald sheen.

Buying and storing

Small oily fish are vulnerable to spoilage: it is best to buy as close to the fishing grounds as possible – or pay a good price to a reliable fishmonger. When buying on the harbour front, test for freshness by dipping a finger in the brine and touching it to your tongue: if the run-off is noticeably salty, the fishermen have waited too long on the tide.

Casting nets over Lake Janit-Zio, Mexico

Medicinal and other uses

The virtues of oily fish are well known: they are rich in protein, vitamins, minerals and those all important omega fatty acids which help in the prevention of heart disease.

Culinary uses

Small fish with a high fat-content deteriorate quickly – a matter of hours rather than days. Until refrigeration was available, ingenuity was needed to make the catch last long enough to get it to market. One solution was salting and barrelling, which led in turn to the sardine-canning industry. The canning-factories of Baja California – made famous in John Steinbeck's stories of Cannery Row – were established to take advantage of the huge hauls of sardines and anchovies landed by the fishermen of the Sea of Cortez. One day, the silvery hoards simply vanished, no one knows where or why, and the industry with it.

Choose the preparation method appropriate to the size. Flour and deep-fry the tiny ones, head, guts, scales and all (sardine and smelt scales slip off easily with a little encouragement under the tap); medium-sized fish can be butterflied: slit the fish down the belly with your thumb and remove the backbone and innards along with the head; anchovies never grow too large to fritter, while large sardines are best kept for the grill.

Pescaítos fritos

(Little fried fish)

Serves 4

A blend of wheatflour and cornmeal produces a deliciously crisp crust, especially if you twice-fry them. The real secret is the absolute freshness of the raw materials: the smaller the fish, the shorter its shelf-life. This treatment is suitable for all fish of any breed so long as they're no longer than your hand: sardines, smelts, squid, snapper, as well as fillets of larger fish.

450g (1lb) fresh anchovies
4 tablespoons flour
1 heaped tablespoon cornmeal
1 heaped teaspoon rough salt
a sprinkling of crushed, dried
  oregano (optional)
Olive or vegetable oil for frying

To serve:
Quartered lemons

Gut the fish (unnecessary if they're tiny) and leave the heads on if the fish are no longer than your thumb. If they're larger, run your finger down the backbone to loosen, and pull it out, leaving the two halves joined. Nip the heads off. Rinse and drain but don't pat dry.

Mix the flour with the cornmeal, salt and optional oregano on a flat plate.

Heat the frying oil in a pan – Hispanic cooks only use as much as will submerge the food to be cooked. When the oil is hot enough to fry (a faint blue haze will rise from the surface), flip the wet fish through the flour one by one and drop them in the hot oil.   Fry in small batches to avoid the temperature dropping and remove while still quite pale. Transfer to kitchen paper to drain. Continue until all are done. Repeat the process to crisp and colour.

Serve piping hot with quartered lemons, a plate of chips and a salad of diced tomatoes, onion and cucumber, just as they do in the harbour-front cafes of Valparaiso.

Pescaítos fritos, crisply jacketed little fried fish

Pejerreyes en vinagre

(Vinegar-pickled smelts)

Serves 4 as a starter

This is a good recipe for the larger sized small fish, caught by the inshore fishing fleets who sell them fast and cheap in the morning market. This – a light pickle – adds at least a week to the shelf-life in a cool larder, even without refrigeration. Start 48 hours ahead.

450 g (1lb) fresh smelts (or anchovies or
  sardines)
150ml (¹/4 pint) white wine vinegar
2 tablespoons water
1 tablespoon salt
2–3 garlic cloves, cut into fine slivers
1 green chilli, de-seeded and finely chopped

To finish:
1 tablespoon olive oil
2 tablespoons flat-leaf parsley

Rinse the smelts and drain thoroughly. Press lightly down the body of the fish to loosen the flesh from the bones. Holding the head firmly between finger and thumb, pull down through the belly towards the tail. The spine and ribs should slip easily through the soft flesh, gutting and splitting all in one movement. Nick the spine at the base of the tail, leaving the tail still attached. Continue until all the fish are gutted and butterflied.

Open each fish flat and lay it flesh upwards in a single layer in a shallow dish. Mix the vinegar with the water and salt and pour over the fish – they should be well-soaked. Sprinkle with the garlic and chilli, cover with foil and leave in the fridge to marinate for 48 hours. (They will keep for a week in the fridge.) To serve, drain and finish with a trickle of olive oil and a sprinkle of parsley.

flatfish

Flounder, sole, brill, turbot, halibut, plaice, dab: a family of many faces – all of which are worn on one side of the head, a convenient arrangement for a fish which feeds on the sea-bed, allowing it to keep both eyes out for predators.

Habitat

Flatfish are bottom-feeders, subsisting on a delicate diet of sand-burrowers.

Appearance and taste

Some flatfish, such as the sole and the flounder, which are dextral flatfish, have their faces on the right side of the body, while others, sinistral flatfish, a group which includes turbot and brill, have theirs on the left. The flesh is pure white and lean in all species, the texture thread-like rather than flaky, though firmness and delicacy of flavour varies.

Buying and storing

Buy on the bone and make sure the flesh is firm and the skin veiled rather than slimy, with the tiny scales still firmly attached. As for quality, let price be your guide: the firmer and sweeter and thicker the flesh, the higher the price.

Culinary uses

Flatfish have, as their name suggests, a long flat skeleton which makes it easy to lift the flesh from the bone once it's cooked. Some flatfish can be filleted easily when raw, while others, the cheaper varieties, are harder. For reasons of camouflage, the top skin is dark and beautifully patterned and the underside is pale; the upper skin is relatively easy to pull off, the underside is harder. This matters little if grilling or poaching the fish whole, but is less convenient when filleting.

Buñuelos de pescado

(Seafood fritters)

Serves 4–6 as a starter

An easy solution to the problem of what to do with the lesser members of the flatfish family – all that skin and bone and very little else. You'll need a whole kilo just (over 2lb) of fish to achieve 4 tablespoons of meat: don't bother to gut or trim, simply poach or bake in foil, then separate the flesh from the rest.

About 4 tablespoons cooked flaked fish
1kg (about 2lb) floury potatoes, scrubbed
1 small onion, very finely chopped
2 tablespoons finely chopped parsley
1 chilli, de-seeded and finely chopped
3 eggs
Salt
A little milk (optional)
Oil for frying

Pick over the fish, discarding any stray bones.

Cook the potatoes until tender in plenty of salted water. Drain, skin and mash well. Beat the fish into the mashed potato with the onion, parsley and chilli. Add the eggs one by one, beating between each addition. The mixture should be so stiff a spoon can stand up in it. Add a little milk if it's too dry and allow to cool completely.

Preheat a panful of oil: a cube of bread should crisp and brown immediately.

Using two wet spoons, shape the fish-mixture into egg-sized patties and drop them directly into the hot oil in batches, no more than will comfortably float on the surface. Flip them over several times to puff and brown. Reheat the oil between batches. Drain on kitchen paper and serve piping hot with a dipping sauce – peanut, chilli, tomato or whatever takes your fancy.

sole, the king of the flatfish tribe

El biche

(Ecuadorian bouillabaisse)

Serves 4–6

A delicate fish soup finished with chopped peanuts, fortified with banana dumplings and new potatoes.

450g (1lb) flatfish fillets
Salt
1.2 litres (2 pints) fish stock (made with a
 fish-head)
4 tablespoons oil
2–3 white onions, finely chopped
1 teaspoon cumin seeds

1 teaspoon crushed hot chilli
450g (1lb) new potatoes

Banana dumplings:
2 green bananas or plantains, grated
3 tablespoons toasted, crushed peanuts
2–3 tablespoons fish stock
1 tablespoon chopped coriander

To finish:
3–4 green peppers, roughly chopped
100g (4oz) peas
4 tablespoons toasted, crushed peanuts
1 lemon, grated zest and juice
2 tablespoons chopped coriander

Salt the fish fillets and set them aside. Strain the fish stock, heat the oil in a big pan and add the onions. Cook gently until the onion softens. Sprinkle with cumin seeds and chilli. Add the stock and potatoes and simmer for 20 minutes.

Meanwhile, work the grated banana with the peanuts, coriander and enough fishstock to make a dozen little balls. Slip the balls into the simmering broth and add peppers and peas.

When all is tender, add the peanuts and stir. Slip the fish fillets into the broth and allow them to become firm and opaque – 3–4 minutes. Taste and season. Finish with lemon juice and zest and a sprinkling of coriander.

oil-rich fish

mackerel, bonito, salmon, kingfish, herring

Pacific mackerel – *sierra* – is plentiful on the west coast, while the eastern seaboard has bonito, shad and Atlantic mackerel. The native salmons are the Pacific chinook and the smaller silver salmon. As stocks in the wild vanish through over-fishing, farmed salmon has become an important export crop and a major source of Chilean fishermen's income. Those who live in the Andean uplands stock their lakes with trout – *trucha* – an alternative method of ensuring a good fish dinner.

mackerel

Appearance and taste

Mackerel is one of the most handsome fish in the ocean: long, slender and silver, with no visible scales and dramatically black-patterned blue-green flanks. Salmon is silver from top to toe with rose-pink flesh, a rich flavour and a fragrance reminiscent of its main food-source, shrimp. Really fresh salmon has a creamy curd between flakes; the flesh is pink and falls into large flakes when cooked. Colour is simply a matter of diet: overly-red flesh in a farmed salmon is a sign of too many additives in its feed; the paler the flesh the more likely it's wild-caught. Farmed salmon can be flabby if not given sufficient space to swim against the current. Mackerel is strong meat, with a distinctively cod-liver-oily flavour and flesh which separates into strings.

Buying and storing

To choose fresh fish in the round (whole fish), check the brightness of its eyes and the colour and scent of its gills – you're looking for a deep crimson with a fresh seaweedy scent.

Medicinal and other uses

Oil-rich fish are a prime source of Omega-3 fatty acids, which are good for our hearts, brains and eyesight. A word of warning: salmon – both wild and farmed – is occasionally infested with tapeworm, and is therefore not recommended for seviches unless preliminary precautions are taken. If you want to use salmon in a seviche, first freeze it for 24 hours.

Culinary uses

Oily fish can be baked, steamed, poached or included in a soup – but grilling and frying suits its character. Fish from the freezer is excellent hot-smoked, treatment for which mackerel and bonito as well as salmon and any large river fish are suitable.

Salmon ahumado

(Hot-smoked salmon)
Serves 6

Hot-smoking – the application of heat and smoke to food in a closed pot or earth-oven – is a technique familiar to the river peoples of the Amazonian basin. In the absence of any form of refrigeration, hot-smoking was used for practical rather than epicurean reasons to add a little shelf-life to the river catch. Since river dwellers had no salt, its addition is a modern refinement.

A whole small salmon, about 1.5kg (3–4lb), cleaned, scaled, with the head left on
4–5 tablespoons salt
Sawdust for smoking (from a camping-shop) or dry rice and green tea

You'll need a fish-kettle or a large turkey-roasting pan with a grill on the base.

Rinse the fish and pat dry. Remove the dark red vein which runs down the bone inside the cavity. Sprinkle with the salt, inside and out. Leave in a cool place for a couple of hours. Let it come back to room-temperature and dust off any excess salt. Line the fish-kettle or roasting tin with foil, shiny side down. Sprinkle in a layer of the smoking-material – sawdust or rice and tea – about ¹/₂cm (¹/₄in) thick. Place the rack on top and settle the fish on the rack. Put the lid on tightly or cover securely with a double layer of foil.

Place the container over a high heat – you'll probably need two burners – and wait until you can smell the smoke. Turn the burners down to medium-heat, open the window and leave the kitchen. Allow 15 minutes for steam to build up and penetrate the fish. Remove (without opening) and set aside – outside would be even better. The fish will continue to cook as it cools. Your reward for a smoke-wreathed kitchen will be moist, succulent flesh with an exquisitely delicate flavour. Serve at room temperature, with a chilli-peanut salsa, baked plantains and roasted sweet potatoes.

Sierra en escabeche

(Hot-pickled mackerel)
Serves 4

As a method of conservation in pre-refrigeration days, a spiced pickle-bath was not only useful but added variety to the diet. A Mexican recipe in the Hispanic tradition.

*2 large or 4 small mackerel, gutted and
  beheaded*
Salt
1 heaped tablespoon of flour
2 tablespoons of olive oil
¹/₂ onion, skinned and finely sliced
1 garlic clove, skinned and crushed
1 mild green chilli, sliced
1 tablespoon chopped parsley
1 bay leaf, torn
6 peppercorns, roughly crushed
3-4 sprigs thyme
*4 tablespoons sherry vinegar (or any other
  good vinegar)*
2 tablespoons water

Chop each mackerel straight through the bone to give 4–6 thick steaks (your fishmonger will do this for you). Sprinkle with salt and dust with flour. Heat the oil in a shallow frying pan and when it has a blue-haze, put in the fish and fry gently until golden and firm (4–8 minutes

depending on thickness). Transfer to a wide shallow dish.

Add the onion, garlic and sliced chilli to the oil remaining in the pan (or a little new oil, if using leftovers) and fry gently for a few moments so that the flavours blend. Add the remaining ingredients and allow the mixture to bubble up. Pour this warm scented bath, unstrained, over the fish. Cover loosely with a clean cloth, and leave overnight, at least, in a cool place. Ready to eat in a day, better in two.

Sierra en escabeche, mackerel steaks marinated in a fragrant vinegar bath

cephalopods

Cephalopod means head-footed, of which two members, squid and octopus, are found throughout the region (cuttlefish are not present). Squid has ten legs, the octopus has eight. Both are highly intelligent predators. While squid are shoal-fish, hunting in packs, the octopus is solitary, hugging the rocks and inlets.

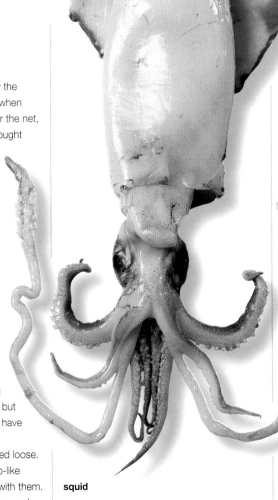

squid

Appearance and taste

Squid is eaten at all stages of maturity from pin-head to more than a metre in length; occasionally giant specimens, kraken, are washed up from the deep. Immature squid can be floured, fried and eaten whole, including their tiny ink-sacs which dye everything jet black and have a faint flavour of violets. When more mature, the flesh is chewy, sweet and white – but only if you take care to remove the ink-sacs (save them to cook with rice). Octopus, whose interior bone has been reduced to a small sharp beak, is a more daunting task since it needs to be thoroughly bashed, although a spell in the freezer has the same effect.

Cleaned squid, Panama

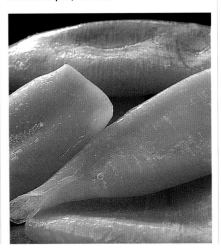

Buying and storing

Squid is a commercial crop landed by the inshore fishing fleets: meet the boats when they dock. The octopus, too canny for the net, is line-caught, a rowing-boat crop, brought home on the tide and thrashed to tenderness against the harbour wall. Buy fresh and cook immediately, or gut, slice and freeze.

Medicinal and other uses

For all practical purposes octopus and squid are fat-free.

Culinary uses

Anatomy is important when preparing the cephalopods. Squid has no bone but a clear plastic-like quill. The tentacles have little circular toe-nails embedded in their suckers which need to be scraped loose. To gut, pull the tentacles from the cap-like outer body, bringing the soft innards with them. Trim off the innards just below the eyes, and discard. Scrape and rinse off the violet membrane which veils the cap. Slice the cap into rings and chop the tentacles – or not, depending on size. Rinse your hands in cold water afterwards so they don't smell fishy.

Pulpo en escabeche

(Pickled octopus)

Serves 6–8

Fishermen don't easily give away their secrets, but here it is: 'First catch your octopus. When you have caught it, throw it forty times against a rock. Fewer times are needed if it's small, more if it's large. First the flesh is hard, but slowly it softens. Now you must rinse it in seawater so that it foams. Unless you do this, it will never soften. ou'll know when it's ready because the tentacles will curl. You must not take off the skin as so many ignorant people do. The skin turns red when you cook it, and this is what tells you it is fresh and good. To prepare for an escabeche, put it in a pan and cook it gently with a ladleful of sea-water until it's perfectly tender. The alternative is a few days in the freezer.

1 kg (2lb) tenderised octopus
300ml (1/2 pint) water
1 tablespoon salt

To dress:
6 tablespoons extra virgin olive oil
Juice 2 lemons
A handful of oregano, leaves only
1 crumbled dried red chilli
Salt and pepper

Cook the octopus in the water with the salt until soft – 30-40 minutes. Keep the water just trembling; don't let it boil. Leave to cool in its broth, then drain and chop into bite-sized pieces. Toss with the dressing ingredients.

Cazuela de calamar

(Squid casserole)

Serves 4–6

A Chilean way with the cephalopod. One of those dishes for which there is a perfect moment: when you dip into a squid shoal, you catch plenty. The recipe can be made with octopus, though the eight-armed sea-monster needs a good preliminary bashing to tenderise.

750g (11/2lb) squid (calamari)
3–4 tablespoons olive oil
4–5 cloves garlic, skinned and chopped
2–3 celery stalks, diced
1 red and 1 green pepper, de-seeded and diced
1–2 fresh yellow chillies, de-seeded and finely chopped
4 tablespoons fresh peas
450g (1lb) small yellow potatoes, scrubbed and diced
1 teaspoon oregano
2–3 bay leaves
1/2 bottle dry white wine
4 tablespoons double cream
Salt

Cazuela de calamar

Pick over and rinse the squid. If preparing your own, see Culinary uses, above.

Warm the oil in a roomy saucepan and put in the chopped garlic. When the garlic begins to sizzle, add the fish. Stir over the heat for a few minutes until the flesh stiffens and turns opaque.

Add the vegetables, herbs and wine, bring to the boil, turn down the heat, cover loosely and leave to simmer gently for about 40 minutes, until all is tender and the juices well-reduced. Taste, season and stir in the cream.

gastropods

Gastropods, that weird company of one-footed sea-creatures which includes abalone, conch, sea-urchins, barnacles, snails and slugs, grow fat and sweet on the transparent pin-head shrimp, shoals which drift through the Straits of Magellan on the icy tides of the Humboldt Current.

Habitat

The rocky cliffs of coastal Chile, which plunge steeply to the depths mirroring the steepness of the mountains above, provide a precarious perch for all manner of sea-creatures, including the prized abalone – most of which goes to the sushi-bars of Japan.

Appearance and taste

Chilean notables are *locos* – giant abalone; *choritos* – small black-shelled mussels; *machas* – razor-shells; *picorocos* ('stick-to-the-rocks'), giant rough-shelled barnacles that taste like lobster; and *ostras* – delicious little cold-water oysters. But the star of the show is the *erizo* or sea-hedgehog, a sea-urchin which achieves an astonishing size: some are as large as a football – one per person is certainly enough; only the females are of gastronomic interest since it's just the five little ovaries which are eaten. Conch, also known as *lambi*, is appreciated in the Caribbean: a large reddish-coloured sea-snail with bright yellow eyes, it lives in a beautiful rose-tinted shell: its meat, when thoroughly beaten to tenderise, is said to be sweeter than clam.

Buying and storing

Freshness is all. Buy live and store in a cool place for the minimum amount of time. Never eat a shellfish which is already dead.

Medicinal and other uses

Shipwrecked sailors can survive for years on a diet of mollusc – as did thousands of coastal-dwellers for centuries. Some people suffer from shellfish-allergies triggered by toxins either inherent in the fish or produced by parasites. Once acquired, the allergy is unlikely to go away.

Culinary uses

Abalone, which must first be tenderised by pounding, can be eaten raw or lightly cooked (long cooking toughens it). It is delicious sliced, dipped in egg and breadcrumbs and fried in very hot oil. The same rules apply to all other shellfish: at its simplest, eat raw with a squeeze of lemon; if applying heat, make it brief and don't reheat.

Mariscal

(Chilean seafood platter with green sauce)
Serves a party

A seafood selection as served straight from boat to plate and opened to order in the picadas – the little harbourside restaurants of Valparaiso and every other coastal town which shelters an inshore fishing fleet. The selection depends on whatever is local – the only constant is that is must be exquisitely fresh.

The shellfish – choose from:
Abalone, beaten to tenderise
Razor-shells or cherrystone clams (steamed or raw)
Mussels, opened
Oysters, opened
Scallops, opened, sand-sac removed
Shrimp and prawns, cooked and peeled

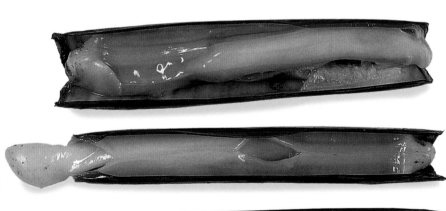

Machas, razor-shells, look strange but taste delicious

Giant barnacles (picorocos), cooked briefly in salted water
Crab claws, cracked
Sea-urchins, snipped round the waist to expose the five little roes

The sauce (for 4)
4 tablespoons finely chopped onion or scallion
4 tablespoons chopped coriander
4 tablespoons chopped parsley
1–2 green chillies, de-seeded and finely chopped
6 tablespoons lemon juice
4 tablespoons oil
1/2 teaspoon salt

To serve (optional)
Ulte or any edible seaweed, cooked to tenderise, chopped

Raw shellfish can be opened by inserting a short, strong, double-bladed knife into the hinge or slipping it round the side; prize the shells apart and serve the meat and the juices on the deeper of the two shells. Crustaceans must be cooked in plenty of boiling salted water for just long enough for them to change colour all over. Sea urchins have to be slit in half to expose the five little roes in a starfish shape – careful, the prickles are sharp. Abalone needs first to be thoroughly tenderised by battering it against the rocks until it froths, then sliced.

Combine the sauce ingredients, taste and adjust the seasoning. More salt? More lemon juice? A pinch of sugar?

Arrange the seafood on a large platter and serve the sauce separately or, if you prefer, spoon a very little into each shell. Napkins and fingerbowls would be a kindness.

Curanto en olla
(Seafood, pork and chicken hot-pot)
Serves 8–10

The *curanto* – the pit-barbecue or earth-oven – was used in pre-columbian times mainly as a method of preserving perishable foodstuffs in times of glut, particularly when more seafood had been

Mariscal, a medley of seafood served with a piquant sauce

gathered than could conveniently be consumed fresh. Modern *chilenos* maintain the tradition in the form of the beach pit-barbecue, a family outing undertaken in much the same spirit as Long Island's surfers set up a clam-bake – although the Chilean *curanto* is likely to include more substantial foodstuffs such as suckling pig, potatoes and sweetcorn. Here, the food – a surf-n-turf blend of shellfish, chicken and pork with potatoes, is cooked in an *olla*: an all-purpose earthenware cooking-pot, heat-proof so it won't crack on an open flame.

2kg (about 4lb) fresh shellfish: razor-shells, prepared abalone, barnacles, etc.
6 tablespoons oil
450g (1lb) shoulder pork, cut into cubes
1 small chicken, jointed
2–3 links chorizo sausage, sliced
1 onion, roughly chopped
1 sweet red pepper, de-seeded and cut into chunks
2 fennel bulbs with their fronds, roughly chopped
24 small new potatoes
1 bottle dry white wine
2 tablespoons finely chopped chilli or chilli paste or red pepper-flakes
2 garlic cloves, finely chopped
2 tablespoons chopped coriander
Salt and pepper

Scrub the shellfish and leave them in a bowl of cold water to spit out their sand.

Heat the oil in a roomy earthenware *olla* which won't crack on a direct flame, or in a roomy stew-pan, and fry the assorted meats until they brown a little. Add the onion and chopped red pepper and fry for a moment more.

Add a layer of chopped fennel and potatoes, pour in the wine and enough water to submerge the meats completely and sprinkle with the chilli, garlic and coriander. Season, bring to the boil, top with a plate so that everything stays submerged, and simmer gently for about 20 minutes, until the potatoes are nearly tender. Arrange the seafood on top, put the lid on again and leave to cook for another 5 minutes, until the shells open.

Serve in deep plates, bathed in its own aromatic broth, with bread for mopping.

bacalão

or bacalhão, salt cod

Salt cod provisioned the wooden ships which made the perilous early Atlantic crossings. Later, it was established as the fast-day food of the Roman Catholic Church. Once cheap and plentiful, it's now a luxury item sold in small quantities, often ready-soaked and vacuum packed.

Appearance and taste

A large kite-shaped sheet of rock-hard fish – though scarcely recognisable as such – salt cod is pungent and mouth-puckeringly salty. When soaked in several changes of water for at least a day and a night, it rehydrates to about three times its volume and loses much of its saltiness. It's a mistake to over-soak: it's nicest when still a little chewy.

Buying and storing

Choose with care. The white of the flesh should be ivory rather than snowy – a sign of chemical bleaching – and check the backbone for traces of pink: an indicator that too little time was spent in the salt. The middle cut is the best; the tail used to be hung up in the dovecote at Christmas for the birds to peck.

Medicinal and other uses

This is not for anyone cutting down their salt intake, for obvious reasons. Otherwise, it is an excellent source of protein.

Culinary uses

Salt cod can be used in any fresh fish recipe, but is most delicious in combination with sweet-sour flavours, such as tomatoes and peppers. Ackee saltfish, the national dish of Jamaica, combines the saltiness of the fish with the blandness of ackee, the fruit of a West African native tree established on the island by Captain Bligh of the *Bounty*, the texture and flavour of which are much like scrambled eggs. The Dominican Republic's *morue en chemise* – saltfish scrambled with eggs – confirms the popularity of the combination. In Brazil, where culinary habit derives from Portugal – the original salt-cod experts – you'll be told it's used in as many ways as there are days in the year.

Salted fish on sale in El Salvador

Fanesca

(Ecuadorian beans and corn with salt fish)
Serves 10–12

A combination of fresh broad beans, corn-kernels and vegetables with salt cod go into this family dish eaten during Easter week – which, in the southern hemisphere, falls in the autumn, at harvest time. It's traditional to send a bowlful of it to the neighbours.

700g (1 1/2lb) fresh broad beans, shelled
700g (1 1/2lb) fresh corn-kernels
700g (1 1/2lb) fresh haricot or cranberry beans
450g (1lb) fresh, mature peas, shelled
450g (1lb) round rice
2 litres (4 pints) milk and water in equal
  proportions
450g (1lb) diced pumpkin
450g (1lb) diced vegetable marrow
1/2 small cabbage, finely sliced
225g (8 oz) salt cod, soaked, de-boned and
  skinned

Refrito:
2 tablespoons butter or oil
3 onions, finely chopped
2 garlic cloves, finely chopped
1 tablespoon color chileno (see achiote,
  p.186), or oil coloured red with paprika
1 teaspoon powdered cumin
Pepper, no salt

To finish:

1–2 chayotes (choko) or courgettes, diced
150ml (¹/₄ pint) double cream
125g (4 oz) roasted peanuts, crushed

To serve (optional):

A handful ready-to-eat lupini (edible lupin
  seeds)
Roasted salted corn-kernels (masitas fritas)
Hardboiled eggs, peeled and quartered
Chopped parsley
Chopped fresh chilli
White cheese in slivers or matchsticks

Cook the broad beans in boiling water without salt for 20 minutes. Drain and slip off the skins when they are cool enough to handle: the beans crumble if skinned when cold. In another pot cook the corn, the haricots and the peas until tender – also about 20 minutes. Drain, reserving the cooking water. Cook the rice in half the milk and water until tender. These preparations can be made the day before.

Next day, cook the diced squash, marrow and cabbage in a tightly-lidded pan in a very little water until tender – 10–15 minutes. Cook the soaked cod in the remaining milk and water. Drain, reserving the cooking liquid, and flake.

Meanwhile prepare the refrito. Heat the oil in a large saucepan or a well-tempered earthenware casserole and gently fry the onion and garlic until soft and a little caramelised. Add the color chileno (or 1 tablespoon paprika mixed with a little oil), sprinkle with the cumin and pepper and fry for another 5 minutes to blend the flavours. Add the reserved bean-cooking water and bubble up. Stir in the reserved beans, corn and rice along with the reserved vegetables and simmer gently for 10 minutes, stirring constantly, to blend the flavours. Stir in the reserved cooking liquid from the salt cod and cook for another 10 minutes.

Finish with the diced chayote, cream, salt cod and crushed peanuts.

Serve hot in bowls, with the optional accompaniments.

Bacalão colorao. Salty flakes of bacalão contrast with the sweetness of the peppers and onion

Bacalão colorão

(Salt cod with red peppers)
Serves 4

A Mexican fasting dish for Lent – very good. Choose middle-cut salt cod and give it no more than 18 hours' soaking, or you'll lose all the flavour.

225g (8 oz) salt cod, soaked in several
  changes of water
150ml (¹/₄ pint) olive oil
6 mild red peppers, de-seeded and cut in
  ribbons
2–3 fresh red chillies, de-seeded and finely
  chopped
1 large onion, finely sliced
4 garlic cloves, chopped
4 tablespoons chopped parsley or coriander

Skin, de-bone and flake the soaked salt cod. If it's still too tough to flake, simmer in water for 5 minutes first.

Heat 4 tablespoons of the oil in a heavy pan and fry the peppers and the chilli. When they're soft and caramelised at the edges, remove and reserve. Fry the onion and garlic (allow it to gild but not brown), remove and reserve.

Fry the soaked cod in the pan drippings until the edges curl and it crisps a little. Combine the salt cod with the pepper and onion mixtures and the parsley or coriander and serve. It is nicest at room temperature.

For a more substantial dish, serve with quartered hardboiled eggs and soft tortillas for scooping.

nuts

The cooks of the region use nuts as thickenings for sauces, to add a little protein to roots and grains, in desserts and to enrich soups and stews. Of the nuts used, two are native, two are shared with other continents, and one is an import – what the botanists call an alien.

Brazil nuts and cashews are both exclusive to the Americas – unknown elsewhere until the arrival of the Old World's colonisers. The peanut, in the New World native to Peru, is also an Old World staple, grown in Africa since the earliest times, and the pinenut – a forest-harvest which fed the Mapuche Indians of southern Chile – also appears as a staple foodstuff of the aboriginal peoples of northern Australia. The coconut, on the other hand, is an imported crop. Although it probably self-seeded on the Pacific coast, drifting from the South Sea islands on the ocean current, the circumstances under which it established itself on the Atlantic coast were grim. The main provision loaded aboard the ships which supplied the sugar-plantations with their workforce, the coconut palms which shade the beautiful beaches of Rio and Bahia and the shores of Cuba and the Caribbean are a by-product of the slave trade. The captives packed into the stinking holds of the trading ships were provided with their own weight in coconuts, a supply intended to serve as both food and water, and at the end of the voyage, the amount of coconuts remaining gave an indication of the mortality-rate of the cargo – evidence, maybe, of carelessness. The leftover coconuts (along, no doubt, with the bodies) were simply tipped overboard to self-seed on the shore.

brazil nut

or nuez de brasil, castanhas do Pará (Brazil)
(*Bertholettia excelsa*)

Brazil nuts are the seeds of one of the most impressive of the Amazonian forest trees, which can reach a height of 50 metres (about 165 feet), topped by a canopy up to 30 metres (100 feet) in diameter.

How it grows

So far the trees remain wild, having resisted all attempts at cultivation. The fruit which contains the nuts is round and smooth-skinned, about the size and weight of a coconut, and falls to the ground when ripe, occasionally causing casualties among the unwary.

Appearance and taste

Each fruit contains as many as twenty nuts arranged like the segments of an orange. Once you manage to crack it, the meat – which has to be prised off the shell – is crisp but tender, and very rich and buttery, thanks to a remarkably high oil content. The nuts of the *sapucaya* or paradise-nut tree, its close relation, though not commercially marketed, are considered even more exquisite.

Buying and storing

Although about a quarter of the crop exported from the Amazonion city of Pará is shelled before shipping, brazil nuts are best bought in the shell. They should be satiny and a little oily: avoid any which look dried out or dusty. Keep them in the fridge, whether shelled or unshelled.

Medicinal and other uses

Brazil nuts are high in protein, with an oil content of nearly 70 per cent. As a prime source of amino acids, Brazil nuts are particularly good for bringing balance to a vegetarian diet; nourishing and fortifying, they are perfect for athletes and anyone involved in hard physical labour. Brazil nuts are not part of the native diet of Amazonia, being too rich and oily for the climate.

Culinary uses

Only crack as many as you need: once extracted from their stone-hard covering, the oily nutmeat rapidly turns rancid.

Crema de castanhas do Pará

(Brazil nut soup)
Serves 6–8

A sophisticated cream soup enriched with brazil nuts and finished with prawns and avocado – sophisticated enough for the salons of Rio.

425ml (³/₄ pint) shelled brazil nuts
1.8 litres (3 pints) chicken stock
50g (2oz) unsalted butter or oil
50g (2oz) plain flour
A pinch freshly-grated mace
300ml (¹/₂ pint) double cream
Salt and pepper

To finish (optional):
1 ripe avocado, diced
125g (4oz) cooked peeled prawns or a handful dried shrimps

Preheat the oven to 200°C/400°F/gas mark 6.

Spread the nuts on a baking tray and roast for 10 minutes – halfway through, shake the tray to turn and toast them evenly. Allow to cool, then rub off the husks. Tip into a processor and grind to a powder. Remove and reserve 2 tablespoons of the powdered nuts, leaving the rest in the processor. Heat the stock, add a ladleful to the powdered nuts in the processor, and process again.

Meanwhile, melt the butter in a roomy soup-pot, sprinkle in the flour, let it sizzle but not take colour, and slowly add the rest of the stock, whisking to avoid lumps. Bring back to the boil, turn down the heat and simmer for 10 minutes to cook the flour.

Stir in the nut-broth, mace and cream and reheat. Taste and add salt and pepper if needed – or maybe a shake of malagueta pepper. Ladle into bowls and finish each serving, if you like, with a little diced avocado, a few prawns and a sprinkling of the reserved powdered nuts.

Pedacinos de chocolate
con nueces de brasil

Pedacinos de chocolate con nueces de brasil

(Brazil nut cookies)

Makes about 18 cookies

Crisp, nutty, chocolatey and delicious with a glass of iced coffee. The basic ingredients make the difference: choose a high-quality cocoa powder and crack the nuts yourself.

125g (4oz) brazil nuts
125g (4oz) plain flour
1 heaped tablespoon cocoa powder
½ teaspoon baking powder
½ teaspoon salt
125g (4oz) softened unsalted butter
125g (4oz) brown sugar
1 egg, forked to blend

Reserve 18 of the best brazil nuts. Crush the rest to a coarse powder and toss with the flour sieved with the cocoa, baking powder and salt.

Beat the butter with the sugar till light and pale. Beat in the egg, then the flour and nuts. The mixture should be soft enough to drop from the spoon, so you may need a little milk.

Preheat the oven to 190°C/375°F/gas mark 4. Butter a baking sheet and sprinkle lightly with flour. Drop spoonfuls of the cookie mixture on the baking sheet. Using a damp finger,press one of the reserved whole brazil nuts into the middle of each cookie. Bake for 10-12 minutes. Allow to cool a little before transferring to a baking rack – they crisp as they cool.

peanut

or maní (Peru), cacahuete (elsewhere), groundnut, monkey nut (*Arachis hypogaea*)

A Peruvian native cultivated by the Incas, and possibly also a native of Equatorial Africa, the peanut is one of the world's major foodstuffs. It is not a true nut but a legume, a member of the pea-family – hence its English name.

How it grows

The peanut's growing-habit is equally interesting: the blossoms appear in the usual way, but the flower-stalks thrust themselves into the ground as soon as the pod begins to develop, ensuring that the seeds – peanuts – are already planted in the earth by the time they mature.

Appearance and taste

The skin which covers the nut can be any colour from pale cream to a reddish brown or even piebald. An oil-nut as well as an eating-nut, the flavour is starchy and beany when raw, developing its delicious nuttiness only when roasted.

Buying and storing

When buying peanuts in the shell, check for dusty patches which indicate the presence of bugs; when buying ready-roasted, if possible taste for freshness before buying.

Medicinal and other uses

With 30 per cent protein and 50 per cent fat, the peanut is the perfect foodstuff – fortifying and digestible. Unfortunately, increasing numbers of people are developing a peanut-allergy, which can, in the worst affected, be fatal.

Culinary uses

To roast peanuts, shell them, spread them on a baking sheet in a single layer and roast them at 170°C/325°F/gas mark 3 for 15–20 minutes; to skin them, shake them vigorously in a sieve while blowing off the papery residue, or rub them with a clean cloth.

Galletas de maní con canela

(Peanut and cinnamon cookies)
Makes about 2 dozen cookies

A basic beaten-biscuit – very easy and delicious. Serve with an exotic sorbet – chirimoya or lucuma.

350g (12oz) plain flour
110g (4oz) crushed peanuts or peanut butter
175g (6oz) butter
110g (4oz) caster sugar
1 tablespoon powdered cinnamon
1 egg
Salt

To finish:
2 tablespoons whole, split peanuts

Sieve the flour and cinnamon with a pinch of salt into a bowl and mix in the crushed peanuts. Beat the butter with the sugar until light and fluffy, then beat in the egg. Work in the flour and nut mixture until you have a ball of soft dough – you may need a little more flour. Cover with clingfilm and leave to rest in the fridge for an hour to firm up.

Heat the oven to 220°C/425°F/gas mark 7.

On a lightly floured board, roll out the dough. Cut out rounds with a biscuit cutter or wine-glass and arrange on a buttered baking sheet. Brush the tops with water and sprinkle with the whole peanuts: push them lightly into the dough. Bake for 15–20 minutes until golden and transfer to a baking-rack to crisp.

Chupe de maní

(Peanut soup)

Serves 4

A simple soup popular in Ecuador and Bolivia. You can use smooth peanut butter if you don't want to grind your own peanuts.

2 tablespoons peanut oil
1 onion, finely chopped
1 floury potato, peeled and diced
1 red pepper, de-seeded and finely chopped
2 dried red chillies, de-seeded and crumbled
1.2 litres (2 pints) strong chicken or beef broth
4 tablespoons finely-ground toasted peanuts
Salt and pepper

To finish:
2 tablespoons chopped coriander
Diced tomato
Extra peanuts for sprinkling

Heat the oil gently in a heavy saucepan. Fry the onion, potato and pepper until soft – don't let them brown. Stir in the chilli and add the stock. Bring to the boil, turn down the heat and simmer gently for 20 minutes, until fragrant and well-blended. Process half the soup to a purée with the peanuts and stir it back into the rest. Taste, season, reheat gently and ladle into bowls.

Finish with a sprinkle of coriander, diced tomato and extra peanuts.

cashew nut

or castanha-de-cajú (Brazil), marañón (Mexico)
(*Anacardium occidentale*)

A relative of the mango and the pistachio, the cashew is the edible fruit and nut of a Brazilian tropical shrub. It was known as *acajú* to the Tupi, the indigenous people for whom it was (and remains) an important foodstuff – hence the name given to it by the Portuguese colonisers.

How it grows

The fruit which contains the seed (the cashew) is suspended beneath a large fleshy apple which is eaten fresh or pulped for its juice and is delicious in puddings – unfortunately, the apple rots within two days, so can only be appreciated in situ.

Appearance and taste

The nut is poisonous when raw and has to be first heated and then shelled: labour-intensive, but a process perfectly understood by the indigenous inhabitants of Amazonia, who are accustomed to the necessity of de-toxifying tropical fruits and roots. The nut-shell contains an oil which irritates the skin, but is useful in waterproofing and is of value to the chemical industry. The nut, which is the shape and size of a large kidney-bean, sweet, white and buttery in flavour, is 45 per cent fat and 20 per cent protein, both of which say the right things to the taste-buds – hence its popularity, particularly when roasted, as a cocktail snack.

Buying and storing

Because they're toxic when untreated, the nuts are never sold in the shell. To check for freshness, look for a clean, clear colour with no sign of powdering.

Medicinal and other uses

Fresh cashew-apple juice is a local remedy for sore throats and upset tummies, including dysentery, The nuts have a high oleic acid content and are recommended for tooth and gum problems and eating disorders (although are not recommended in combination with starches, particularly bread).

Culinary uses

Bahian cooks pound the nuts for thickening sauces or for infusing in water to make a nutmilk (refreshing on a hot day), as well as powdering them for inclusion in cakes and pastries. The apple can be conserved in syrup – the only way it ever appears on the export market – and is delicious with vanilla ice cream.

Sango de quinua y marañón

(Cashew nut and quinoa risotto)
Serves 6

A combination of grains and nuts from Ecuador's Amazonian highlands – perfect as a vegetarian party dish.

350g (12oz) quinoa, picked over and rinsed
1.2 litres (2 pints) water
2–3 tablespoons peanut oil
225g (8oz) cashew nuts
1 onion, finely chopped
2 garlic cloves, finely chopped
1 yellow chilli, de-seeded and chopped
Salt and pepper
2–3 tablespoons cream

To finish:
Quinoa or spinach leaves, wilted in a covered pan with a little peanut oil
Salt and chilli flakes

Rinse the quinoa in a sieve under a tap until the water runs clear, transfer to a heavy pan with the water, bring to the boil, turn down to simmer and cook for about 20-30 minutes, until the water has completely evaporated and the grains are soft and fluffy.

Meanwhile, heat a tablespoon of the oil in a frying pan and fry the cashews for a few minutes, stirring until lightly browned, then

Sacks of nuts in a Mexico City market

remove and reserve. Add the remaining oil, onion and garlic to the pan and fry until soft – don't let them brown. Add the chopped chilli, fry for a minute, then stir in the cream and bubble up. Stir in the cooked quinoa and all but a tablespoon of the browned cashews, roughly crushed, and toss it all together over a gentle heat for another 5 minutes. Season.

To serve, top each portion with some of the greens and finish with a sprinkling of the toasted cashews tossed with salt and chilli flakes.

Horchata de cajú

(Cashew nut milk)

Makes 1.2 litres (2 pints)

A refreshing nutmilk, a legacy of the Moorish occupation of Iberia that was imported as a chilli-taming thirst-quencher.

225g (8oz) powdered cashews
1.2 litres (2 pints) water

2 tablespoons sugar (more if you like)
Short stick cinnamon

Stir the ground nuts into the water and leave to infuse overnight. Next day, strain the milky liquid into a saucepan, stir in the sugar and add the cinnamon stick. Bring to the boil and leave to cool. Refrigerate, removing the cinnamon stick just before serving.

Serve well-iced, in tall glasses.

Horchata de cajú

pinenuts

or piñones (*Araucaria araucaria, A. angustifolia, Pinus cembroides*)

Chief of the native pinenuts are seeds extracted from the cones of the araucaria or monkey-puzzle, a close relative of the Australian bunya-bunya tree. This pedigree makes it, along with the peanut, one of the few botanical candidates which support the theory that all the continents once formed part of the same landmass.

Buying and storing

Use your nose: the scent should be sweet and resinous, with no powdery residue to indicate the presence of small uninvited guests. The flavour deteriorates once the nuts are shelled, so keep them in a sealed jar in the fridge and use within the month.

Medicinal and other uses

A miraculous foodstuff. Forget fillet steak: a handful of pinenuts a day supplies all the protein and fat a body needs. The Latin American varieties are particularly rich in vitamins and minerals.

Culinary uses

All pinenuts – including the pinenuts of commerce, the seeds of the Mediterranean stone-pine (*Pinus pinea*) – are interchangeable for culinary purposes. They are traditionally used throughout the territory in nut-thickened sauces of Mediterranean origin as well as in indigenous pre-Columbian dishes.

Araucaria trees in Cani National Park, Chile

How it grows

A pine tree which grows to a remarkable size, the araucaria is a native to southern Chile and has a prodigious life-span – around fifteen hundred years – which makes it one of the oldest living things on earth. The nuts remain an important foodsource for the south Chilean Mapuche Indians – the 'people of the land' – for whom the trees are sacred. Unfortunately, only vestiges of the once vast forests remain, and even these are vanishing with alarming rapidity. In Brazil, a similar gastronomic niche is filled by the Parana pine (*A. angustifolia*); in Mexico, the seed-cones of *P. cembroides* provided the Mayas and the Incas with a high-protein foodsource.

Appearance and taste

Commercially sold pine-kernels are pre-shelled, and with good reason. As I well remember from childhood holidays in the Andes, you need a pair of heavy stones and a great deal of patience to crack even a small handful. The Mapuche of southern Chile harvest the cones in the autumn and store them underground through the winter as a source of protein during the cold months, cracking them to order and eating them raw, or toasting and milling them for flour, or cooking them and fermenting the pulp to make a form of chicha.

Locro con piñones

Torta de piñones
(Pinenut tart)
Serves 6–8

When crushing the nuts, don't reduce them to a powder or they'll go oily. The sugar sounds a lot, but it makes the nut filling gorgeously chewy. This is also good made with Chilean hazelnuts, *Gevuina avellana*, a relation of the macadamia, which grows wild on the snowline and is usually sold ready-roasted, like peanuts.

Pastry:
225g (8oz) flour
1 teaspoon powdered cinnamon
50g (2oz) sugar
175g (6oz) butter
1 egg yolk, mixed with 1 tablespoon cold water

Filling:
110g (4oz) pinenuts, roughly crushed
75g (3oz) granulated sugar
1/2 teaspoon crushed allspice
1 eggwhite, whisked until stiff
1/2 pint double cream, half-whipped

Make the pastry first: mix the flour with the cinnamon and sugar, rub in the butter, then work in the egg and enough water to give a soft, firm dough – use the tips of your fingers and don't overwork, just press it together lightly until it forms a ball. Cover with clingfilm and leave to rest for 30 minutes.

Preheat the oven to 200°C/400°F/gas mark 6.

Roll out the pastry into a disk and use it to line a 18cm (7in) tart tin. Prick the base, and slip it into the oven for 10 minutes (no need to fuss with beans and foil) to set the pastry.

Meanwhile, mix the filling ingredients together. Spread the mixture in the pastry case, return it to the oven and bake for another 30 minutes or so, until the filling is set and the pastry crisp.

Locro con piñones
(Potato soup with pinenuts)
Serves 4–6

A winter soup from the cold uplands of Chile's altiplano fortified with monkey-puzzle pinenuts, though any pinenuts will do. On the other side of the Andes, the cowpokes of Argentina make their stock with the roasted bones left over from the *asado* – but if water is all that's available, water will do.

1kg (2lb) mature potatoes, peeled and thickly sliced
2.5 litres (about 4½ pints) bone-stock or water
1 large clove garlic, chopped
2 small onions, finely chopped
Salt and pepper

To finish:
100g (4oz) pinenuts
1 tablesoopn finely chopped garlic
Coriander or spring onion

In a roomy pan, cook the potatoes in the stock or water with salt, garlic and onion for about 30 minutes, till completely mushy. Mash roughly (don't process).

Meanwhile lightly toast the pinenuts in a dry pan, stir in the garlic and crush the mixture if using plain water, leave whole if using stock. Stir this aromatic panful in the soup and simmer for another 10 minutes. Taste and adjust the seasoning.

Serve steaming hot in bowls, with sprigs of coriander or spring onion.

coconut

or nuez de coco (*Cocos nucifera*)

The coconut is the fruit and seed of the coconut palm, a cultivar which probably originated in Malaysia and the islands of Polynesia. A primary foodsource – sometimes sole foodsource – throughout the tropics, it self-seeded in the Americas by way of Africa.

How it grows

The coconut palm, as is usual with a native of the tropics, crops constantly, blooming and seeding all year.

Appearance and taste

In spite of the dismal circumstances under which it was introduced to the New World, this is a crop of many useful parts. The fibre – coir – is used to make matting and baskets; the outer-shell when hard and dry provides fuel for the cooking fire; young buds, known as pine-cabbages, are eaten as a vegetable; the leaves can be used as fans and for roofing-material; the nut can be eaten ripe or unripe and yields a clear, highly perfumed oil; the flower-buds are infused and fermented to make an alcoholic drink; the shell, when green, is full of clear, slightly nut-flavoured water much appreciated as a refreshing drink, while the unripe flesh is a soft neutral-flavoured jelly; and the nutmeat, when ripe, can be eaten immediately or stored. Once the coconut has been cracked and exposed to the air, keep it in the fridge.

Buying and storing

When buying a whole mature coconut, shake it: you should hear a sloshing sound which tells you it's fresh and full of liquid. Check the three little dimples – the 'eyes' which give it a face like a monkey (*coco* in Spanish) – for signs of damp or mould. To crack a coconut, shove a sharp instrument through the dimples and drain off the liquid. Then tap with a heavy hammer all around the circumference until it cracks, or drop it onto a concrete floor, or heat it in the oven at 180°C/350°F/gas mark 4 for half an hour, after which a light tap will do the trick. Remove the meat from the shell, bag it up and keep it in the fridge. Eat within a week, or grate and de-hydrate in the lowest possible oven and store in an airtight jar.

Medicinal and other uses

Coconuts are high in iodine, making them useful in the treatment of thyroid conditions. In the form of milk, its chemical balance is comparable to mother's milk. The oil extracted from the ripe flesh has been used for centuries for cooking; in its natural state, coconut fat is easily digested and appears not to cause weight-gain. When refined – the odourless colourless state in which it usually comes to market – it's more than 90 per cent saturated fat, even higher than butter or lard. In this form, it's extensively used in commercial cream-preparations, such as ice creams, 'dairy' whiteners and whips, to which it delivers an instant cholesterol-hike. Unrefined oil goes rancid quickly, but is lovely as a cosmetic rub, particularly good as a hair-conditioner and wonderful for repairing stretch-marks after pregnancy.

Related products

Coconut milk and cream are both available in a tin, boxed, and as a block. To make your own: measure 8 tablespoons of grated coconut (fresh or dried) into 600ml (1 pint) hot but not boiling water, process in the blender and strain. Repeat, adding another 600ml (1 pint) water to the same coconut. Mix the two strainings to give coconut milk; the first straining gives you cream. For an even richer cream, allow the liquid to settle and skim off the top layer as if it were cow's milk.

Culinary uses

Puerto Rican piña colada is made with fresh coconut milk, pineapple juice, sugar syrup and rum. The milk is delicious in rice puddings and milky desserts; in Brazilian and Colombian cuisines coconut cream is used to enrich soups and sauces, particularly those with chicken or fish.

Enyucado de coco

(Cassava coconut cake)
Serves 8–10

A deliciously moist coconut cake from the Caribbean coast of Colombia. Bake it in a ring mould for a celebration – it is delicious with a fresh fruit salad, a tropical combination of papaya and lime or banana and passion fruit.

1.3k (3lb) peeled cassava
1 large fresh coconut
450g (1lb) white cheese (cheddar is fine)
A little salt
2 egg yolks
250ml (a scant half pint) milk
225g (8oz) sugar
4 tablespoons softened butter
1 teaspoon aniseeds, lightly toasted and crushed

Enyucado de coco, a moist coconut and cassava cake

Grate the cassava, the coconut and the cheese into a bowl. Add the remaining ingredients and mix together to make a smooth soft dough. Set it aside for an hour to swell.

Preheat the oven to 150°C/300°F/gas mark 2.

Transfer the dough to a buttered baking tin – a large loaf tin is perfect – and bake for an hour, until firm to the finger, well-risen and browned. Surprisingly light and moist – it is delicious with fresh pineapple.

Ximxim

(Bahian chicken and prawns with coconut milk)
Serves 6–8

Pronounced chim-chim, this is the classic one-pot stew of Bahia, Brazil's most populous province. The combination of poultry and seafood with coconut milk is particularly delicious – wonderful food for a party.

1 free-range chicken, jointed into bite-sized
* pieces*
2 limes
450g (1lb) fresh prawns or large shrimp
8 tablespoons oil (olive and dende is perfect)
2 mild onions, diced small
2 garlic cloves, finely chopped
1 mild red pepper, de-seeded and diced
1 mild green pepper, de-seeded and diced
450g (1lb) ripe tomatoes, chopped
1 malagueta or habanero chilli, de-seeded and
* diced*
2 heaped tablespoons crushed, toasted
* cashews*
2 heaped tablespoons crushed, toasted
* peanuts*
2 heaped tablespoons dried shrimp (see p.142)
1/2 teaspoon grated fresh ginger
Salt and pepper

To finish.
4 tablespoons finely chopped leaf-coriander
150ml (1/4 pint) unsweetened coconut milk
2 tablespoons dende oil, or vegetable oil
* coloured with achiote (see p.186)*

Pick over the chicken pieces and trim off excess flaps and any whiskery feathers. Season with salt and pepper and toss with the juice of one of the limes. Leave to marinate for half an hour.

Pick over the prawns – if they are large, peel, removing the heads and leaving the tails, and de-vein (remove the dark intestine which runs down the back). Season with salt and pepper, toss with the juice of half the remaining lime, and leave to marinate as above.

Heat half the oil and fry the chicken pieces until nicely browned. Push to one side and add the prawns – they'll only take a minute or two. Remove and reserve both the chicken and prawns. Fry the onion, garlic and chopped red and green peppers in the remaining oil added to the pan-drippings. Allow to soften but don't let them brown. Add the tomatoes and chilli and bubble up, squashing down to make a sauce. Add a glass of water, bubble up again and return the chicken to the pan. Cover loosely and simmer for 20–30 minutes, until the chicken is perfectly tender. Stir in the nuts and dried shrimp, well pounded. Bubble up again, add the ginger and simmer for another 5 minutes. Stir in the chopped coriander, coconut milk and dende oil, lay the prawns on top and reheat gently.

Delicious with white rice, a sprinkling of farofa and a drop of malagueta pepper sauce. Now pour yourself a caipirinha and shake those hips.

the store cupboard

When considering the Latin American store-cupboard, it's worth remembering that before the arrival of the Europeans, salt was not available – neither mined nor produced by evaporation. For many centuries, the main method of conservation was through prolonged cooking in an earth-oven (with or without the addition of smoking), plus, sometimes, an additional plant-based anti-bacterial substance such as allspice or cassareep. Freeze-drying was known to the Incas, who used the method to conserve potatoes; meat – in those areas where the climate was not too damp to prevent the quick dehydration essential without salting – was preserved by air-drying.

Such a diet, lacking the savour of salt, needed enlivening with chillies, chocolate, vanilla and many other flavourings of local interest. Notable plant-based additives include achiote (annatto seeds, used as a colourant), allspice (for its fragrance) and angostura, valued both for its medicinal properties and its palate-stimulating bitterness.

As for those things whose function is to sooth, stimulate or give pleasure, a wide variety of infusions – tisanes – are enjoyed for their medicinal or stimulant properties. Maté, a tea brewed from the leaves of a member of the holly family, is the most popular, taking the place of chocolate in the southern parts of the region. In the tropical lands of the region, coffee – an Old World import which found its natural habitat in the New World – swiftly became both locally popular and economically important as a crop for export.

The people of the pre-Columbian civilisations were perfectly familiar with the pleasures of strong drink, preparing fermented beverages from a wide variety of raw materials. Among these, a Mexican beer – *pulque* – is remarkable for being made from the collected juice of a desert cactus; it is famous in its distilled form as tequila, a colourless odourless white brandy.

cocoa

or chocolate, cacao
(*Theobroma cacao*)

The tropical tree which produces this valuable crop is highly temperamental. Dependent on a tiny mosquito for pollination, it refuses to flower at all unless provided with year-round moisture and a temperature which never falls below 18°C (64°F), confining itself to no more than 20 degrees on either side of the equator. The tree is singularly wasteful of its creamy little blooms, since only one in every hundred bears fruit.

How it grows

Theobroma cacao is a lower-canopy tree indigenous to equatorial America, whose pods, born on the main trunk rather than the extremities, vary in colour as they mature from ochre to red. Inside are rows of pale beans, much like corncobs embedded in soft white fluff. The harvesters split the pods and heap them under damp leaves to ferment, a natural process which develops the flavour as well as inhibiting sprouting. The beans are then exported to the manufacturing country, where the raw materials undergo their metamorphosis into chocolate bars and cocoa powder.

Buying and storing

Among bean varieties, the *criolla*, the original bean of the Maya, is held to be the best: fruity, fragrant, with a touch of palate-tickling acidity. The *forastero*, the wild bean native to the forests of Brazil – now extensively cultivated in equatorial Africa – is considered a little on the bland side, needing high roasting to intensify the flavour. The *Trinitario*, the Caribbean bean, is a hybrid of the two: mellow, with flavours of oak, honey and hay. Most chocolate is a blend of all three. When assessing the quality of dark chocolate for cooking purposes, read the label: the cocoa-solid content (included by law) should be at least 70 per cent. When

unwrapped, the surface should be glossy and smooth. A reddish tinge is good: dark chocolate should be a deep mahogany, never black. When breaking, listen for the crisp snap and look for a tree-bark texture in the break. Melt a small piece on the tip of the tongue: the taste should be clean (aromas as for wine: caramel, hay, fruit, flower, spice); the texture creamy rather than oily (a quick melt indicates high cocoa-butter content); the 'finish' (aftertaste) should be long, as for wine. To store, keep wrapped in a cool, dry place.

Medicinal and other uses

Among the Aztecs and their predecessors, cocoa was an all-purpose cure-all. As an aphrodisiac, its consumption was confined to the emperor who was expected, quite literally, to father the nation by the most obvious means of all. To his priests, it was a panacea for stomach pains, an antidote to any form of poisoning, a disinfectant for cuts and a balm for burns; for the ordinary mortal, it provided a form of currency – exchangeable throughout the empire for goods and services. This is the form in which it was first encountered by the Spanish colonisers.

A harvest of fresh coca leaves in Peru

Culinary uses

Cocoa is bitter tasting in its raw form and, like coffee, must be fermented and roasted. In the civilisations of the Maya and the Aztecs, beans were prepared in much the same way as they are today: dried in the sun and fermented in their pods, then ground over a fire to a powder and formed into pellets for storage. In this form, the taste is bitter and must be balanced by the sweetness of honey, a thickening of sweet cornmeal and a flavouring of vanilla or chilli or both. This aromatic blend was then stirred into boiling water and beaten until foamy. Today, the cocoa butter is heat-extracted and the shells are ground to produce plain cocoa or, alternatively, extra cocoa butter and sweeteners are added to the ground shells to make a solid chocolate block. Cocoa is best used in its unsweetened form in savoury dishes, although high-quality bitter chocolate will do well enough.

Mole negro de guajalote

Mole negro de guajalote
(Turkey in chocolate and chilli sauce)
Serves 10–12

One of the great dishes of the Mexican kitchen, said to have been invented by the nuns of a convent in Oaxaca. Don't be intimidated by the length of the ingredient list – the cooking's easy.

1 whole turkey breast, on the bone
1 large onion, chunked
3 cloves and 3 allspice berries
6 peppercorns
2-3 sprigs thyme
2-3 sprigs dried marjoram
Salt

The sauce:
250g (8oz) dried medium-hot chillis,
  de-seeded and torn
6 tablespoons rendered pork fat or oil
6 garlic cloves, roughly chopped
1 onion, finely sliced
1 maize-flour tortilla, torn in small pieces
4 tablespoons roughly chopped peanuts
2 tablespoons pumpkin seeds

2-3 tomatilloes (or ordinary tomatoes),
  chopped
4 tablespoons raisins
50g (2oz) unsweetened cocoa or grated
  black chocolate
1 teaspoon orange-zest
1 teaspoon powdered cinnamon
Salt

Simmer the turkey breast with the aromatics and a little salt in enough water to cover for 1½-2 hours, until perfectly tender – the poaching liquid should tremble rather than bubble. Strip the meat from the bones and reserve. Strain the broth and reserve.

Toast the chillis in a dry frying-pan for about a minute, until they change colour, then put them in a bowl with enough boiling water to cover.

Heat half the fat or oil in the pan and fry the tortilla crumbs till crisp and brown, then tip into a blender. Toss the nuts and pumpkin seeds in the hot drippings and stir over the heat till they toast a little, then add to the blender. Fry the tomatoes (you may need a little more oil) until soft and soupy, stir in the raisins and bubble up, then add

to the blender. Add about 300ml (½ pint) of the reserved broth, and process all to a thick purée.

Fry the garlic and onion in the remaining lard or oil till soft and golden. Add the contents of the blender and bubble up, then turn down the heat and leave to simmer gently for 15 minutes.

Meanwhile, tip the soaked chillies with their water into the blender and process. Add to the sauce in the pan and bubble up. Stir in the chocolate, cinnamon and orange zest. Add another 600ml (1 pint) of broth and bubble up again. Add the reserved turkey meat and simmer for 20 minutes till the oily sauce begins to pool a little. Taste and add salt.

Heap the mole on a pretty dish and finish with extra pumpkin seeds and a few more curls of orange zest. Serve with black beans, white rice, a freshly made guacamole and soft tortillas for scooping.

Chocolate con vainilla
(Hot chocolate with vanilla)
Serves 4

A cup of steaming hot chocolate fragrant with vanilla is the best pick-me-up after a night on the tiles.

50g (2oz) best-quality dark chocolate (look for
  70 per cent cocoa solids)
600ml (1 pint) hot water (not boiling)
The seeds from a 2.5cm (1in) vanilla-pod
1 egg yolk or 1 teaspoon cornflour slaked in a
  little cold water
4 tablespoons unsweetened evaporated milk
  (or single cream)
Honey to sweeten
Chilli flakes or powder (optional)

Break the chocolate into small pieces and soften very gently over a low heat with 150ml (1/4 pint) water. As soon it liquefies, whisk in the rest of the hot water. Add the vanilla seeds and whisk until perfectly smooth. Remove from the heat. Use a fork to mix the egg-yolk or cornflour with the milk or cream, and whisk it into the hot liquid. Whisk over the heat until silky and smooth, removing it just before it boils. Add honey to taste and sprinkle with a few flecks of the optional chilli.

vanilla

or vainilla, vainica (*Vanilla planifolia, V. fragrans*)

The vanilla bean is the seedpod of a tropical tree-orchid native to Central America, known to both the Mayas and the Aztecs, who used it as a flavouring for drinking-chocolate. The first pods were brought back to the Spanish court by Hernán Cortes – the blue-eyed, blond-haired Conquistador who, somewhat misguidedly as it turned out, was hailed as a god when he entered the Aztec capital.

How it grows

A high-canopy orchid, it has cream-coloured, rather lily-like blooms and flourishes 50 metres off the forest floor. When grown commercially, the orchid is treated as a climbing vine and trained up poles in long rows. Each flower opens only once a year and, in the absence of insect-pollinators must be hand-pollinated. The pods are harvested when still yellow and unripe, when they have neither fragrance nor flavour. They are then subjected to a lengthy curing process, a form of fermentation, which triggers the development of enzymes which allow the beans to acquire their characteristic fragrance. The traditional method of achieving this is by drying the beans under cover for several weeks, then laying them out on woollen blankets to heat in the sun; at night they're wrapped in their blankets and taken under cover to sweat; when the beans have turned from brown to black, they are left to dry out for another two or three months before being bundled up for storage or export. The curing-process takes a total of 3–6 months. The main Latin American vanilla-producing countries are Mexico, Guyana, Puerto Rico, Guadalupe and Dominica. West Indian vanilla is extracted from a different species, *Vanilla pompona*.

Appearance and taste

Properly-prepared vanilla pods are a luscious deep brown in colour, shiny and dark and exuberantly freckled with tiny crystals of vanillin, a chemical developed as a result of the curing-process. The flavour is complex, as at home in the perfumery as in the kitchen. It is both flowery and fruity – tuberose and mango is the closest I can manage – while the scent is fragrant but never cloying. Mexican vanilla has a pleasantly sharp edge not found in other vanillas.

Buying and storing

The best vanilla comes as a whole pod in a container – glass or clear plastic – which excludes air and through which you can see the goods. Look for the characteristic dusting of vanillin crystals on the pods. Fresh pods will always have a better flavour than even the most carefully prepared essence – made by steeping the pods in alcohol over several months. Price and packaging will tell you if you're buying the real thing, so it's wise to distrust anything sold loose or cheap. You can re-use the pod if all you have done is immerse it in a custard: just rinse it carefully, wipe it dry and store it in the sugar-jar, where it'll perfume the sugar. On the other hand, in a creamy dessert, the tiny seeds are irresistible for their crunchiness as well as the beauty of the tiny black freckles, adding another layer of pleasure. Avoid synthetic vanilla – usually based on euginol, a substance which occurs naturally in clove oil but is also to be found in soft-wood pulp used for paper-making. Cloying and sickly rather than fresh and sweet, it lacks the subtlety as well as the spirit of the real thing.

Medicinal and other uses

A liver-stimulant, vanilla assists in the production of digestive enzymes. It also has a considerable reputation as an aphrodisiac, a virtue not unallied to its digestive properties.

Culinary uses

Vanilla delivers sweetness as well as fragrance, although since it's usually used in combination with sugar, this is not often apparent.

Chucula de vainilla

(Vanilla and guava cream whip)
Serves 4–6

A creamy Ecuadorian dessert perfumed with vanilla seeds – deliciously fragrant against the gentle background of guava and banana.

1 short length vanilla pod
2 ripe bananas, thickly sliced
150ml (1/4 pint) water
2–3 ripe guavas, quartered, skinned and cored
3–4 tablespoons caster sugar (or cane-sugar syrup)
300ml (1/2 pint) cream, whipped

Scrape the seeds from the vanilla pod and reserve. In a small covered pan, cook the bananas in the water with the scraped vanilla pod. Remove from the heat as soon as the fruit softens – 5 minutes or so. Add the guavas, put the lid on again and cook for another 5 minutes. Remove the vanilla pod. Liquidise the fruit with the sugar and vanilla seeds and fold in the whipped cream. Leave to cool – or lightly freeze, if you prefer – and serve piled in pretty glasses.

Chucula de vainilla, a vanilla-perfumed fruit fool

Ponche de vainilla

(Vanilla rum punch)

Serves 6

An eggnog, a pick-me-up – the classic remedy for the morning-after. You'll find variations on the same theme throughout the region. Here's the Mexican version.

600ml (1 pint) creamy milk (or single cream)
4 tablespoons castor sugar
$^1/_2$ vanilla pod
6 egg-yolks
300ml ($^1/_2$ pint) pale rum

Put the milk, sugar and the vanilla pod in a heavy pan, heat gently until almost boiling, stirring until the sugar dissolves, turn the heat right down and simmer gently for 15 minutes, until the vanilla has imparted its fragrance to the milk. Remove the vanilla pod.

Whisk the yolks until white and light. Whisk in the hot milk a little at a time, return to a gentle flame and cook, stirring, until it thickens enough to coat the back of a wooden spoon. Allow to cool before blending with the rum. Bottle and cork. It is ready to drink in a day or two – unless the hangover can't wait. As an elegant apéritif, serve chilled from the fridge or pour over ice.

honey

or miel

liquid honey

honeycomb

The foodstuff which sustains the bee-grub in the hive; although honey is the original sweetener, it is also used throughout the region to season meat and other savoury foods.

Manufacture

South American bees have a well-deserved reputation for ferocity and irritability. Fortunately, their honey is delicious – particularly when gathered in the wild and sold in great glittering, bee-buzzed combs in the market.

Appearance and taste

The grubs as well as the honey are appreciated in the region – the flavour of a combful of bee-grubs is rather like caramel and cream. The forest honeys of Mexico and Guatemala are particularly dark and high in vitamins and minerals. Especially delicious and well-endowed with minerals are the pine-flavoured honeys of the Andean uplands.

Buying and storing

Local honeys reflect the diet of the bees which produce them, passing on toxins – including anti-biotics and pesticides – as well as fragrances and other desirable attributes. When buying locally, take advice: some honeys are very strong, almost medicinal in flavour; some, if the bees have been pollinating certain blossoms, can even be toxic. Honey will keep virtually for ever: it will crystallise over the course of a year, but can be brought back to a liquid state by popping the jar in simmering water. A honey which has been heated up to 145°F/63°C can still be labelled uncooked, although the flavour and vitamin content begin to alter at 104°F/40°C.

Medicinal and other uses

Raw honey is antiseptic and laxative; stirred into an infusion of thyme, it clears sinuses; in combination with vinegar or lemon, it sooths coughs; when applied topically, it heals wounds. As a foodstuff, honey is metabolised more slowly than sugar and the darker honeys are usually richer in minerals than light honeys. The comb-washings go to make a fermented liquor, the wax to make holy candles to mollify the saints who inhabit the churches and whose temper is uncertain, just like the old gods who ruled from the ancient temples on which the churches were built. With or without the intercession of a priest, the saints have an insatiable appetite for candles.

Beekeeping in San Martín, Mexico

Culinary uses

You need about 30 per cent less honey than sugar to sweeten something. The flavour of a particular honey which has not been blended with other honeys is best appreciated in its simplest form, stirred into the preferred infusion of the region: drinking-chocolate in the lands of the Maya and the Aztec, and maté, a mildly stimulant tea popular in southern Brazil, Uruguay, Paraguay and the Argentine. Honey can be boiled down to make a thick, toffee-like sauce – delicious poured over vanilla icecream, or as a stuffing for doughnuts, churros. Since sweetness is associated with pleasure, honey-sweets take pride of place at weddings and the seasonal celebrations of the church, particularly those associated with the Virgin Mary.

Turrón de miel de abejas

(Honey nut meringue)

Serves 6

A Chilean dessert derived from the Spanish *turrón*, who had the idea from the *halvas* of the Moors. Very light and exquisite, particularly if served with something sharp – a sorbet or a fresh fruit-salad made with shredded pineapple and strawberries or, if you happen to be in Chile, shiny black murtilla berries, dark-juiced, with a flavour of sour cherries.

6 tablespoons honey
6 tablespoons dry white wine
4 large eggwhites
Pinch salt
2 tablespoons toasted pine-kernels

Bring the honey and the wine gently to the boil in a small enamel saucepan, stirring to blend. Stop stirring as soon as the mixture boils, turn down the heat and simmer for 5–10 minutes, until the syrup thickens to the small-ball stage: 130°C/250°F.

Meanwhile, whisk the eggwhites with the salt until stiff enough to hold soft peaks – don't overbeat or they'll go grainy. Pour the hot syrup in a steady stream onto the whisked whites, beating until cool and shiny. Spoon into pretty glasses and finish with a sprinkling of toasted pine-kernels.

Cachapas con miel

(Venezuelan fresh maize pancakes with honey)

Makes a dozen

Deliciously light little pancakes which include both fresh corn and cornmeal, wonderful with a dark forest honey.

350g (12oz) sweetcorn, stripped from the cob
50g (2oz) cornmeal (or fine-ground polenta)
50g (2oz) plain bread-flour
1 level teaspoon baking powder
Pinch salt
175ml (6fl oz) buttermilk
1 large egg

Cachapas con miel, breakfast pancakes drenched with honey

To serve:
A small jug of warm honey

Drop all the pancake ingredients in the blender and process to a smooth batter. Heat a griddle or heavy iron pan and grease lightly. As soon as it's hot enough to toast a sprinkle of flour to a rich brown within 10 seconds, it's ready to bake.

Wipe the surface with a buttery or oil-soaked scrap of linen. Drop tablespoons of the batter on the hot surface to make small round pancakes no bigger than a coffee saucer. Wait until bubbles form on the upper surface – a minute, no more – and flip the cakes over to brown the other side. Pile in a clean cloth to keep warm. Continue until the mixture is all used up and serve with the warm honey.

sugar cane

or caña de azúcar (*Saccharum officinarum*)

Sugar cane was imported into the Caribbean and Brazil as a commercial crop worked by a labour-force supplied though the slave-trade. It's still, in spite of the proliferation of sugar beet, the world's most important sugar-crop.

Crude brown sugar on sale in a Quechua market in the Peruvian highlands

How it grows

Sugar cane grows in tall, bamboo-like clumps and is ready for cutting to extract the juice after the first year's growth. After that, it throws up successive clumps of canes known as ratoons, although these decrease in productivity each season.

Buying and storing

Sugar cane was a treat I enjoyed as a child: buy fresh cane in short lengths when it comes into the market at the beginning of the season, peel back the green skin and suck the fibres to extract the juice.

Related products

Rum, the main derivative of the sugar industry, was at the beginning a back porch industry, a distillation of the washings from the sugar cane extraction. It is a colourless, odourless liquor which needs outside assistance to acquire distinction. Jamaican rum goes to make a Planter's Punch: orange, grapefruit and pineapple, sweetened with grenadine, well-iced and fortified with rum. The Puerto Rican piña colada is a blend of coconut milk, pineapple juice and rum. The daiquiri, containing equal amounts of lemon juice and rum, well-iced, was named for a small copper-mining town in northern Cuba where it was first popularised.

Medicinal and other uses

Sugar is the world's favourite pick-me-up, either in processed form or simply chewed straight from the cane. It delivers the fastest energy-buzz, though very little else, as I expect you know. It's this quick-fire delivery combined with the body's reluctance to give itself more work than necessary which makes it addictive.

Appearance and taste

The darker the sugar, the less processed it is and the better the flavour – within reason: raw sugar as imported for processing in sugar refineries is full of a great many things you wouldn't want to eat.

raw, unrefined sugar

rum

sugar cane

Culinary uses

West Indians add sugar to meat when they fry it in oil, giving it a deliciously deep caramelised flavour which not only tastes good but makes a small amount of a valuable ingredient go further. Another unusual technique peculiar to the region is that of boiling milk and sugar together until it becomes granular and caramelised: *dulce de leche* (see p.104).

Trinidad Pepper Pot

Serves a party (even better the next day)

This is a sweet-and-sour Sunday hot-pot, seasoned Caribbean-style with sugar, vinegar and chilli. The pot can be kept simmering on the back of the stove for months, with something new in the way of meat or fowl added each day. Serve with white rice or plain boiled potatoes or yams, and maybe a relish of sliced mango and ripe plantain dressed with lime juice. The Guyana pepperpot includes cassareep, a syrupy, spicy preparation based on bitter cassava, whose value as a meat-tenderiser was particularly useful when cooking what the hunter caught, the only meat available before the Europeans introduced their domestic animals.

Trinidad pepper pot, spicy, sweet and hot

900g (2lb) chicken joints
1 pig's trotter, scrubbed and split (optional)
1.3kg (3lb) stewing pork or beef, cubed
2–3 red peppers, de-seeded and sliced
2 onions, thickly sliced
1–2 habanero chillies, de-seeded and chopped
1 short length cinnamon stick
3–4 cloves
A sprig of thyme
1–2 tablespoons vinegar
1 tablespoon Worcester sauce
2 tablespoons dark brown sugar
Salt

Put all the ingredients in a large stewpot with enough water to submerge everything, bring to the boil, turn down the heat, cover and simmer for at least 2 hours – longer if you like – until the meat is perfectly tender. Add more water if necessary. If you prefer to use the oven, allow the same length of time at 150°C/300°F/gas mark 2.

Taste and adjust the seasoning, adding a little more sugar or a touch more vinegar, if you wish. That's all. Good today, it's even better tomorrow.

Caipirinha

(Lime and rum highball)
Serves 1

Brazil's national drink. When made with white rum instead of Brazilian *cachaça* – sugar-cane rum – it becomes a *caipirissimia*. On second thoughts, who cares? The only rule is that you make only one at a time.

1 lime, cut into small chunks
Caster sugar (to taste)
A shot of cachaça or white rum
Ice cubes

Pack the lime, pulp-side uppermost, into a tumbler – short and fat is better than long and thin. Add the sugar and crush into the limes with a pestle – don't bruise the skin or the lime-oil will make the drink bitter. Add the rum and stir, then add the ice cubes.

allspice

or pimento de Jamaica, Jamaican pepper
(*Pimento dioica/P. officinalis*)

A small brown berry a little larger than a peppercorn, allspice is the fruit of the West Indian pimento tree which is also found in Central and South America. It gets its name from the complex bouquet of spices it delivers.

How it grows

The pimento tree is a small forest-tree native to the Caribbean but particularly prolific in Jamaica, which produces most of the world's supply of allspice. As with many aromatic substances (including black peppercorns and vanilla pods) the berries are picked green and spread in the sun to dry and brown, a process which allows them to ferment a little, intensifying the flavour.

Appearance and taste

Unlike peppercorns, allspice berries are variable in size. Intensely fragrant with a scent of nutmeg, cinnamon and clove, they have a peppery undertone which makes them suitable for both savoury and sweet dishes.

Buying and storing

Choose clean, clear-coloured berries with no powdery residue. They are at their most fragrant when freshly ground – buy whole rather than powdered allspice from a store which serves a Caribbean population. Store in an airtight tin, and never for longer than a year.

Medicinal and other uses

A digestant, performing the same function as mint by preventing the formation of gases in the upper intestinal tract (hence the after-dinner mint). A decoction of pounded berries can be used as a pain-relieving muscle-rub and the oil can be applied topically to relieve toothache.

A Belize plantation of allspice trees

Culinary uses

A warm spice, allspice adds depth and balance when used in savoury dishes in combination with chillies. Its main use, however, is in cakes and desserts, to which it contributes a stimulating pepperiness as well its complex blend of fragrances.

Jerked chicken with allspice

Serves 4–6

Jerk-seasoning is available ready-mixed, or you can make a quantity of it and store until needed. It is perfect with pork – delicious rubbed on a boned-out shoulder to be roasted on the barbecue (leave it overnight to take the flavour). For a marinade for fish, blend the seasoning with the same volume of coconut milk rather than lime juice and give the fish just an hour in the marinade.

Jerk-seasoning:
1 tablespoon ground allspice
1 tablespoon ground ginger
1 tablespoon dried thyme, crumbled
1 tablespoon dried onion, finely chopped
1 teaspoon sea salt
1 teaspoon cayenne pepper or chilli powder
1 teaspoon sugar
1/2 teaspoon ground white pepper
1/2 teaspoon ground cinnamon

The chicken:
About 900g (2lb) chicken joints (drumsticks and wings)
Juice of 2 limes
2 cloves garlic, crushed
2 tablespoons oil

Mix the seasoning thoroughly. Pick over the chicken joints and remove any stray feathers. Mix 2 tablespoons of the seasoning with the lime juice, crushed garlic and oil and rub it thoroughly into the chicken. Marinate in a cool place for 3–4 hours – overnight if possible.

Preheat the grill or light the barbecue. Grill the chicken joints for 7–15 minutes, browning all sides – drumsticks take twice as long as wings. Serve with baked plantains (see p.206).

Jamaican allspice and banana milkshake

Serves 3–4

The natural pepperiness of allspice lifts the blandness of a vanilla and banana milkshake. The subtle warmth of the berries works well with the soft cool flesh of the banana, the fruit of the winter months in non-tropical lands, but available all year in Caribbean markets.

4 ripe bananas
4 scoops good vanilla ice cream
600ml (1 pint) creamy milk
Sugar to taste
1/2 teaspoon freshly ground allspice

Put all the ingredients in the liquidiser and process until perfectly blended. Serve in tall glasses, with an extra sprinkling of freshly ground allspice.

achiote

or annatto, roucou (West Indies), urucu (Brazil)
(*Bixa orellana*)

Achiote is the collective noun applied to the berries of a small tree, originally gathered by the native Brazilians of the Amazon rainforests who used the red juice to decorate their bodies. When the Africans arrived in Brazil, they found a new use for the dye: missing the flavours and colours of home, they used the berries to give ordinary oil the same colour as their beloved dende or palm-tree oil.

Appearance and taste

When fresh, the berries are bright brick-red with a very light rose-petal fragrance.

Buying and storing

Buy in small quantities (from West Indian shops). As the seeds age, they go brown, losing both their ability to colour as well as their elusive scent.

Medicinal and other uses

As a natural dye, achiote is a safe and effective food colourant. It is used by commercial cheesemakers and – traditionally – by the buttermakers who supply the Caribbean market from the ship-victualling port of Cork on the west coast of Ireland.

Culinary uses

Used as a food colourant throughout the region, it is particularly popular in Chile, the Caribbean and Brazil, where the seeds – hard and not very palatable – are infused in oil, and strained out.

Related products

To make *color chileno*, warm $1/2$ cup achiote (annatto seeds) with 2 tablespoons pork-lard and cook gently for 5 minutes. Strain off the fat and reserve. Reheat the achiote with another 2 tablespoons lard, strain and reserve with the first batch. Repeat the process twice more, making four batches in all. The blending of the batches produces a very concentrated colour: ¼ teaspoon will tint a dish for 4.

For oil coloured like dende, add 3 tablespoons annato seeds to 300ml (½ pint) vegetable or olive oil and leave to infuse overnight, or heat over a low flame for 5 minutes, until it turns a sunny orange. Strain and use as required.

Huevos revueltos con color chileno

(Chilean scrambled eggs)
Serves 4

Chilean chorizo comes in short fat links, like pork sausage, and has plenty of luscious red fat. If you can only find it in a plastic pack from the supermarket, skin it and crumble or chop.

2–4 tablespoons olive oil (depending on the fat in the chorizo)
110g (4oz) chorizo or any other paprika-spiced dried sausage, sliced
1 small fresh red chilli, de-seeded and finely chopped
$1/4$ teaspoon color chileno
6 eggs, mixed lightly with a fork
Salt

Heat the oil in a small frying pan and add the sliced chorizo. Fry until the sausage browns a little and the fat runs. Add the chilli, stir over the heat for 1 minute, then add the color chileno, and finally the eggs.

Stir the mixture with a fork as it sets so the eggs scramble in little hanks. Salt lightly – the chorizo is salty anyway. As soon as the eggs begin to set, remove the pan from the heat and transfer to a warm plate. Serve with warm arepas or toasted country bread over which you have poured the pan-drippings.

The achiote plant growing in Brazil

Patatas bravas chilenas

(Chilli potatoes)

Serves 4 as a starter

The colder the winter, the hotter the dressing.

700g (1¹/₂lb) small potatoes

To dress:
2 garlic cloves, finely chopped
2–3 dried chillies, crumbled
1 teaspoon dried oregano
1 teaspoon cumin seeds
2 tablespoons fresh pork lard
¹/₂ teaspoon annatto seeds, crushed
450g (1lb) tomatoes, grated or chopped
1 tablespoon pitted black olives

To serve:
Cos lettuce
Pickled jalapeño chillies

Cook the potatoes until tender in plenty of salted water. Drain and toss over the heat to dry and split the skins a little.

Meanwhile prepare the dressing. Crush the garlic, chilli, oregano, cumin and annatto seeds to a paste with the salt in a mortar. Heat the lard in a frying pan and fry the paste gently for 2–3 minutes until it softens. Add the tomatoes and bubble up, squashing down to make a thick sauce. Stir in the olives and fold in the potatoes, turning to coat thoroughly.

Serve with cos lettuce leaves for scooping and pickled jalapeño chillies on the side.

angostura

Angostura is a flavouring ingredient which contains quinine – the earliest effective treatment for malaria – extracted from the bark of a South American native tree (*Galipea officinalis*).

Manufacture

It is sold in the form of bitters, made to a secret formula and industrially bottled in Trinidad.

Appearance and taste

Angostura bitters are a pinkish brownish liquid with a spicy flavour and fragrance in which can be identified cloves, mace, nutmeg, allspice, cinnamon, citrus peel, prunes, quinine and rum.

Buying and storing

You have no choice: Angostura bitters come in a small bottle and one bottle can last a lifetime.

Medicinal and other uses

Angostura bitters were originally formulated up the Orinoco river in the Venezuelan town of the same name (now renamed Ciudad Boliva) by a certain Dr Siegart, whose patients found the preparation effective in the reduction of fever.

Culinary uses

In their exported bottled form, Angostura bitters are best known as an addition to gin, which they colour pink – hence, pink gin. In the Caribbean and in Bolivia, Peru and Ecuador they're used as a flavour-enhancer. A few drops are added to creamy desserts or offered as an alternative to chilli with fresh fruit. They're also sometimes included in marinades and sauces, perhaps because of their similarity to cassareep, a syrupy preparation made with bitter cassava, traditionally used to tenderise meat.

Coctel de gambas angostureño

(Angostura prawn cocktail)
Serves 4

This is a tomato sauce with a touch of bitterness which works well with the sweetness of the prawns. It is good with any plain-cooked fish – steamed, baked or grilled.

450g (1lb) cooked, peeled prawns (tails left on)
3 large ripe tomatoes, scalded, skinned and chopped
1 garlic clove, peeled and chopped
2 tablespoons toasted pinenuts
2 red peppers, roasted, de-seeded and skinned
1 fresh green or red chilli, de-seeded and chopped
100ml (4fl oz) olive oil
1/2 teaspoon Angostura bitters

the familiar angostura bottle and its contents

Pisco sour

1 teaspoon salt
A pinch sugar

To finish:
Shredded lettuce leaves

Drop all the ingredients except the prawns in the liquidiser and process to a purée. Taste and adjust the seasoning: more sugar, a little lemon juice? Dress the prawns with the sauce, saving the best for decoration, and pile on shredded lettuce leaves.

Pisco sour
Serves 1

The bitterness of the Angostura bitters makes this a particularly grownup cocktail. It is properly made with pisco, the Peruvian brandy which, though basically no different from any other distilled grape-liquor, is matured in paraffin-lined barrels, so is both odourless and colourless. The pisco sour is equally appreciated in Ecuador and Bolivia.

A shot of pisco
1 teaspoon eggwhite
1 tablespoon caster sugar
1 tablespoon lime juice
6 ice cubes

To finish:
Angostura bitters

Shake all the cocktail ingredients together until they foam. Strain into a chilled whisky sour tumbler. Finish with three drops of Angostura bitters. That's all.

coffee

green coffee beans

(Coffea arabica)

Coffee beans are the berries of a small tree native to the highlands of Ethiopia but grown widely throughout the tropical Americas. Its natural habitat is volcanic soil, and the higher it's grown, the better the flavour. The main coffee-grower of the Americas is Brazil, the world's largest producer – though, with the exception of the deliciously aromatic Santos, a lot of it is not much good; Colombia is the second largest in quantity but is unsurpassed in quality – look for Medellín, Manizales, Libanos, Bogatoas and the deliciously named Buccaramangos; Costa Rica produces relatively small amounts of highly aromatic beans; Peru and Ecuador produce in limited quantities, mostly used in blends; Guatemala is distinguished by particularly fragrant beans with a mellow flavour grown at altitude – look for Cobán and Antiquas; Venezuelan beans rival Colombia's finest but are even more delicate – look for Meridas and Caracas; of the

mellow and mild Caribbean coffees, the most famous (and absurdly expensive because the production is so small) is Jamaica's Blue Mountain; Cuba, Dominica and Haiti also produce high-quality coffees.

brown coffee beans

How it grows

The leaves are glossy and lance-shaped; the flowers are white, sweet-scented and grow in bracelets along the branches. The blossoms drop to form berries – called cherries – which consist of an outer skin, a layer of pulp, an interior membrane and a pair of inner seeds which grow face to face (a few grow only one: a peaberry). The berries ripen from green to red, the stage at which they're cropped. The processing involves a preliminary light fermentation in damp conditions, followed by drying in the sun (these days, the sun is often replaced by more reliable mechanical driers). Although high-value beans are still harvested by hand, lesser qualities are plucked by mechanical grabber.

Appearance and taste

Raw coffee beans vary in colour from grey-green to yellowy-brown and come encased in a fine papery covering which rubs off when they're roasted. This is the form – the raw but treated state – in which they're stored or exported. When freshly roasted, the beans are light to dark brown, and have a strongly aromatic scent and deep rich flavour which is further released by milling to a fine powder before infusing in water.

Coffee pods ripening on the tree

Buying and storing

You can buy your coffee-beans at one of three stages – green, ready-roasted, or ready-roasted and ground. If you buy green beans, they can be kept in an airtight tin almost indefinitely (aged coffees command a premium).

To roast your own, stir carefully in a pan over an even heat till a rich brown toasty colour is a achieved, a process much like making popcorn. The process of roasting the beans releases and develops the aromatic oils which deliver the flavour; the degree to which they're roasted – light, medium, dark (very dark if coated with a little sugar right at the end) – determines the final flavour; once roasted, store in a sealed packet in a cool place, and the sooner they're used the better. Once the beans are ground, the oils and their fragrance evaporate quickly. If you drink coffee regularly, you'll find it's well worth acquiring a small electric grinder of your own.

Medicinal and other uses

The active ingredient in coffee, caffeine, is stimulant, diuretic and laxative – highly desirable properties. In its pure state, unless consumed in the kind of levels which indicate addiction, there's no medical evidence the caffeine acts harmfully. When adulterated with other substances – flavourings, processings and the like – the reverse may be true.

Culinary uses

To make a perfect cup of coffee of the simple sort most frequently encountered in the region, all you need is a jug and sieve and two tablespoonsful of medium-ground coffee per person. Put the coffee in the jug, pour in 300ml (½ pint) boiling water per person, allow to steep for 5 minutes, give it a stir with a cold spoon to settle the grounds, then strain into warmed mugs.

La Belle Josephine

(Caribbean coffee and cream)
Serves 4

This is a delicious confection which commemorates the beauty of Josephine Baker, star of the Folies Bergères in Paris in the Twenties. It is also known in the French Caribbean as *Negresse en Chemise*: **Black Beauty in a White Petticoat. Exquisite, by whatever name.**

350g (12oz) white curd cheese: ricotta or
  fromage frais
150ml (¹/4 pint) cream
1 coffee cup very strong black coffee
1 coffee cup dark Barbados rum
110g (4oz) black chocolate, grated

To finish (optional):
Sliced banana
Crushed walnuts
Cinnamon

Push the cheese through a sieve and then beat it with the cream. Gently heat the coffee with the rum, then stir in the chocolate, whisking until dissolved. Set aside for an hour at room temperature for the flavours to develop.

Drop a spoonful of each of the mixtures in individual bowls into which you have, if you wish, dropped a few slices of banana. Swirl together without blending completely. Finish with crushed walnuts and cinnamon – delicious!

maté tea

or yerba mate, Paraguay tea, yerbamá
(*Ilex paraguayensis* – main species)

A shrubby plant, maté comes from a species of holly native to South America, whose lance-shaped leaves are used to make a stimulant infusion popular in pre-Columbian times, later adopted by the Hispanic colonists. After coffee and tea, its popularity in the region makes it the most widely used stimulant infusion in the world.

Gathering & preparation

The shrub's branches are picked and dried over a fire. Afterwards, the narrow, toothed leaves are beaten off with sticks, dried in ovens, and then powdered.

Appearance and taste

A touch of bitterness makes maté very refreshing. Some people say it tastes like wet haystacks – though I suspect this is mainly because the modern palate is used to more aggressive flavours. The flavour is mild and delicate, but once a taste for it is acquired, it's addictive. For the export trade, the leaves are baked twice to darken the colour and strengthen the flavour.

Buying and storing

Select as you would dried herbs. The scent should be clean and sweet, the colour greenish and fresh-looking. Store the leaves in an airtight canister away from direct sunlight.

Medicinal and other uses

Stimulant, with less tannin than tea, maté is not, as is sometimes supposed, caffeine-free. In its land of origin, it is considered suitable for all ages. As a schoolgirl in Montevideo, for my tenth birthday, my mother's cook presented me with a maté-gourd of my own, inscribed with my name in poker-work, complete with a *bombilla*, a silver straw with a perforated bobble on the end which acted as a strainer. On my return from school, she'd fill it for me from the kettle, and drop in a lump of burnt sugar, held in a flame until it caramelised and smoked. I would suck it slowly – taking care for the first few sips not to burn my lips on the hot metal – sitting on the steps outside the kitchen, my favourite vantage-point as well as a convenient spot for the receipt of cookies hot from the oven.

Culinary uses

To prepare, simply infuse a tablespoonful of dried maté leaves in a mugful of boiling water. Possible additions are a slice of lemon or a splash of milk, honey or sugar. In summer, it's delicious iced, with or without a sprig of mint.

A gaucho enjoying his maté tea, Argentina

Yerba mate dulce con hielo

(Iced maté with honey)

Serves 4

Maté, while usually brewed black and taken without embellishment, is delicious in the summer, well-iced, with cream and honey. Serve hot in winter.

4 tablespoons yerba mate
1.2 litres (2 pints) water

To finish:
Cream
Honey
Ice cubes

Heat the teapot by swirling a little boiling water around inside it. Boil a litre of fresh water and pour it over the yerba mate in the pot. Stir, steep for 5 minutes, and strain it into a jug with cream and honey to taste. Allow to cool completely. Pour into long glasses over ice cubes.

blue agave

or maguey, octli (Aztec) (*Agave* spp.)

A spiky-leaved desert-plant which looks like an enormous jagged-leafed blue-green tuft of grass; the juices from the tall bud which shoots from its heart are used to make tequila.

Agava tequilana growing in the Oaxaca valley, Mexico

How it is processed

The Aztecs made a beer with the juice which accumulates in the hollow when the cactus bud is cut out just after it forms before it reaches maturity. The monks who arrived in the wake of the Conquistadores distilled the beer to produce tequila – a white brandy named for the town in which it was first manufactured. Modern distilleries grow the cacti in serried ranks in the fields and apply modern methods to the collection and fermentation of the juice.

Appearance and taste

Pulque, the beer made from the juice, has a strong vegetable flavour, as I well remember from a few years back – rather more than I care to admit – when the maguey grew wild in the dessert, and it was simply a matter of waiting seven years for the plant to form a bud. The bud was then chopped out with a machete and the ladies of the village were summoned to suck the juice from the wound with a straw, passing it through the mouth and directing it into a receptacle – a gourd, as I remember – delivering an intoxicating beverage within the hour. Female saliva, chemists interested in this oddity have recently confirmed, is more effective in hastening the conversion of plant-sugars to alcohol than the saliva of the male. I can vouch for this through personal experience, insofar as I can remember anything at all – being only seventeen at the time and having drunk rather too deeply in order not to offend my generous hosts.

Buying and storing

Tequila, the white brandy distilled from the fermented cactus mash, is odourless and colourless in its natural state. Mescal is a refined tequila from Oaxaca which often includes a cactus grub in the bottle, though the good stuff dispenses with any such garnish. It is best drunk with a suck of lime and a lick of salt or in any way which suits you. *Tequila añejo* is aged tequila which has had time to take colour and flavour from the barrel. Store in a cool cellar – although it's unlikely to deteriorate over time whatever you do.

Sorbete margarita

(Margarita sorbet)
Serves 6–8

A delicate sorbet made by freezing the raw materials of a margarita. The alcohol keeps the sorbet relatively soft: serve it in a long glass so you can drink the dregs.

225g (8 oz) white sugar
600ml (I pint) water
Juice of 6 lemons
1 eggwhite, mixed with a fork until it froths
2 tablespoons tequila

Dissolve the sugar in the water in a small pan and bring gently to the boil, stirring to make sure all the crystals have melted. Allow to cool and stir in the lemon juice.

If you're using an ice-cream maker, mix in the eggwhite and tequila and freeze as usual. If you use, as I do, the ice-making compartment of the fridge, take it out when solid, beat it thoroughly while incorporating the eggwhite and tequila, and re-freeze.

In the Mexican town of Tequila, family-run distilleries have been producing tequila spirit from the agave cactus for over a century

Filete azteca

(Aztec steak)

Serves 4

Serve with the full Mexican complement of white rice, tortillas, fried peppers, raw onion and black beans.

450g (1lb) cubed pork, dusted with flour
A little oil for frying
2 tablespoons tequila
1 tablespoon parsley, finely chopped
1–2 chillies, de-seeded and sliced
Salt and pepper

The sauce:
450g (1lb) green tomatoes
3–4 spring onions, finely chopped
1 garlic clove, finely chopped
1 tablespoon epasote, finely chopped or crushed
1 green chilli, de-seeded and chopped
2 tablespoons double cream

Dust the meat with a little flour and fry in the oil until lightly browned and perfectly firm. Pour the tequila over the meat and bubble up. Finish with the parsley and chilli and keep warm. Liquidise all the sauce ingredients except the cream, but not too thoroughly. Tip into the oily frying pan, bubble up, turn down the heat, lid loosely and simmer gently for 15–20 minutes, until the sauce is reduced and concentrated. Stir in the cream, bubble up again and pour over the pork. Serve with all the trimmings.

herbs

thyme

basil

oregano

coriander

mint

Four herbs usually identified with the cooking of the Mediterranean were used in pre-Columbian times: basil, oregano, thyme and mint, and a fifth, coriander, achieved instant popularity when the Europeans arrived. Although the New World's species are not botanically identical to those of the Old World, and in any event vary throughout the region, for all culinary purposes (and most of the medicinal) they're interchangeable. Basil – *basilio* – is much used in Colombia and Chile in combination with sweetcorn; thyme – *tomillo* – is the essential flavouring in the Argentine's *chimichurri*, an oil-and-vinegar sauce which accompanies barbecued beef; oregano appears in the marinades of Mexico and Central America; and several varieties of mint – *menta* – were popular throughout the lands of the Maya and Aztecs for medicinal as well as culinary purposes. Coriander – *cilantro* – though unavailable in pre-Columbian times, has become an essential ingredient in many Mexican dishes, particularly guacamole and green chilli sauces, as well as in the cooking of Costa Rica and Dominica, where a herb with a similar flavour, *Gerinium foetidum*, is also known as coriander.

Buying and storing

Oregano and thyme, both dry-leaf herbs, lose none of their power when dehydrated – the very reverse, the essential oils appear to intensify – and are best bought in dried form, stored in an airtight container and replaced at the beginning of each growing season. Basil and coriander are both volatile soft-leaf herbs which don't survive drying and must be bought fresh. They are best kept in a cool place with their stalks in water and used within a day or two. Mint is certainly more fragrant when used fresh, but develops more complex flavours when dried, becoming more like its close relations, oregano and basil.

Medicinal and other uses

Mint is digestive, antiseptic, stimulant and clears the sinuses; basil is anti-spasmodic and assists with flatulence (something of a problem among bean-eaters); marjoram is a stomach calmative and expectorant; thyme is an all-purpose natural tranquiliser; and coriander naturally aids digestion and can be used topically as a poultice to relieve itching.

Culinary uses

Apart from their intrinsic value as flavouring-herbs, thyme, oregano and mint are all effective bacteria-suppressants useful to cooks in the days when refrigeration was not an available option. Basil is used to discourage flies, and coriander is simply the world's most popular herb.

A profusion of herbs in Copacabana market, Rio de Janeiro

Crema de elote con basilio

(Cream of sweetcorn with basil)
Serves 4–6

A Chilean recipe for a sunny yellow soup enriched with butter and milk, finished with fresh basil.

2 tablespoons butter
1 smallish onion, finely chopped
850 ml (1¹/₂ pints) sweetcorn kernels (fresh or frozen)
600ml (1 pint) chicken broth
300ml (¹/₂ pint) creamy milk
Salt and pepper

To finish:
Large handful fresh basil leaves
1 tablespoon oil
¹/₂ teaspoon salt

Melt the butter in a roomy soup pot and soften the onion – don't let it brown. Add the sweetcorn and broth, bring to the boil, turn down to simmer and cook gently for 10 minutes. Add the milk and process to a purée. Reheat and season with salt and pepper. Finish with the basil leaves processed to a purée with the oil and salt.

Sopa de albóndigas con oregano

(Meatballs in broth with oregano)

Serves 4

Miniature meatballs bulked with a little rice in the Hispanic style, flavoured with oregano and poached in a clear broth. One of Mexico's favourite mid-morning snacks – perfect for hangovers, invalids and toothless old grandads.

The meatballs:

1 tablespoon rice

350g (12oz) finely minced meat (pork and/or beef)

1 egg, mixed with a fork

1 garlic clove, very finely chopped

1/2 onion, very finely chopped

1 tablespoon chopped or crumbled oregano

1/2 teaspoon ground allspice

1 teaspoon finely-chopped fresh chilli or 1/2 teaspoon chilli flakes

Salt

The broth:

1.2 litres (2 pints) strong chicken, beef or marrow-bone broth

1–2 habanero or malagueta chillies

1–2 sprigs dried oregano

To finish:

Chopped tomato

Put the rice in a small bowl with enough boiling water to cover, and leave to soak and swell for about 20 minutes. Drain the rice and put it in the processor with the rest of the meatball ingredients. Process all to a paste. With wet hands (keep a bowl of warm water handy for rinsing your fingers), form the mixture into about 24 bite-sized balls.

Bring the broth to the boil with the chilli and oregano (tied into a scrap of muslin for ease of removal). Slip in the meatballs and bring back to a simmer. Put the lid on loosely and leave to cook gently until the meatballs are tender – 20–25 minutes. Serve in bowls, finished with a little chopped tomato.

Tortitas de papa con cilantro

(Potato cakes with coriander)
Serves 4 as a starter

Coriander-flavoured potato cakes with a pleasantly rough texture, eaten with a fierce little coriander/chilli/avocado salsa.

The cakes:
4 medium potatoes, boiled in their jackets and skinned
2 tablespoons finely chopped fresh coriander
2 tablespoons grated cheese
1 large egg, mixed with a fork
1 teaspoon chilli flakes
1 teaspoon salt
Oil for shallow frying

The salsa:
2 tablespoons chopped fresh coriander
1 avocado, stoned, skinned and roughly chopped
2 green (jalapeno) chillies, de-seeded and finely chopped
3–4 spring onions or 1 mature onion, finely chopped
4 tablespoons lemon juice
1 teaspoon salt

Mash the potatoes roughly with a fork in a bowl. Using your hands and without crushing out all the lumps, work in the coriander, cheese, egg, chilli and salt.
Heat the oil in a wide heavy frying pan and combine all the salsa ingredients. When the oil is lightly hazed with blue, drop in tablespoons of the potato mixture, patting it roughly into little cakes. Fry, turning once, until golden and crisp. Remove and drain on kitchen paper. Serve topped with a spoonful of the green salsa, or hand it around separately in a bowl.

Chimichurri

(Argentinian thyme and garlic relish)
Makes 1 wine-bottleful

A thyme-infused, garlicky, oil-and-vinegar dressing, this is the ketchup of the pampas, a must with barbecued beef – an *asado*, a young bullock roasted gaucho-style on a sharpened pole stuck at an angle over the evening's campfire. And if the meat's to be spared for another day, the sauce works wonders with a potato baked in the embers.

3–4 springs fresh thyme (the drier the better)
1 large onion
6 cloves garlic
4 tablespoons flat-leaf parsley
150ml (1/4 pint) wine vinegar
425ml (3/4 pint) olive oil

Pop the thyme sprigs in an empty wine bottle along with the onion, garlic and parsley. Add the vinegar and oil, shake it up and leave to infuse for a couple of days. Ready when you are. Keep it in the fridge.

Mojito
Serves 1

Unlike rum-and-coke – *Cuba Libre* – this is the politically acceptable tipple in Castro's Havana.

Juice of half a lime
1 teaspoon sugar
2–3 sprigs fresh mint
A shot of white rum
Crushed ice
Soda water

Mix the limejuice with the sugar in highball glass until it dissolves. Drop in the mint and add the rum and ice. Stir. Top up with soda. Finish with another sprig of mint.

fruit

The fruits of the region are a wild and wonderful mixture of the exotic, the weird and some which are so hard to obtain you can only taste them once a year, and then only in the particular place where they're grown. Many of the more familiar fruits are used in unfamiliar ways: in unripe form as vegetables, or ripe but dusted not with sugar but with chilli, while many of the more exotic and perishable jungle fruits and tropical berries are yet to be discovered outside the territory. Aware of this, whenever possible I have tried to give alternatives which, although they can never be quite the same, are the kind of substitutes a native of the region might use when trying to recreate the taste of home.

The traveller will have better luck. Anyone unfamiliar with the botanical riches of a particular area can easily sample them in the form of freshly squeezed *liquados, sorbetes* and *batidos* – iced and frothed with cream, or topped with condensed milk – offered for sale by roadside vendors in screws of paper or plastic cups. This service, though taken for granted by the natives, is a constant source of pleasure for the visitor, as well as providing much-needed refreshment. The surprise is the offer of a drop of chilli-sauce along with the sugar-shaker.

pineapple

or anana, piña, abaxi (Brazil) (*Ananas comosus*)

Several species of this oddly constructed fruit, both large and small, are native to the Brazilian lowlands. The Spanish Conquistadors first came across it in the Caribbean and decided it reminded them of a pinecone – *piña*. The name did not travel throughout the region: elsewhere it's more commonly known as *anana*, a Tupi word for delicious.

Fresh pineapples in transit

Medicinal and other uses

The pineapple is recommended for arthritis and stiffness in the joints. But be careful when handling the fresh fruit: the juice is so corrosive that pineapple-canning factories have to provide their workers with protective clothing.

Culinary uses

The presence of bromalin, a powerful protein-digesting enzyme, makes pineapple useful as a meat-tenderiser. For the same chemical reason, a jelly made with fresh pineapple won't jell if the setting-agent is an animal-derived gelatine, as most of them are. The bromalin is neutralised when heated, so canned fruit or pasteurised juices don't have the same effect.

Galinha assado com abacaxi
(Roast chicken with pineapple)
Serves 4–6

The pineapple tenderises the chicken as it roasts to make this deliciously juicy and delicately perfumed dish. It is even better with guinea fowl, an African bird which has claimed its perch in the barnyards of Brazil.

1 free-range chicken or guinea fowl
1 smallish pineapple, skinned and diced (save the juices)
1 onion, coarsely chopped
2 tablespoons oil or butter
1 teaspoon ground allspice
Salt
1 teaspoon malagueta pepper sauce (see p.51) or 1 teaspoon chilli powder

How it grows

The pineapple is not one but many little fruits clamped together round a single stem, topped by a tuft of narrow spiky leaves.

Appearance and taste

The fruit, which has a rough exterior with a prickly pinecone structure, ripens to a rich red-gold; the exterior roughness is reflected in the interior flesh, which is chewy rather than soft, striated like soft wood but tender, juicy and very fragrant, its sweetness balanced by sourness – thrilling on the palate.

Buying and storing

The fruits don't ripen any more after picking, so it must be perfectly mature when harvested. Brazilian gourmets – and pineapple-appreciation is a high art in the markets of Rio and Bahia – will tell you the flesh is sweeter at the stalk-end. Look for firmness with no sign of withering and a strong fragrance with no hint of fermentation; to check for ripeness, pull out one of the little leaves from the top-knot – if it comes out easily, the fruit is mature.

Preheat the oven to 200°C/400°F/gas mark 6.

Wipe the bird inside and out and place it breast-side down on a roasting tin. Tuck the chunks of pineapple and onion inside the cavity. Trickle with the oil or slip the butter under the skin of the breast and sprinkle with the allspice, salt and pepper sauce or chilli.

Roast for 30 minutes, turn the bird breast side up, baste with the reserved pineapple juice and the drippings in the pan, turn down the heat to 180°C/350°F/gas mark 4. Roast for another 30 minutes, until tender and beautifully brown.

Joint neatly and serve with the onion and pineapple handed around separately.

Flan de piña, a fragrant pineapple caramel custard

Flan de piña
(Pineapple caramel custard)
Serves 6

Egg and sugar confections, a legacy of colonial rule, were the specialities of the convents, which make these little caramel custards with pineapple juice instead of milk.

For the caramel:
2 tablespoons caster sugar
2 teaspoons water
Juice of half a lemon

For the custard:
300ml (1/2 pint) pineapple juice
225g (8oz) granulated sugar
6 large egg yolks (another 2 if the eggs are small)

You will need 6 little moulds or 1 large one, and a roasting tin to use as a bain-marie. Preheat the oven to 180°C/350°F/gas mark 4.

Make the caramel first. Melt the ingredients together in the pan, turning it over a high flame until the sugar caramelises a rich golden brown. This will take only a moment or two. Tip it into the moulds and roll it around to coat the base. Set aside to cool. To make the custard, put the juice and sugar in a heavy pan, and heat gently until the sugar dissolves. Boil for about 20 minutes, until reduced by a third. Stir with a wooden spoon: it's ready when the syrup trails a transparent string when you lift out the spoon.

Meanwhile whisk the egg yolks thoroughly. Pour the hot syrup into the eggs, beating vigorously. This will begin the thickening process. Pour the mixture into the mould(s). Cover with foil and transfer to the roasting tin. Pour in enough boiling water to come halfway up the moulds. Bake for 30–50 minutes, depending on the size of the container. It's ready when firm to the finger. Allow to cool and shake well before unmoulding – the caramel makes a deliciously dark sticky sauce.

banana

or platano (*Musa* spp.)

An ancient cultivar of Asian origin, the banana is naturalised throughout the tropical and sub-tropical zones of the Americas. Plants of the family Musaceae are not actually trees but grasses, with a rhizome rather than a root, and a trunk formed from its own overlapping leaves (see Plantain, p.206, additional culinary uses).

How it grows

The fruits develop from the small female flowers which ring the seed-head, a long stalk tipped by a single scarlet blossom whose petals peel back to expose a pointed ivory bud, the male. The weight of the bud draws the stalk downwards, allowing the fruits, semicircular 'hands' which circle the stem like elegant emerald bracelets, to point upwards. Left to its own devices, the plant can grow to over 9 metres (30 feet), although the insecurity of its footing and the weight of the fruit – as many as 200 per stalk – can cause it to topple before its time.

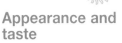

Appearance and taste

The banana is the earliest convenience food: it not only tastes delicious – smooth and creamy with a vanilla-citrus fragrance and a delicately spicy flavour – but fits neatly in one's hand, ripens in the pocket and can be slipped easily out of its skin. These virtues have made it the most-widely consumed fruit in the world, much of which gets its supplies from the Americas.

Buying and storing

Caribbean bananas grown on the steep slopes of the Windward Islands are smaller, sweeter and juicier than the big 'dollar bananas' of the Central American mainland – so called because they are grown on lowland plantations controlled by the two US-based monopolies. In Brazil, popular varieties include *banana de agua*, lady-fingers, which are small, thin-skinned and sweet, and preferred for frying to accompany meat or fish. Another popular variety is the red or apple banana which is juicy and lemony when ripe; when green, it fries to an exquisite crispness. Bananas are exported green, the state in which they usually come to market. If the banana doesn't snap easily from the stalk for peeling, it's not ripe, a process which turns the fruit from a bright sunny yellow to a deep gold lightly freckled with brown, the moment of perfection. To slow down the ripening process, refrigerate: the skin will turn brown but the fruit will remain perfect.

Medicinal and other uses

The banana is an excellent all-rounder, fortifying, easily assimilable, and high in fibre and essential vitamins and minerals – particularly potassium. It's also a bowel stimulant, a remedy for ulcers and a stomach-calmant, as well as inducing sleep and encouraging the production of hormones.

Culinary uses

The red-skinned banana, floury and fragrant with pale orange flesh, cooks well: it is delicious roasted in the skin, then split and sprinkled with powdered cinnamon and brown sugar. When very ripe, it develops a bronzed skin and soft dark flesh – perfect for banana bread. The application of heat to the ripe fruit emphasises its natural starchiness, making the flavour more robust, the flesh more chewy. When mashed before cooking, it quickly collapses to a soft mush, an advantage in baking, when the combination of starchiness and sweetness makes it an excellent cake ingredient.

Banana plantation, Honduras

Banana bread

Banana bread

Serves 6–8

Not only every island but every household in the Carribean has a favourite recipe for banana bread. It is good for breakfast and tea and perfect for the midday break. My little granddaughters love it.

450g (1lb) very ripe bananas (3 large ones),
  skinned
110g (4oz) honey
2 medium eggs
110g (4oz) butter, softened
110g (4oz) light brown sugar
225g (8oz) self-raising wholemeal flour
1 level teaspoon baking powder
1 teaspoon freshly grated nutmeg

To finish:
1 banana, skinned and quartered lengthways

Preheat the oven to 180ºC/350ºF/gas mark 4. Butter and line a 23 x 15cm (9 x 6in) loaf tin with buttered greaseproof paper or butter paper (banana bread is a bit of a sticker).

Purée the bananas thoroughly with the honey and the eggs in the liquidiser or food processor. Beat the butter with the sugar until light and white, then beat in the banana mixture, alternating with the flour sifted with the baking powder and spice, and blend thoroughly. Drop the mixture in the loaf-tin, spreading it well into the corners. Top with the finishing bananas.

Bake for an hour, until the cake is shrunk from the sides, well-risen and springy in the middle – it may need a little longer, in which case turn the oven down a notch and bake for another 10–15 minutes. Tip it out onto a baking rack to cool. It's all the better for a few days in the tin.

Doce de banana

(Sugared Brazilian banana)
Serves 4

A very sweet, sticky, spicy, jam-like banana compote. Take your time – it's the long, slow cooking which turns the fruit a beautiful mahogany. Try with soured cream.

4–6 ripe bananas (depending on size), skinned
  and thickly sliced
450g (1lb) soft brown sugar (palm-sugar, for
  preference)
600ml (1 pint) water
3–5 cloves
1 short stick cinnamon

Put all the ingredients in a heavy pan. Put the lid on loosely and cook over a gentle heat until the fruit turns a rich dark red and the juices thicken to a rich clear syrup – 30–40 minutes. Allow to cool before serving. Keeps well in the fridge.

plantain

or plátano (*Musa* spp.)

The plantain is not, as might be supposed, a separate species of fruit from the sweet banana, but a description applied to a green unripe banana which is usually, but not always, of a variety specially grown for its virtues as a vegetable. Just to confuse matters, the name is sometimes applied to an unripe sweet banana. As if that were not trouble enough, platano is the Spanish name for both varieties.

Appearance and taste

The purpose-bred varieties are mouth-puckeringly bitter when raw; when cooked, they're starchy and bland, more like a root than a fruit. The plantain is grown as a staple vegetable in those places – such as tropical jungles – where grain-foods cannot thrive.

Buying and storing

The purpose-bred varieties are longer and more angular in shape than the sweet banana, often narrowing to form a short horn at the non-stalk end. the colour starts a bright green and ripens to yellow streaked with brown.

Medicinal and other uses

The plantain is indigestible and constipating when raw, though both problems are solved by cooking.

Related products

The leaves of both banana and plantain – which are actually gigantic blades of grass – are used throughout the region as a wrapper to protect delicate foodstuffs from the direct heat of the fire, or to keep food moist during prolonged steaming in an earth-oven. A little preliminary preparation is needed: wilt the whole fresh leaf over a wide-based heat-source – a charcoal barbecue or a gas-flame – until the surface begins to look oily and the colour changes from bright emerald to dark green. Cut out the central rib and snip the rest into sizes suitable for wrapping the food – chicken, fish, meatballs, whatever – and package in whatever way suits the recipe. The leaves give a particular distinction to the cooking of the Yucatan on the Caribbean coast of Mexico, where both fish and chicken are cooked in banana leaves, imparting an exquisite viscosity and delicate citrus flavour to the juices.

'Open market' in São Paulo, Brazil

Culinary uses

To serve plantains or green bananas as a vegetable, roast in the jacket, boil, bake or slice and fry. Use a sharp knife to peel them – or follow the instructions in the Patacones recipe below – the skin is virtually welded to the flesh. To make plantain chips, choose firm green fruits, slice thinly, skin and deep-fry until crisp. To grill or barbecue plantains as the street-vendors do in Jamaica, cut them in half horizontally without peeling them, brush the cut side with oil and start with the skin side towards the heat. Grill for 5 minutes and turn, allowing another 2 minutes for them to soften and crisp.

Baked plantains
Serves 4

The perfect recipe for over-ripe plantains. Serve like baked potatoes in their jackets: finger-licking good with spicy jerk chicken (see allspice, p.184).

4 ripe plantains

To serve:
Butter

Preheat the oven to 230°C/450°F/gas mark 8.

Arrange the plantains on a baking sheet and bake for 20–30 minutes, until cooked right through. To serve, split right down the middle with a sharp knife, mash the flesh a little, and drop in a knob of butter.

Patacones
(Plantain fritters)
Serves 4–6

These twice-cooked fritters – fried once to soften, a second time to crisp – are known in some places as *tostones*, in others as *patacones* – notably in Ecuador and Colombia, where you can buy special little wooden presses for squashing them flat.

2 firm plantains or 3 green bananas, thickly
  sliced (2 fingers' width)
Salt
Oil for deep-frying

Soak the plantain slices in salted water for half an hour, until you can push the edible disks out of their skin; drop them back in the water to stop them browning until you're ready to cook.

Heat a panful of oil to the point just before it hazes with blue.

Pat the plantain slices dry. Drop them in the oil a few at a time and fry gently until softish but not yet crisp. Remove to kitchen paper, cover with clingfilm and punch down with a butter-pat to reduce the slices to half their thickness – as mentioned, Latin-American cooks can buy a special little wooden press for the purpose.

You can do this in pairs, overlapping one slice over the other and flattening both together. Either way, the soft diaphragm spreads to make a pretty broken edge which browns deliciously.

Reheat the oil, this time to chip-frying temperature. Fry the flattened slices, a few at a time, until brown and crisp on the outside and still meltingly soft on the inside.

Treat as tortilla chips: as a scoop for a seviche, a soupy bean-dish, guacamole, or a savoury stew. Or serve as dessert with fresh curd cheese, honey and nuts.

guava

or guayaba (Spanish), goiaba (Portuguese)
(*Psidium guajava*)

A Peruvian native, the guava was already established in Mexico at the time of the Hispanic conquest.

Guava tree, Cuba

How it grows

A smallish tree, about the size of an apple-tree, the guava has large smooth-edged leaves and white flowers from which develop somewhat pear-like fruits.

Appearance and taste

The fruits are very variable in size and colour with skin which runs the gamut from pale green through yellow to (sometimes) scarlet when ripe. The flesh varies from creamy-white to bright pink and has an outer and inner section, the inner section being scattered with gritty little seeds in a circular pattern round the core, although some seedless varieties are grown.

Buying and storing

The fruit should yield a little to light pressure, and have a strong flowery fragrance; it ripens very rapidly – making export a problem. Choose firm fruits, discarding any which feel spongy or show signs of bruising. Store in the fridge and use within a couple of days.

Medicinal and other uses

The musky, spicy fragrance of a ripe guava indicates the presence of eugenol, an essential oil found in cloves, effective as a remedy for toothache, also used as a stimulant for the lymphatic system.

Related or similar fruits

The pineapple-guava (*Feijoa sellowiana*) or feijoa is the fruit of a small evergreen tree native to southern Brazil but also found in northern Argentina, Uruguay and Paraguay. Fruits are egg-shaped, about the size and appearance of a kiwi fruit but without the fuzzy jacket. Yellow when ripe, when cut, they reveal a rim of flesh surrounding a hollow centre filled with a soft pulp which holds lots of tiny seeds. The flavour and fragrance are complex: strawberry/guava/pineapple. The pineapple-guava ripens quickly – in nature, as soon as it drops from the tree – becoming more fragrant as it develops. Eaten raw when the first of the crop comes in, it is used for juice and jellies later. To prepare, peel off the soft skin, then slice and sprinkle with lemon juice to avoid discolouration. When ready to eat, the scent should be fresh and flowery – fruit picked when immature will be bitter even when ripe – and should have a slight give, like a pear. Medicinally, the pineapple-guava is particularly rich in iodine. It can replace apples in pies and compotes and is also delicious raw in a fruit salad.

Culinary uses

The large, pale-fleshed, pear-shaped guavas are considered the best for eating, while the small, pink-fleshed varieties such as the strawberry guava, *P. cattleianum* – a Brazilian native which ripens to a deep purple – make the best jelly.

Mermelada de guayaba
(Guava jelly)

A clear garnet-pink jelly with a flowery scent and delicate flavour.

900g (2lb) guavas
About 900g (2lb) golden cane sugar
Juice of 2 lemons or 3 limes

Rinse and roughly chop the guavas – skins, pips and all – and put them in a roomy saucepan with enough water to cover. Bring to the boil and cook for 20 minutes, until the fruit is soft and mushy. Dump the contents of the pan in a clean jelly-cloth and hang on a hook set over a bowl. Leave to drip overnight.

Mermelada de guayaba, a clear guava jelly

Next day, measure the juice (save the pulp for the next recipe) and return it to the pan with its own volume of sugar and the lemon juice. Bring to the boil, skim off the foam which rises and boil steadily, uncovered, for 35 minutes or until setting-point is reached. To test, drop a little on a cold saucer and push it with your finger: when it wrinkles like skin, it's ready. Pot it up in well-scalded jelly jars. Keep in a cool larder away from direct sunlight.

Membrillo de guayaba
(Guava cheese)
Makes about 900g (2lb)

A thick, slightly grainy fruit paste – very delicious. The Christmas treat, the New World version of the Old World's quince paste, guava cheese is traditionally made into little palm-leaf parcels and given by the host to wedding guests to keep the memory of the encounter sweet.

900gk (2lb) guava pulp (freshly stewed, or left over from the guava jelly recipe)
450g (1lb) golden cane sugar

Push the pulp through a sieve, discarding the skins and pips. Put the sieved pulp in a pan and beat in the sugar. Cook very, very gently for at least an hour until the pulp and sugar have formed a soft, dark, dryish mass, or spread on a baking tray and leave in the lowest possible oven overnight. It'll set to a firm paste as it cools. Wrap in paper and keep in a warm dry place – never in the fridge. Delicious with cheese.

musk cucumber

or sicana (Peru), cassabanana (Puerto Rico), calabaza melón (Mexico), cojombro (Nicaragua), melocotón de bresil (Guatemala), cura (Brazil) (*Sicana odorifera*)

The musk cucumber is a member of the watermelon family native to Brazil.

How it grows
An ornamental vine, as decorative as it's useful, the musk cucumber is cultivated in its land of origin not only as a fruit but also for the beauty of its foliage and flowers.

Appearance and taste
The fruit looks like a large fat cucumber with a smooth shiny skin which can be red, black or purple. The flesh is yellow to orange and very melon-like in flavour and texture, centered around a hollow cavity packed with rows of flat seeds embedded in a cotton wool-like fibre.

Buying and storing
Look for the cassabanana in markets which serve Central American communities, particularly Puerto Rican ones. Tap gently – the hollower, the riper. A good keeper, the musk cucumber is so deliciously perfumed that Puerto Rican housewives tuck a couple in the linen-cupboard to scent the sheets.

Medicinal and other uses
In Puerto Rico, the juice, well sugared and slightly fermented, is used as a cold cure. The Brazilian name for it is *cura*: cure-all.

Culinary uses
When preparing it as a vegetable, peel with a sharp knife and chop. It's eaten as a vegetable when unripe, in soups and stews, in much the same way as the vegetable marrow or summer squash. When ripe, it can be eaten raw, though it's more usually converted into a sticky preserve popular at Christmas.

Sopa de sicana
(Musk cucumber soup)
Serves 4–6

The Peruvian way with this most fragrant of gourds. If you can't buy them or grow them, a similar culinary effect can be achieved by replacing the main ingredient with chayote and a splash of rose-water. Not the same of course – but good enough to fool the neighbours.

900g (2lb) unripe musk-cucumbers, peeled, de-seeded and roughly chopped
900g (2lb) tomatoes, scalded, peeled and roughly chopped
450g (1lb) onions, skinned and chopped
1 stick celery, washed and sliced
1 pint home-made stock or plain water
A handful of fresh basil leaves

To finish:
150ml (1/4 pint) double cream

Put all the ingredients except the cream into a roomy saucepan, bring to the boil, put the lid on and turn down to simmer for 30 minutes, until the vegetables are all soft and soupy.

Mash everything down hard with the potato masher and finish each plateful with a swirl of cream.

A portable Bethlehem scene, belén, displayed at Christmas in Peru

Dulce de cassabanana puertoriqueño
(Candied musk cucumber)
Serves 6

In Puerto Rico, Christmas wouldn't be the same without this very sticky, exquisitely fragrant preserve, traditionally offered on the best glass dish in tiny portions to guests so their visit may be all the sweeter. It's delicious with soured cream and walnuts, and a little goes a long way.

1.4kg (3lb) ripe cassabananas, peeled and
  de-seeded
350g (12oz) sugar
6 tablespoons water

To serve (optional):
Walnuts, coarsely chopped
Sour cream

Either scoop into balls with a melon-baller (pretty and appropriately festive) or dice into bite-sized pieces. Layer the fruit and sugar in a heavy saucepan and add the water.

Set the pan on a very low flame, put the lid on tightly and simmer gently for 50–60 minutes, until the fruit is tender and the syrup thick and shiny. You may need to splash in more water, or you may need to boil it down with the pan uncovered – it all depends on how watery it was when it started.

Leave to cool in the pan in its syrup before you pot it up as a preserve, making sure there's enough syrup to submerge the fruit completely. Or serve immediately, sprinkled with walnuts, and hand the sour cream around separately.

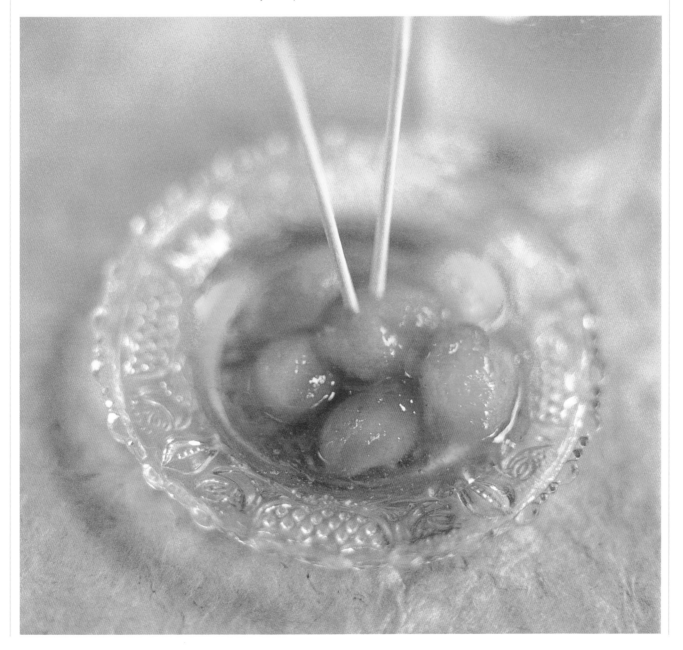

papaya

or melón zapote (Mexico), fruta bomba (Cuba), lechosa/lichisa (Puerto Rico), mando or mamão (Brazil) and paw-paw – sometimes, but not to be, confused with cherimoya (p.226) (*Carica papaya*)

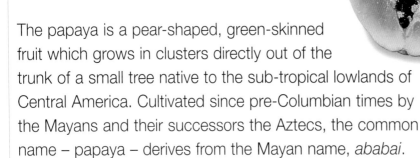

The papaya is a pear-shaped, green-skinned fruit which grows in clusters directly out of the trunk of a small tree native to the sub-tropical lowlands of Central America. Cultivated since pre-Columbian times by the Mayans and their successors the Aztecs, the common name – papaya – derives from the Mayan name, *ababai*.

Medicinal and other uses

Papaya is digestive and stomach-settling – but be warned, don't let the corrosive juices anywhere near sensitive or broken skin, and wash your hands thoroughly before you change a baby's nappy.

Related products

The central cavity is filled with small black seeds slicked with sticky juice in a soft gloop. These seeds, though very hard, can be cracked and eaten: crushed or milled, they taste a little like grain-mustard and are good in a salad-dressing. The leaves can be used as a food-wrapper, imparting a delicate flavour as well as acting as a tenderising agent.

Culinary uses

Delicious ripe and raw with just a squeeze of lime juice, papayas can be included in meat stews and marinades as a tenderiser. All parts (fruit and leaves) contain papain, a protein-digesting enzyme used in commercial meat-tenderising powders. For this reason, it won't set as a jelly if the setting-agent is gelatine of animal origin.

How it grows

A fruit of variable size in its land of origin, the papaya can be as large as a honeydew melon. The export trade prefers smaller fruits weighing no more than a pound which can be sold as suitable for a single portion or, at most, for sharing between two people.

Appearance and taste

When ripe, the flesh is pink, tinged with orange, and is tender and fragrant, with a flavour of strawberry and banana. Growing in popularity commercially is the *chamburo* or *babaco* (*C. pentagona*), a deeply ridged, five-sided seedless papaya of Ecuadorian origin – a hybrid of a native fruit, unknown in the wild – which has sweet, juicy, fragrant, vanilla-scented, ivory-white flesh which, lacking the hard little seeds, is edible throughout.

Buying and storing

Look for a fruit which yields to gentle pressure in the hand and feels heavy for its size, with an unwrinkled, unblemished skin blushed with yellow ripening to red (the non-sun side remains green). Regional names are a minefield: the traveller or anyone attempting to buy the fruit in a market serving ethnic communities would be wise to exercise caution. In Cuba, *papaya* is slang for the female reproductive organs; elsewhere, eyebrows will be raised at the use of the word *lechosa*. The problem lies in the mind of the beholder, having to do with the colour of the cut flesh (a beautiful orangey-pink), its softness and succulence, and the exuberant amount of small, jelly-coated seeds. I'm sure you get the picture.

Papayas and watermelons on sale in Panama

Picante de papaya

(Devilled papaya)

Serves 4

A marriage of two perfectly compatible fruits – one dense and buttery, the other juicy and fragrant – given a sinful little twist with a chilli-infused syrup. Roadside vendors who sell prepared fruits blended to order and ladled into plastic cups will always offer a sprinkle of chilli along with the sugar-shaker.

Juice of 1–2 limes
6 tablespoons sugar
1 hot red chilli
1–2 papayas, peeled, de-seeded and diced
1 small ripe melon, de-seeded and diced

Put the lime juice and sugar in a small pan with its own volume of water. Bring gently to the boil, stirring to dissolve the sugar crystals. Add the chilli, remove from the heat and leave to infuse and cool. Combine the prepared fruits in a bowl and dress with sugar-syrup. Top with the infused chilli as a warning to the unwary.

Guiso de chivo con papaya

(Kid or lamb stew with papaya)

Serves 4–6

A Mexican shepherd's stew, equally good made with a well-grown kid or the sinewy little lambs of the Hispanic tradition, left to cook gently overnight in the embers of the campfire, and reheated the next day.

About 1.3kg (2½lb) kid or lamb on the bone, cut into chunks
1 medium-sized, unripe, green papaya, cut into chunks
Juice and zest of 1 bitter orange, or half lemon, half sweet orange
1 teaspoon chilli powder
Short length cinnamon, broken up
1 tablespoon sugar
1 teaspoon salt
2 tablespoons oil
2 onions, finely sliced
2 garlic cloves, skinned and chopped

Mix the meat with the papaya, citrus juice and zest, chilli, cinnamon, sugar and salt in a bowl, cover and leave for 3–4 hours to marinate.

Warm the oil in a roomy casserole and fry the onions and garlic gently for 8–10 minutes, until soft and golden. Add the meat and papaya, put the lid on tightly and leave on a gentle heat for 2–3 hours until perfectly tender and deliciously gluey. Or bake: it'll take about the same amount of time in the oven at 150°C/300°F/gas mark 2.

Picante de papaya

passion fruit

or purple granadilla, grenadilla, maracujá (Brazil), curuba (Colombia), parcha (Venezuela and Puerto Rico), ceibey (Cuba), couzou (West Indies) (*Passiflora edulis*)

Passion fruit – *grenadilla* – is the fruit of a flowering vine native to the rainforests of Brazil but naturalised throughout the region, including by the Aztecs in Mexico.

How it grows

While the fruits are not particularly noticeable, the blossoms are of an astonishing beauty, as intricately-chiselled as the carvings on an Aztec altar. Spanish missionaries, seeking images to assist them in their preaching, declared it a holy flower. They named it for the passion of Christ and carried it into the pulpit as a metaphor for their message: twelve petals for the Apostles, five stamens for the five wounds, three styles to symbolise the three nails and the corolla for the crown of thorns.

Appearance and taste

On the vine, the fruit looks like a purply-brown hen's egg, smooth when ripening and crinkling a little when ready to eat, with a leathery skin whose colour bleeds carmine into the soft white pith which lines the carapace and

protects the interior seeds. These – small and crunchy and without any particular flavour – are encased in a soft, exquisitely fragrant, sweet-sharp, pineapple/guava-flavoured jelly which drips with juice.

Buying and storing

Choose fruits which weigh heavy for their size. When ripe, the skin crinkles up like an elderly prune: if it looks only a little bit shrunk, store at room temperature until it crumples.

Medicinal and other uses

High in vitamin C, the passion fruit is valuable as a cold-cure.

Related or similar fruits

The sweet calabash, *P. maliformis* – a smallish, yellow-skinned passion fruit native to Amazonia – is particularly esteemed for its exceptionally fragrant, sweet-sour pulp: a spoonful will perfume ten times its own volume of cream.

The sweet granadilla, *P. ligularis*, is a native of Mexico whose pretty orange skin acquires, when ripe, a dusting of snowy freckles. The water-lemon, *P. laurifolia*, also called

Jamaican honeysuckle and yellow granadilla, is a Caribbean native which looks, as you might expect, like a small smooth-skinned lemon, but in all other respects serves the same culinary purpose as other passion fruits.

The banana passion fruit, *P. molissima,* is known as *curuba* in Colombia, *tacso* in Ecuador, *parcha* in Venezuela and *tumbo* in Bolivia and Peru.

Giant or royal granadilla, *P. quadrangularis* – known as maracujá in Brazil – is one of the largest of the genus, up to 20cm (8in) long. It ripens from green to gold or crimson and looks rather like a small mango. Next to the skin is a thick lining of pinkish, melon-like flesh – also edible – as well as the usual pulp-and-seed arrangement. For all its popularity (and the vine is widely planted throughout Asia as well as the tropical Americas) the flavour doesn't match the fragrance. Although acceptable raw for its juices and the odd combination of textures, the giant granadilla is disappointingly bland and is best combined with more sharply defined flavourings such as pineapple, lemon and bitter orange.

Red granadilla, *P. coccinea*, is an Amazonian native popular in Guadaloupe, which has scarlet blossoms and speckled yellow-green fruits; *P. alatta*, the wing-stemmed passionflower, is mostly cultivated for the beauty of its blossoms though the fruits are edible (check your gardeners' catalogue); as is *P. caerulea*, the blue passionflower, whose fruits are bland but edible.

The Brazilian jungle-plum or ciriguela is a fruit of Amazonia which looks not unlike a kumquat, with thin, sharply flavoured skin and soft aromatic flesh around a shiny black kernel. A Christmas fruit, it comes to market in December, after the rains.

Culinary uses

To eat passion fruit raw from the hand, use your teeth to make a small hole in the leathery skin and suck out the seeds and sweet-sour juices. As a flavouring, push it through a sieve to extract the seeds (or not, as you please): it is sensational in creams, mousses and soufflés and wonderful in fruit salads, delivering the same acid punch as a squeeze of lemon. Use undiluted as the acid-bath when preparing a seviche. Each fruit yields one mouthful of seed-laden jelly – the aril. It takes 100 fruits to produce a litre of thick juice whose viscosity comes from a high starch-content. Happily, the flavour is remarkably concentrated and can be generously diluted.

Caipirinha de maracujá

(Passion fruit and rum cocktail)
Serves 1

A mouthful of sheer pleasure, tart and exquisitely fragrant – served at every fashionable Brazilian cocktail party. Make one at a time.

1 passion fruit
1 tablespoon caster sugar
2 tablespoons cachaça or white rum
Ice cubes

Squeeze the contents of the passion fruit into a short fat tumbler. Crush the sugar into the pulp. Add the cachaça or rum and enough ice cubes to fill the glass. Stir and serve.

Baba de maracujá

(Little passion fruit mousses)
Serves 6–8

The flowery fragrance of the fruit makes each of these lightly-set honeycomb mousses a mouthful of sheer pleasure. Condensed milk delivers the authentically Brazilian flavour, though some might consider fresh cream to be even better. Delicious with a crisp little biscuit.

12 ripe passion fruit
2 sheets clear gelatine or 1 tablespoon powdered – enough to set 300ml ($^1/_2$ pint) of liquid
300 ml ($^1/_2$ pint) unsweetened condensed milk or fresh double cream
4 eggwhites
6 tablespoons caster sugar

Scoop the pulp from 8 of the passion fruit and reserve the remaining 4 fruits. Push the pulp through a sieve to separate the juice from the seeds. Tear the gelatine into bits and put to soak in a little cold water for 10 minutes or so, until it softens. If using powdered gelatine, follow the directions on the packet. In a small pan, mix the soaked gelatine with half the passion fruit juice and dissolve it over a gentle heat, whisking to blend. Whisk in the condensed milk or the cream.

Meanwhile whisk the eggwhites until they hold their shape, then whisk in the sugar spoonful by spoonful to make a soft meringue. Fold in the warm passion fruit cream and spoon into whatever receptacles you like – small or large. Finish with the reserved passion fruit – juice and seeds – halved and squeezed over.

cape gooseberry

or physalis, uvilla (little grape, Colombia), capuli (Bolivia/Peru), topotopo (Venezuela), chuchuva (Venezuela), bolsa de amor (love-bag, Chile), cereza de Perú (Mexico), ciriguela de Peru (Brazil) (*Physalis peruviana*)

Physalis – a group which includes the tree-tomato and tomatillo as well a number of cherry-like fruits of the genus Solanaceae – is a Peruvian vine-fruit, a member of the potato-tomato family. It was exported north to Mexico, where it was appreciated by both the Aztecs and the Mayas, and early Portuguese colonisers established it as a crop on the Cape of Good Hope – hence its name.

How it grows

Cape gooseberries are the fruits of a perennial vine; they hang down like little lanterns where the leaves meet the stalk and are enclosed in a papery calyx. The berry-like fruits of its close relation, the decorative garden plant known as the Chinese lantern, though smaller, are interchangeable for culinary purposes.

Appearance and taste

While the flesh has a similar structure and texture to the tomato, the seeds are smaller and crunchier and the flavour is distinctly fruity: sweet-sour, fragrant and refreshingly sharp.

Buying and storing

The fruits start green and ripen to a brilliant yellow-orange. Buy them ripe – don't worry if the husks look a bit dingy. Stored in a sealed container in a dry place, they'll keep for months.

Mayan temple façade, Yucatán, Mexico

Medicinal and other uses

Avoid unripe fruits: they're poisonous.

Related or similar fruits

The sweet cucumber (*Solanum muricatum*) or *pepino dulce* is the fruit of a small bush native to the Andean regions of Peru and Chile, also cultivated elsewhere throughout the temperate zones. One form which grows on a vine looks a bit like a small cucumber – hence the name – but more usually the shape and colour is that of a small, pale-skinned eggplant. The smooth golden skin is freckled with green or violet and, like the eggplant, is usually sweet but can occasionally be bitter. When ripe, the texture and appearance of the flesh – golden and juicy – is somewhere between a honeydew melon and a ripe pear, with a fragrance of vanilla and honeysuckle. The seeds and skin are both edible, though the latter is best removed since it's a little tough.

Other vine-fruits of the same group, particularly *P. pruinosa*, are known as *cereza de suelo* – ground-cherry – and are of local rather than commercial interest.

Naranjilla (Peru) or naranjilla de Quito (Ecuador), lulún (Mexico), toronjo (Colombia) (*Solanum quitoense*) is a furry little orange berry native to Peru, Ecuador and Colombia, in all respects similar to the phsyalis, apart from its hairy brown jacket which can easily be rubbed off. It is particularly esteemed for its juice, for which it is grown commercially.

Culinary uses

The papery calyx – inedible and mildly toxic – must be removed and discarded: when serving, just peel it back to make a feathery handle. Delicious raw (even better when dipped into a thick fondant icing) the cape gooseberry makes a fine jam, though it lacks sufficient pectin to set a jelly.

Canjica com ciriguela de Peru

(Hominy porridge with cape gooseberries)
Serves 4

A favourite Brazilian dessert, even better at breakfast. The acidity and juiciness of the fruit contrasts beautifully with the blandness and softness of the hominy, and is balanced by the richness of the coconut milk. If using dried rather than canned hominy, cook it like a porridge in double the volume of coconut milk – allow about 30 minutes at a steady simmer. Remember that you need hominy: lye-treated, skinned, pre-cooked and dried corn-kernels; untreated corn-kernels or popping-corn never soften.

450g (1lb) can white hominy
600ml (1 pint) coconut milk
2 tablespoons white sugar
*8 physalis (Cape gooseberries), hulled and
  quartered*
1 thick slice pineapple, thickly shredded

To finish (optional):
Honey or guava jelly

Drain the hominy. Bring the coconut milk to the boil with the sugar, stir in the hominy and cook for 10 minutes, until most of the coconut milk has been absorbed. Allow to cool to finger-temperature, toss with the fruit and finish, if you like, with a spoonful of honey or guava jelly.

**Canjica com ciriguela, a delicious
breakfast porridge**

Mermelada de lulún

(Cape gooseberry jam)
Makes about 2.25 kg (5lb)

A deliciously tart jelly – unusual and well worth the trouble, since you won't find it sold commercially.

*1.35k (3lb) cape gooseberries (or related
  berries)*
Juice of 2 lemons
1.35kg (3lb) preserving sugar

Hull and rinse the berries and put them in a large pan with the lemon juice and about half a litre (roughly a pint) of water. Bring to the boil, turn down the heat and simmer gently for half an hour, stirring occasionally to prevent sticking, until the fruit is quite soft. Meanwhile set the sugar to warm in a low oven.

Stir the sugar into the berries and keep stirring over a low heat until the crystals are completely dissolved. Boil for 10 minutes, or until setting-point is reached. To test, drop a little of the jam on a cold saucer and push it with your finger: when it wrinkles, it's ready. Pot up in clean sterilised jars and store in a cool dark cupboard.

tamarillo

or tomate de arbol, tree-tomato, Peruvian tomato (*Cyphomandra betacea*)

The tamarillo – its name in the USA and when commercially grown – is the fruit of a small tree native to the Amazonian highlands, capable of surviving at high altitudes, whose self-contained habit allows it to be grown as a decorative plant in pots.

Tree tomatoes from Colombia on sale in Panama City

Culinary uses

The purple variety is preferred for eating raw, but the yellow has a more pronounced flavour, with a subtle rather carroty sweetness and a richly spicy flavour which intensifies in the cooking process – it is wonderful in sauces and pickles.

How it grows

The fruit are drop-shaped, about the size of a small egg, and hang together in clusters.

Appearance and taste

The fruit ripens in the wild to a sunny scarlet but is captive-bred to produce yellow and dark purple varieties. When cut, it looks like a tomato, revealing small black seeds clustered round a central pillar of flesh. The flavour is wonderfully rich and spicy, with the sweetness balanced by a satisfying acidity which is underlined by a strong fragrance of sun-ripened tomato.

Buying and storing

Look for firm fruits which weigh heavy for their size. The yellower they are, the sweeter. If they're still hard, allow them to ripen at room temperature.

Medicinal and other uses

The skin of the tamarillo is inedible, so always peel it whether eating it raw or cooked. Never cut it on a wooden or any other absorbent surface: the juices stain anything they touch, and you'll never be able to remove the mark.

Tree tomatoes growing on the eastern slopes of the Andes, Bolivia

Salsa de tamarillo

(Tamarillo sauce)
Serves 4

The flavour of this close relative of the tomato deepens and becomes spicier as it cooks – a remarkable process which can be enhanced by the inclusion of cinnamon and ginger, the warm spices. Serve in the Andean style, with arepas for scooping, or as a sauce for chicken or fish (it is particularly good with grilled prawns).

900g (2lb) red tamarillos, scalded, skinned
  and chopped
1 red onion, finely chopped
1 fresh yellow chilli, de-seeded and chopped
1 teaspoon powdered ginger
1 teaspoon powdered cinnamon
1 teaspoon sugar
Salt and pepper

To finish:
1 tablespoon oil

Put all the ingredients in a small pan with a glass of water. Bring to the boil, put the lid on loosely enough to allow a little steam to escape, turn down the heat and simmer gently for 20–30 minutes, until it is richly concentrated. Taste and adjust the seasoning. Stir in a spoonful of oil and serve at room temperature, as a dipping-sauce.

Mermelada de tamarillo

(Tamarillo chilli jam)
Makes about 2kg (4 one-pound jars)

A chilli-spiked jam to eat with bolillos – dense-crumbed bread rolls baked fresh every day for breakfast – thickly spread with cream cheese. Or use as a piquant stuffing for a tamale.

A fresh-flavoured tamarillo salsa

900g (2lb) ripe tamarillos, skinned and chopped small
1 orange, zest and juice
1 lemon, zest and juice
1 teaspoon powdered cinnamon
1 teaspoon freshly-grated allspice
2 small dried chillies, de-seeded and torn
About 900g (2lb) granulated sugar

Put the fruit in a roomy pan with the zests, spices and chillies, add half a glass of water, bring to the boil, turn down the heat, put the lid on loosely and simmer gently for 20–30 minutes, stirring occasionally, until completely pulped. Weigh and return it to the pan with its own weight of sugar, add the two juices and bring gently to the boil, stirring until the sugar dissolves. Let it bubble, stirring to stop it sticking, until it reaches setting-point – put on a cold saucer, it will wrinkle when you push it with your finger. Bottle up in warm sterilised

prickly pear

or nopalito (leaves), higo chumbo, tuna, Barbary pear, Indian fig, cactus pear (*Opuntia* spp.)

The prickly pear is the fruit of a cactus of Central American origin now naturalised in many parts of the world – including the Mediterranean – where the prickly plant does double duty as a source of food (both fruits and young paddles are eaten) and as a protective thicket for enclosing livestock.

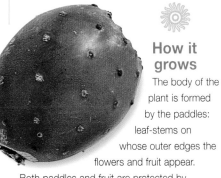

How it grows

The body of the plant is formed by the paddles: leaf-stems on whose outer edges the flowers and fruit appear. Both paddles and fruit are protected by clusters of vicious thorns which are very hard to remove once embedded in the fingers.

Appearance and taste

Technically a berry, the fruits are oval, small enough to cradle in the palm of the hand – which would be unwise as they're covered in evenly-spaced bunches of needle-sharp thorns. They ripen from green through yellow to scarlet, darkening in some species to a deep purple-black, while others remain a brilliant yellow. The flesh is studded with small tender seeds and varies in colour from shocking pink to soft cream, while the flavour and texture is somewhere between a strawberry and a banana, though it lacks acidity, rather like watermelon. Juicy, but without a strongly-defined character, the prickly pear is at its best when combined with a more sharply-flavoured fruit or juice or with a shake of Angostura Bitters.

Buying and storing

When ripe, the fruits vary from dark green to a deep magenta and should be a little soft; handle with care when buying, as a few short transparent prickles will inevitably be left behind. Check for mouldy spots, a sign of trouble within, and don't buy if the skin looks faded. Darker fruits are the sweetest. Mexican children deal with the problem of the prickles by picking the fruit in the early morning when the dew has softened the thorns, and rubbing them in dry sand to scrape them off. When the fruits are offered for sale in the marketplace as a ready-to-eat snack, you'll notice a bucket of water set beside the seller, who soaks the fruit and scrapes it before peeling it fresh for each purchaser. If you buy unripe fruit, allow it to soften at room temperature and eat it as soon as it is ripe.

Medicinal and other uses

Very rich in minerals, vitamins and protein, the prickly pear is truly manna in the desert.

Related or similar fruits

Two other fruit borne of cacti which are locally appreciated are the Barbados gooseberry, the fruit of *Pereskia aculeata,* a West Indian native – the fruits ripen through yellow to red and the flesh is sharp – and the strawberry-pear or *pitaya,* the fruit of *Hylocereus undatus*, a cactus native to Central America but widely cultivated in Florida and the West Indies. The fruit is roughly the same size and shape as the prickly pear but the skin is divided into smooth cones tipped with spines, rather like small pineapples. The flesh is white, sweet and succulent, speckled with tiny black seeds – it is excellent eaten chilled, halved and scooped out with a spoon.

Prickly pear growing above a shrine to Our Lady of Guadalupe, Mexico

Culinary uses

To eat the fruits raw, serve them ready-peeled on ice, with quartered limes, lemons or passion fruit for squeezing; warn everyone about the seeds which are perfectly edible but a little hard. Hand sugar around for those who like it and chilli-flakes for the sophisticates. In its land of origin, the fruit pulp is spread in the sun and dried as a paste for winter storage.

Nopalitos en chile rojo

(Cactus paddles with red chilli)
Serves 4

Make these with the tender young cactus paddles that appear on the edges of last year's growth in the spring. At this stage, when bright green and newly sprouted, they can be eaten raw, when the flavour is somewhere between fresh asparagus and young green beans. Wear gloves when scraping off the spines. As with asparagus or palm-hearts, you can buy them tinned – cut into matchsticks and blanched.

3–4 nopalitos (young cactus paddles), scraped
  and cut into matchsticks
Salt

The sauce:
150ml (¹/4 pint) de-seeded, torn, dried chillies
  (a mixture of mild and hot)
4 tablespoons olive oil
1 large mild onion, finely chopped
4 garlic cloves, finely chopped

Put the nopalito matchsticks in enough boiling water to cover, salt lightly, bring to the boil and cook for about 15 minutes, until tender. Drain and reserve, saving the cooking water.

Meanwhile make the sauce. Lightly toast the chillies in a dry pan for a minute or two – only until they change colour – and be careful not to inhale the fumes. Remove and reserve. Heat the oil in a heavy pan and gently fry the onion and garlic till it softens and gilds – about 10 minutes. Add the toasted chillies and 300ml (¹/2 pint) of the reserved nopalito cooking water. Bubble up, turn down the heat to simmer and

Dulce de tunas con mango

cook for 10 minutes until the sauce thickens. Stir in the reserved nopalitos and cook for another 5 minutes, to reheat and marry the flavours. Taste and adjust the seasoning. Nopalitos in red chilli are traditionally served with dried-shrimp fritters (see p.41).

Dulce de tunas con mango

(Prickly pears with mango)
Serves 4

A sophisticated fruit salad which combines the flavours of the desert and the jungle.

4 prickly pears with their spikes rubbed off
1 orange, juice and zest
3 tablespoons fresh lime juice
1 tablespoon tequila (optional)
3 tablespoons runny honey
1 large mango or 2 smaller ones, diced

Carefully remove the skin of the prickly pears – avoiding any little bumps which might conceal left-behind spines – and mash the flesh with the two juices, the tequila and the honey, simmered for 10 minutes in a small pan with the orange zest. Serve spooned over the diced mango.

pine-strawberry

or fresa de piña, fresa chilena (*Fragaria chiloensis*)

This big-berried, very sweet strawberry native to Chile and the Argentine has long been naturalised throughout the territory, and was cultivated by the Aztecs of Central America, who traded with the Incas.

How it grows

The pine-strawberry thrives in the wild on the Andean uplands. Once cultivated and crossed with the smaller but more acid Virginian strain and the tiny European wood strawberry, it became the mother of the deliciously fragrant, juicy, modern hybrids which are now the universal cultivar.

Appearance and taste

In its land of origin, there are red, yellow and white varieties of the pine-strawberry. Though named for its pineapple flavour, it lacks the depth of fragrance and distinctive floweriness of the modern hybrid.

Buying and storing

The berries should be firm, sun-ripened and without a trace of mould, with a bright colour and strong fragrance; avoid any with green or white tips as these will not have been allowed to ripen properly and can cause the skin allergy known as hives. Check the hulls for signs of withering and the skin for mould or bad patches. Store in the fridge, eat as soon as possible and bring up to room temperature before serving.

Medicinal and other uses

An easily digestible berry, the pine-strawberry cleanses the blood and clears toxins; it is recommended for cardiac problems and is a source of the anti-cancer compound, ellagic acid. When pulped and applied topically, it is a remedy for skin complaints.

Culinary uses

To enjoy its fragrance and flavour, you will do best to eat it raw with a sharp little dressing. Since the fruit is low in pectin, jams will always be runny, so take care not to overcook.

The home of the pine-strawberry, the Andean uplands of Ecuador

Tamales negros de fresa
(Black tamales stuffed with strawberries)
Makes about 24 – serves a party

A steaming pile of honey-sweetened fruit-stuffed tamales (cornmeal dumplings) is the star of any tamalada, a tamale-party held to celebrate weddings and other joyful occasions. Montezuma, last emperor of the Aztecs, was said to prefer a strawberry-stuffed tamale to all others; the Guatemaltecos like their festive tamales coloured and flavoured with chocolate – the combination is irresistible.

The filling:
450g (1lb) ripe strawberries
Juice of 1 bitter orange or lime

The dough:
450g (1lb) masa harina
2 heaped tablespoons cocoa powder
A scrape of seeds from a vanilla pod (optional)
1/2 teaspoon salt
3 tablespoons soft butter or fresh white pork lard
Warm water
3 tablespoons honey

The wrappers:
12 pieces banana leaf cut into 30cm (12in) squares
or maize husks, dried or fresh
or squares of foil

Prepare the strawberries: hull, cut them in quarters if large, and turn with the juice. Work the masa harina with the cocoa powder, optional vanilla, salt and butter or lard. Add enough warm water to make a smooth, slightly sticky dough and knead thoroughly: the grain swells as you work.

Lay the wrappers on a clean cloth, shiny-side up if using banana leaves (hold them in a flame for a second to make them more bendable); if using maize husks, brush lightly with oil; if using foil squares, place shiny-side up. Dampen your hands and break off a plum-sized lump of dough. Work it into a ball, place it on a wrapper and pat it flat to make a rectangle the length and width of your hand. Drop a strawberry in the middle. Continue with all.

Fresas con naranja amarga y miel

To wrap, fold one of the long sides of the wrapper over to enclose two thirds of the filling (the husk will bring the dough with it), fold over the other long side, then fold over the short sides to complete the enclosure. Use a wet finger to seal the cracks. Fold the wrappers to make little torpedo-shaped parcels, long sides first, tucking the short sides under. Secure with a strip of husk or string.

Arrange the tamales in the steamer – a sieve set over a large saucepan will do – and fill the lower level with boiling water (it shouldn't make contact with the upper deck). Cover with a layer of wrapper, and steam, with the lid tightly on, for an hour, until the tamales are perfectly firm, adding more boiling water to the steamer as necessary. As with any steamed pudding, the more even the cooking-temperature, the lighter the dumplings.

Fresas con naranja amarga y miel
(Strawberries with bitter orange and honey)
Serves 4

Very simple and very delicious. Lemon juice or sherry vinegar can replace the bitter orange juice.

450g (1lb) big strawberries
4 tablespoons dark forest honey
2 bitter oranges, strips of zest and juice

Hull the strawberries and wipe them, but don't wash. Heat the honey in a small pan with the orange juice and zest and simmer for about 10 minutes, until the honey thickens and acquires the flavour of the orange. Dress the strawberries with the honey.

mango

The mango, though native to India and the forests of South East Asia, arrived in the tropical Americas during the seventeenth century and has been perfectly at home ever since.

Growing mangoes in Panama

How it grows

The tree is a handsome evergreen – at first glance, not unlike a narrow-leaved magnolia, with a smooth grey trunk and dark green foliage. The fruits, green globes, are suspended from the branches on short vegetable ropes, like Christmas baubles, and do not ripen until they drop. The shape of the fruit is simplicity itself: a smooth-skinned sphere, elongated and slightly flattened, some ending in a little point where the flower-head was. Mango groves are found throughout the tropical belt, including Cuba and the Caribbean, though Puerto Rico and Brazil are the main exporters.

Appearance and taste

When ripe, the skin-colour can be green or yellow or blushed with scarlet, according to its breeding; the flesh ripens from translucent green to a soft yellow, some varieties deepening to a beautiful orange. The texture of a ripe mango is juicy, buttery and soft, a little fibrous round the hard brown stone, with an apricot/peach/pineapple flavour. When unripe and green, the stone is white and soft, the skin tender and the flesh much like that of a sharp green apple, refreshing and fragrant.

Buying and storing

The mango gives off practically no smell at all until almost overripe – as a fruit which ripens only after it falls and which needs to spread its seed beyond the confines of the tree's canopy, it waits for the perfect moment before attracting potential sowers. To test for ripeness, cradle the fruit in the palm of your hand and give it a gentle squeeze, looking for a slight movement in the flesh. If it is very soft, or the skin is mottled with black spots, it's already over the hill. Store in the fridge.

Medicinal and other uses

A powerful disinfectant, the mango is valuable in the treatment of kidney complaints and digestive problems. Applied topically, it is a skin healer and pore-cleanser.

Culinary uses

The fruit is eaten at all stages of ripeness, even when green and hard: the stage when it's particularly high in pectin and can be used to set a jelly. To remove the stone, just place the fruit on its narrowest edge and slip a knife between the flesh and the stone, following the curve which mirrors the shape of the stone; repeat on the other side, then deal as neatly as you can with the margins. If the variety is particularly fibrous, roll it in your hand to soften the flesh, make a small hole in the stalk end and squeeze out the pulp.

Downtown juice bar in Rio de Janeiro

Cebiche de mango verde y aguacate

(Green mango and avocado seviche)
Serves 4–6 as a starter

A refreshing Ecuadorian vegetarian seviche: the crispness of the green mango is balanced by the softness of the avocado.

1 large red onion, thinly sliced into half-moons
Salt
2 small or 1 large green mango, stoned, skinned and diced
2 small or 1 large avocado (ripe but not mushy), stoned, skinned and diced
1 firm tomato or 1 chayote, diced
1 fresh chilli (ají – green or yellow), de-seeded and finely chopped
2 tablespoons chopped coriander
1 tablespoon pitted green olives, sliced
Juice of 2 lemons
1 teaspoon sugar

Soak the sliced onion in salted water for half an hour – until it goes limp and pink – to soften the flavour. Drain and pat dry. Fold the onion with the mango, avocado, tomato, chilli, coriander, olives and lemon juice. Taste and adjust the seasoning, adding the sugar if required. Chill until needed – overnight is fine.

Serve with toasted maize kernels, popcorn and bread rolls for scooping.

Coconut parfait with mango purée

Serves 4

A deliciously delicate ice perfectly partnered with smooth mango. A sophisticated recipe from the Dominican Republic.

The parfait:
2 small cartons (400ml) coconut cream
2 egg-whites, lightly whisked
75g (3oz) castor sugar

The purée:
1 fresh ripe mango, skinned and stoned
A little lemon juice

Pour the coconut cream into a bowl and use a fork to blend: it should be about the consistency of single cream. In another bowl set over a pan of simmering water, whisk the eggwhites with the sugar until you have a thick shiny meringue which just holds its shape. Remove from the heat and continue to whisk until cool.

Fold it into the coconut cream. Divide between small metal moulds, cover with clingfilm, and freeze until firm – 4–5 hours. About 20 minutes before serving, unmould onto pretty plates: a parfait is best if left to soften a little.

Meanwhile, process the mango flesh to a smooth golden purée with a little lemon juice. Pour this round the parfaits and serve it before it melts. Taste the sunshine.

Coconut parfait with mango purée

cherimoya

or custard apple, chirimoya, soursop, anona blanca, graveola (Brazil), guanabana blanca (El Salvador), zapote de viejas (Mexico), pox (Mexico), chirimorriñón (Venezuela), sinini (Bolivia) (*Annona cherimoli*)

The cherimoya is the fruit of a tree native to Ecuador and Peru. The Incas gave it its name – ice-seed in Quechua – either for the snow-white flesh (all the brighter for the contrast with the jet-black seeds) or for its remarkable ability to survive the harsh winters of the Amazonian uplands.

Custard apples in Cuba

How it grows

The fruits sprout (as do many other jungle-fruits) on the trunk, branches or twigs of the tree.

Appearance and taste

Spherical and dimpled at the stalk end like an apple, the custard apple is about the size of a grapefruit, though some can be much smaller or considerably larger, weighing up to a kilo. It is marked more or less obviously with irregularly-spaced facets – fingerprints – which give it the appearance of a large, jade-skinned pinecone. The flesh when ripe is soft, creamy and deliciously fragrant, with a pineapple/banana/vanilla flavour and enough acidity to stimulate the taste-buds. The texture is grainy and rather pear-like close to the skin, graduating to fibrous and pineapple-like where it cradles the seeds. 'Deliciousness itself,' declared Mark Twain on tasting the fruit for the first time.

Buying and storing

In all varieties, the soft leathery skin remains more or less green when ripe. Choose a fruit without brown patches or signs of mould round the stalk end. Cradle the fruit in the palm of your hand and squeeze gently: though firm, the flesh should yield a little under the pressure. Handle gently as it bruises easily. To ensure a good proportion of pulp to seed, look for fruits with large scales (fingerprints): each of these indicates the position of a seed, of which the fewer the better.

Medicinal and other uses

The custard apple is liberally endowed with vitamins A, B and C as well as assorted minerals.

Related or similar fruits

Soursop or guanabana, guana agrio or prickly custard apple (*Annona muricata*) is a dark green, avocado-like fruit, curved on one side but flattish on the other (the sunny side grows faster than the shady side), and is distinguished from the cherimoya by the smoothness of its skin which, though lacking the pinecone effect, is fuzzed with soft spines. One of the largest of the family, it can weigh up to 5kg (11lb). The skin is leathery in appearance but quite tender and the flesh is white and rather cottonwoolly, tangled up with a few large black seeds – leave them alone, they're toxic. At its best – and it's very variable in quality – the fruit is fragrant, succulent, astonishingly juicy and deliciously sharp, sometimes so acid it needs sugaring. It makes a refreshing drink. A native of the Caribbean and northern South America extensively cultivated in Mexico.

Sweetsop or bullock's heart (*A. reticulata*), a cherimoya native to the Caribbean, has particularly large, bland-flavoured fruits which

**Manjarblanco de cherimoya,
a smooth, creamy dessert**

ripen to russet on the sunny side and yellow on the other. As its name indicates, the flesh is sweet but lacks acidity, nevertheless, it has been cultivated since pre-colombian times throughout Central America, from where it was exported to Africa and thence to Asia, where its tolerance of climate and prolific fruiting habits made it suitable rootstock for many modern cherimoya hybrids.

Sugar apple, the fruit of *Annona squamosa*, a tree native throughout the American tropics (also known as the sugar apple or scaly custard apple for the impression of scales which cover the soft green pale-bloomed skin) is much appreciated in Brazil where it's known as the count's apple after the Conde de Miranda who cultivated the trees in his garden in Bahia. The creamy yellow flesh is fragrant, sweet and succulent, with a flavour, observed the early colonisers, of rosewater; it's rarely exported since it's fragile and apt to fall to bits if roughly handled. Its counterpart, the countess's *applebiriba*, the fruit of *Rollina mucosa*, another Amazonian native, ripens to a soft yellow and has ivory flesh, fragrant and succulent.

Ilama (*Annona diversifolia*), a Mexican native tree, is of more elongated shape and has an unmarked skin – rough or smooth, bloomed with white – which ripens to any colour from green to pink to purple; the flesh of the pinker varieties is satisfyingly acid, while that of the green ones is as sweet and bland as the sugar apple.

The atemoya is a delicious new sweetsop–cherimoya hybrid which combines the vanilla/banana sweetness of one with the pineapple/citrus sharpness of the other.

Culinary uses

For custard apple purée, halve the fruit, scoop out the pulp and push it through a sieve to separate the seeds from the flesh. To eat raw, cut the fruit in half and eat with a spoon. If you don't want to eat it immediately, sprinkle it with lemon juice to stop it browning.

Manjarblanco de cherimoya

(Custard apple blancmange)
Serves 4

A sophisticated Chilean dessert which combines an egg-thickened *dulce de leche* with creamy cherimoya. Finish with summer fruits of which Chile has more than its share, including its own variety of blackberry, *murtilla*, described by the Spanish Conquistadors as the queen of all fruits.

1 large can (14oz) sweetened condensed milk
1 large can (12oz) evaporated milk
2 large eggs, separated
1 large ripe cherimoya, de-seeded and mashed

To finish:
Whipped cream
Diced cherries, plums or berries

Combine the two milks in a heavy saucepan and cook gently, stirring steadily, over a medium heat for 20–30 minutes, until it is as thick as double cream and lightly caramelised. Allow to cool in a bowl.

Beat in the yolks, place the bowl over a panful of simmering water and whisk until it thickens to a custard – about 10 minutes. Remove from the heat and fold in the eggwhites, well-whisked. Fold in the cherimoya pulp. Serve well-chilled in pretty glasses, topped with whipped cream and whatever berries take your fancy – strawberries, being native to Chile, would be perfect.

Sorbete de cherimoya

(Custard apple sorbet)
Makes about 1 litre (2 pints)

The fruit's natural viscosity makes it the perfect candidate for a sorbet – looking and tasting like an ice cream but without the cream.

900g (2lb) custard apples (2 fruits)
125g (4oz) castor sugar
300ml (1/2 pint) water
Juice of I lemon

Quarter, skin and de-seed the custard apples. Boil the sugar and water together for 5 minutes and allow to cool. Liquidise the flesh of the custard apples with the sugar syrup and the lemon juice. Freeze until quite solid. Turn out, liquidise again and refreeze.

Defrost for half an hour before serving: this is quite a creamy sorbet with a very subtle flavour and should not be served rock-hard. Delicious with a long cool glass of iced maté tea.

barbados cherry

Cherries growing in Chile

or acerola (Puerto Rico), garden cherry, cereza de Jamaica (*Malpighia punicifolia*)

The fruit of a small tree native to sub-tropical America, the Barbados cherry is particularly appreciated in Puerto Rico and the West Indies.

How it grows

This thin-skinned three-sided berry, scarlet when ripe, has yellow flesh surrounding three smooth, brown, close-fitting stones. It is a member of the jungle-berries group, which includes myrtles as well as some of the less familiar members of the lychee family. All bear small cherry-like fruit.

Appearance and taste

This particularly delicious fruit looks like a cherry, tastes like a raspberry and mutates into sharp green apple when cooked.

Buying and storing

Try before you buy, though you are more likely to find Barbados cherries in the garden than the market. Keep them in a cool dry larder; jungle-fruits have a remarkably long shelf-life.

Medicinal and other uses

Cherry-fruits and jungle-berries of all types are loaded with citric acid, delivering as much vitamin C as the rose-hip. In Venezuela, mamoncillo seeds are roasted and pounded with honey as a cure for diarrhoea.

Related or similar fruits

The Brazilian jungle-berry or *Japoticaba myciaria* (formerly *Eugenia*) *cauliflora*, a member of the myrtle family, is particularly esteemed in the markets of Rio de Janeiro. The fruits look like black cherries and grow directly from the trunk and branches of a large tree. They are mostly eaten fresh, though they're also made into jams and jellies.

The small round Brazilian cherry or grumichama (*Eugenia brasiliensis*) is the fruit of a tree belonging to the aromatic myrtle family which is native to Brazil and Peru. The pulp is variable in colour – it can be crimson, yellow or white – but all varieties are considered equally delicious. It is usually eaten raw.

Pitomba (*Eugenia luschnathiana*) is the small, round, orange, cherry-like fruit of another Brazilian native tree which is also a member of the myrtle family. The flavour and texture are much like that of an apricot; the fruit is usually eaten fresh, but is also used locally in preserves.

The Surinam cherry or pitanga, pendanga (Venezuela), cereza de cayena and cereza quadrada (Colombia) (*Eugenia uniflora*) is the fruit of a berry-bearing shrub of the myrtle family native to Amazonia. It is grown in Brazil and Peru (and elsewhere) as an ornamental garden plant and bears deeply-ridged four-sided berries which ripen to a brilliant scarlet. The flesh is fragrant but a little bitter, centred on a single resinous seed (remove the seed and chill the flesh to neutralise the resin). It is usually eaten raw, sprinkled with sugar.

The honeyberry or mamón, mauco, mamoncillo, genip and grosella de miel (honey gooseberry, Mexico) (*Melicocca bijuga*) is a large tree of the lychee family. A native of Colombia and Venezuela, the honeyberry is also found in Caribbean gardens. In Barbados, it is considered interchangeable with ackee. The fruits hang from the branches in clusters of what look like miniature limes. It is sour when unripe but juicy, crisp and sweet when ripe – translucent, pale green and a little fibrous. The single seed is edible. To eat in the hand, bite a small hole in the skin and suck out the juices. For a refreshing summer cordial, peel, cook and push through a sieve to extract the juice.

An alternative source of winter-time vitamin C is provided by a refreshing scarlet tea prepared from the dried or fresh flower buds of the roselle (*Hibiscus sabdariffa*), a small tree native to North Africa but naturalised throughout the Caribbean and Central America, where it blooms exuberantly down the verges of the State highways. The infusion, known as sorrel in Jamaica and Jamaica-water in Panama, is very tart and usually drunk chilled. The flavour is bitter-cherry, the colour a festive ruby-red: Christmas in the Caribbean wouldn't be the same without it.

Orinoco apple or cocono and tupiro (*Solanum sessiliforum*), a jungle-berry of the same family as the naranjilla, is very fragrant and sweet, with cream-coloured flesh and a jelly-like yellow heart.

Culinary uses

The Barbados cherry is good in pies and jams. Small fruits such as these with tough skins and large stones can be skinned, simmered in water to extract the flavour, then pulped or strained for use in syrups and sweet sauces. If the seed is edible, roast it and crush it for inclusion in a pastry or crumble.

Pastelitos de acerola

(Barbados cherry tartlets)
Makes a dozen tartlets

Deliciously sweet-sour, with a flavour and fragrance not unlike a ripe raspberry, the Barbados cherry is perfect in a tart.

The almond pastry:
175g (6oz) plain flour
50g (2oz) ground almonds
1 tablespoon caster sugar
1/2 teaspoon salt
150g (5oz) butter
3 tablespoons cold water

The filling:
450g (1lb) Barbados cherries, stoned (squeeze through the stalk end)
4–6 tablespoons caster sugar (depending on the cherries' acidity)
Juice of an orange and a lemon
1 teaspoon cornflour mixed with a little water
2–3 tablespoons custard or soured cream

Toss the flour with the ground almonds, sugar and salt in a bowl. Cut the butter into the flour with a knife and then rub it in lightly with your fingertips until the mixture looks like fine breadcrumbs. Sprinkle in the water and press into a firm smooth ball of dough, still using your fingertips. Put the pastry aside to rest in a plastic bag in a cool place for 30 minutes to swell and gain elasticity.

Preheat the oven to 220°C/425°F/gas mark 7.

Roll the pastry out with a floured rolling pin – use small light movements: the pastry is fragile. Use a wine-glass or pastry cutter to cut rounds of the right size for your tartlet tins. Place the pastry rounds in the tins and prick the bases with a fork to prevent any bubbles forming. Bake for 15–20 minutes – the almond pastry will first whiten and then turn golden. Remove to a baking rack to crisp and cool.

Meanwhile, put the stoned cherries in a pan with the sugar and the juices diluted with their own volume of water. Bring to the boil, turn down the heat and simmer for 10-15 minutes, until the cherries are tender. Remove with a slatted spoon and reserve. Allow the syrup to cool a little, then stir in the cornflour, reheat and bubble up for a moment to thicken.

Put a teaspoonful of the custard or cream into the base of each tartlet, arrange a few cherries on the top and finish with the thickened syrup.

Acerola and raisin relish

A Barbadan sweet and sour chutney which can be eaten as a dip. It is very good with cold meats, particular pork.

450g (1lb) Barbados cherries, stoned and roughly chopped
4 tablespoons raisins
2 tablespoons shredded coconut
1 teaspoon ground allspice
1 teaspoon chopped fresh ginger
1 finger-length cinnamon stick, broken
300ml (1/2 pint) vinegar
225g (8oz) dark brown sugar
1 teaspoon salt

Put all the ingredients in a large saucepan and add a teacupful of water. Stir, bring to the boil, bubble up, turn down the heat and simmer, stirring to avoid sticking, until all is perfectly tender and the fierce taste of the vinegar has mellowed – 40 minutes or so.

Pot in sterilised jars in the usual way.

Pastelitos de acerola, Barbados-cherry tarts

mamee apple

or mamey, St Domingo apricot, abricozeiro, abricó do Pará (Brazil) (*Mammea americana*)

How it grows

The fruit of a tropical tree, the mamee apple is a member of the same family as the mangosteen of South East Asia. Originally native to Brazil, it is now cultivated throughout the region but rarely exported. It is delicious eaten fresh from the hand, in a *liquado*, or sliced into a fruit salad with cream and sugar.

Appearance and taste

This round, russet-coloured, tough-skinned, winter fruit is about the size and shape of a large peach, coming to a point at the base. The skin is bitter but the yellowy-orange pulp, embracing three smooth, ivory-coloured inedible stones, is sweet and fragrant, with a scent of caramel and vanilla. The texture varies from crisp and firm to soft and rather custardy.

Buying and storing

To test for ripeness, use your nose: the scent should be vanilla/caramel with no hint of fermentation. Hold the fruit in the palm of your hand and squeeze gently, rejecting any which feel soft rather than yielding. When over-ripe and lacking acidity, the flesh is woolly and sickly-sweet.

Medicinal and other uses

Medicinally, the mamee apple has some antibiotic properties, but a few might experience digestive problems. If you're eating it for the first time, try a small slice only.

Culinary uses

To prepare the mamee apple for eating or cooking, score the skin from top to bottom and peel it off in segments. Then scrape off the whitish membrane beneath to expose the soft orange flesh (the membrane which encloses the stones is also bitter); it is delicious in a fruit salad with cream. Unripe fruits are best for cooking and have enough pectin to set a jelly.

Mamee apple smoothie

Mamee apple jelly
Makes 8–10 jars

Choose firm fruits and prepare them carefully: score the skin from top to bottom and peel it off in segments, then scrape off the whitish membrane beneath to expose the soft orange flesh, discarding the skin, the stone and the bitter membrane which encloses the stone. Unlike other fruits, mamee apple jelly is prepared with the pulp only. If you have trouble achieving a set, add a bottle of pectin.

2.75kg (6lb) prepared mamee apple
Juice of 4 bitter oranges or lemons
3–4 cloves
About 2.75kg (6lb) preserving sugar

Put the mamee apple pulp, lemon juice and cloves in a deep preserving pan with a mugful of water to moisten, and cook down to a mush. Tip everything in a jelly bag (or clean cloth pinned on the legs of an upturned stool). Set a bowl beneath to catch the juice and leave to drip overnight.

Next day, measure the cloudy juice (don't press the pulp), return it to the pan and stir in an equal volume of sugar. Stir gently over the heat until the sugar dissolves, then boil rapidly until a drop poured onto a cold saucer forms a skin when pushed with a finger – 20–40 minutes. When cool, pot up in clean jars, top with a little circle of greaseproof paper dipped in rum, and seal or cover in any way which will exclude the air.

Mamee apple smoothie
Serves 4

Fresh fruits puréed with milk – *liquado* – are prepared to order for the passer-by at roadside stands throughout the region. For the traveller this is one of the best ways to savour the delicate flavour of unfamiliar, rare or exotic fruits.

2 ripe mamee apples, skinned and de-seeded
600ml (1 pint) fresh creamy milk
2 tablespoons sugar

Drop the mamee pulp with the sugar and milk in the liquidiser and purée until smooth.

red mombin

or jocote, xocote (Mexico and Guatemala), cajá or hobó (Brazil), ciruela roja (red plum – Cuba), Brazilian plum (*Spondias purpurea*)

The fruit of a small tree native to Amazonia, the red mombin is found throughout the tropics from southern Mexico through Peru and northern Brazil.

Appearance and taste

The fruits are round or oval, about the size of a damson, thin-skinned and rather like a small mango, ripening to a sunny yellow or even scarlet. The flesh is sharp-flavoured and spicy, with a hard, nut-like core which can be cracked and eaten.

Buying and storing

Try before you buy: the flesh should be soft and juicy, sweet and not too sharp. Store in the fridge for no more than a couple of days.

Medicinal and other uses

The juice is drunk as a diuretic and to lower a fever.

Related or similar fruits

Yellow mombin or ciruela amarilla (Cuba) or hog plum (*Spondias pinnata*) is the fruit of a tree native to the American tropics, much appreciated by pigs as well as humans –

though, being only mildly acidic and on the watery side, and therefore less distinctive in flavour, it is considered less good than the red mombin.

The Brazilian greengage or imbu or umbu (*Spondias tuberosa*) is the fruit of a Brazilian native tree; oval or roundish, ripening to a yellowy green, with much the same shape and size as a greengage, it is generally held to be the most delicious of the genus. Its skin is thickish and quite tough, the flesh soft, fragrant and spicy; acidic when unripe, the flesh sweetens as it ripens. It makes excellent jelly.

The South Seas ambarella (*Spondias dulcis*), a larger fruit of the same family, was planted in the West Indies and is much sought-after in the markets of Trinidad, where it's used unripe in relishes and ripe in jams.

Culinary uses

If eaten fresh, the Brazilian plum is best served chilled – it looks pretty on a bed of ice. To eat the nuts, crack the stones and extract the kernels.

Picante de jocote

(Devilled Brazilian plum)
Serves 4

A tart little relish for serving with bean dishes. Sour plums or damsons can replace the mombin.

450g (1lb) mombin, stoned and diced
3–4 spring onions, chopped with their green
1 teaspoon honey
Juice of 1 lime
1 red or green chilli, de-seeded and finely chopped

Toss the diced plums with the spring onions, dress with honey and limejuice, and finish with a sprinkling of chopped chilli.

sapote

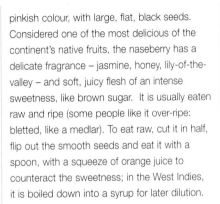

or zapote, lucuma (Peru), sapote de carne (flesh-sapote, Colombia), mamey (Cuba), chachas (Mexico) (*Pouteria* – formerly *Lucuma* – *sapota*)

The sapote is native to southern Mexico and is found in the wild as far south as Nicaragua; it is widely cultivated throughout the region (and also in South-East Asia).

How it grows

The winter-maturing fruit of a small shrubby tree, the sapote is one of several soft-fleshed, thin-skinned, winter-maturing fruits of a group which, though not necessarily of the family Sapotaceae, bear an identical or similar name – a word derived, as it happens, from the Aztec zpotl, which simply means 'soft'.

Appearance and taste

The fruits are large, oval and up to a handspan long, with reddish skins and pinky-orange, soft, sweet flesh with a banana/pineapple/vanilla fragrance and flavour.

Buying and storing

As a winter fruit, the sapote should be tree-ripened, so avoid any which are not fully mature – they should be fragrant and yield a little when cradled gently in the palm.

Medicinal and other uses

Of the sapote and the following related fruits, some – particularly the sapote – are soporific; the star-apple is recommended for laryngitis and to clear lungs affected by pneumonia.

Related or similar fruits

The canistel or yellow sapote, huicón, kanis, costiczapotl (Mexico) and egg-fruit (West Indies) (*Pouteria campechiana* – formerly *Lucuma rivicoa*) looks rather like a small mango: round but tapers to a point. The skin is smooth and thin, ripening to a smooth shiny orange and the flesh – sometimes likened to a hard-boiled egg-yolk with the flavour and texture of sweet potato – softens towards the centre which contains the large black, shiny seeds. The skin and flesh both ripen to a sunny yellow.

The naseberry (West Indies) or sapodilla or sapote chico (*Manilkara zapota*) is the fruit of an evergreen tree native to central America and the Caribbean, also known as the chicle tree since the sap – *chicle* – is the raw material of chewing gum. The fruit itself, a round yellow-skinned berry covered in brown fuzz, is about the size of a plum; when cut, the flesh looks grainy, like a pear, and ripens to a sunny apricot or

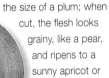

pinkish colour, with large, flat, black seeds. Considered one of the most delicious of the continent's native fruits, the naseberry has a delicate fragrance – jasmine, honey, lily-of-the-valley – and soft, juicy flesh of an intense sweetness, like brown sugar. It is usually eaten raw and ripe (some people like it over-ripe: bletted, like a medlar). To eat raw, cut it in half, flip out the smooth seeds and eat it with a spoon, with a squeeze of orange juice to counteract the sweetness; in the West Indies, it is boiled down into a syrup for later dilution.

The white sapote or zapote blanco (Mexico), matasano (elsewhere in South America) and Mexican orange (*Casimiroa edulis*) is a native of Mexico which has never really been popular anywhere else. The small round fruit is a member of the citrus family (Rutaceae) and has an orange skin, the characteristic citrus interior and a mild pear-like flavour. Its last name – *matasano* or kill-health – is a reference to suspected soporific properties.

Black sapote or zapote negro, zapote prieto or sapodillo (*Diospyros ebenaster*) is a winter fruit which ripens on the branch after the leaves have fallen and looks rather like a slightly flattened tomato. A member of the persimmon family, it is about the size of a large tangerine with a thin, greenish skin and soft, sweet, almost black flesh with small seeds.

Star-apple or cainito (*Chrysophillum cainito*) is an ancient Central American cultivar, probably native to the West Indies. A soft-fleshed fruit about the size of a small apple, the star-apple is pointed at the flower end, with a thin skin and a star-shaped, jelly-like heart in which are buried flat brown seeds. The fruit needs to ripen on the tree, making it difficult to export. When mature the flesh is a soft ivory (*cainito blanco*) or a deep purple (*cainito morado*). It is usually eaten fresh, but is also made into jam.

Culinary uses

The skins and seeds of all these winter fruits are often toxic. Take no risks: when eating raw, use a spoon to scoop out the soft pulp, and skin and core carefully before cooking.

Sorbete de lucuma

(Sapote sorbet)

Makes about 1¹/₂ pints

Peru's favourite ice cream. The lucuma gives it a creamy texture and a maple-syrup/vanilla flavour. In Chile as well as Peru the pulp and juice can conveniently be bought canned – ready for a smoothie or a sorbet.

1 can (12oz) evaporated milk
4 egg-yolks
600ml (1 pint) sapote pulp

Make a custard with the milk and egg-yolks: put the two in a bowl set over simmering water, and whisk until it thickens to a custard which will coat the back of a spoon.

Let the custard cool. Stir in the pulped sapote. Freeze as usual – easier if you have an ice-cream machine. If all you have is the ice compartment of the fridge, you will have to take the ice out when it is nearly solid and beat it thoroughly to incorporate as much air as possible. Move it from the freezer into the fridge half an hour before you are ready to eat. Serve with crunchy cookies flavoured with cinnamon and cloves: *revolución caliente*, a political reference to the struggle for independence.

Matrimonia

Serves 2 – of course

A marriage of two juices, Jamaican-style, one smooth and flowery, the other sharp and citrussy.

300ml (¹/₂ pint) sapote juice
300ml (¹/₂ pint) orange juice

Mix the two juices and pour over ice. Sit under a palm tree and sip it in the sun.

Matrimonia

index

Author's acknowledgements
First and foremost, I owe a deep debt of gratitude to Francine Lawrence, not only for her skills as a photographer but for her foresight in abandoning the editorship of *Country Living* to explore some of the lesser known corners of what is, after all, a dauntingly vast, ethnically diverse and sometimes inaccessible continent. Without her collaboration – no other word will do – along with the sparkling styling of Susi Hoyle and the help of Brent Darby and Jon Day on long days spent between camera and stove, this book might never have blossomed. My thanks are also due to Helen Woodhall, Caroline Taggart, Esme West and the meticulous Robina Pelham Burn for unflagging support and patient editing from first bud to final fruit, and to designer Geoff Hayes for creating order out of chaos. And to Kyle Cathie for proposing and piloting the project, Michael Bateman for confirming her choice, and my beloved agent Abner Stein for making the whole thing happen.

Among sources consulted during the course of research, I have sought both inspiration and information from the work of Diana Kennedy, Elisabeth Lambert Ortiz, Nitza Villapol, Michelle O. Fried, Alan Davidson, Jessica B. Harris, Sophie Coe, Heidi Cusick, Cristine Mackie, Christopher Idone, Antonio Montana, Himilice Novas and Rosemary Silva, Michael Bateman, Maricel Presilla, Marlena Spieler, Lourdes Nichols and contributors to the small but brilliant Petits Propos Culinaires.

The author, publishers and photographer would like to thank the following for their contributions to the book:
Fired Earth Ltd,
Twyford Mill,Oxford Road, Oxon OX17 3HP.
Telephone: 01295-814-300

The Spice Shop
Spices, herbs from all over the world
1 Blenheim Crescent, London W11
Telephone: 020 7221 4448

Sean Miller
Colourful ovenproof and dishwasher safe pottery
108 Dewsbury Road, London NW10 1EP
Telephone: 0208 208 0148

Ceramica Blue
Brightly coloured plates and bowls
10 Blenheim Crescent, London W11
Telephone: 020 7727 0288

Fired Earth
Tiles from Mexico and South America
117 Fulham Road, London SW3
Telephone: 0207 589 0489

The Denby Pottery Company Ltd
Denby, Derby DE5 8MX
Telephone: 01773 740700

Photographic acknowledgements
Key: GPL – Garden Picture Library; SAP – South American Pictures; APA – Andes Press Agency; RH – Robert Harding; TI – Travel Ink; ICL – Impact Colour Library; FY – Francesca Yorke; (t) – top; (m) – middle; (b) – bottom; (l) – left; (r) – right

All photographs by Francine Lawrence except the following pages:
1 ICL/Adrian Sherratt; 2–3 SAP/Marion Morrison; 6 FY; 9 FY; 10 ICL/Rhonda Klevansky; 11 APA/Anna Gordon; 12 TI/David Forman; 14 SAP/Robert Francis; 15 SAP/Jason P Howe; 16–17 FY; 18–19 FY; 20 ICL/Robert Gibbs; 24 ICL/Peter Menzel; 26 SAP/Robert Francis; 28 TI/Abbie Enock; 32 GPL/Gary Rogers; 34 SAP/Tony Morrison; 38 APA/Carlos Reyes-Manzo; 40 RH/Robert Frerck; 42 GPL/Brigitte Thomas; 44 FY; 47 APA/Carlos Reyes-Manzo; 48–9 SAP/Charlotte Lipson; 51 SAP/Charlotte Lipson; 56–7 SAP/Tony Morrison; 58 SAP/Tony Morrison; 60(m) ICL/Nancy Bravo; 60(b) APA/John Curtis; 62 ICL/Susan Campbell; 64 APA/Carlos Reyes-Manzo; 65 TI/Grazyna Bonati; 66 ICL/Rachel Morton; 72(t) FY; 72(b) Julie Dixon; 74 SAP/Tony Morrison; 78 ICL/Piers Cavendish; 80 APA/Carlos Reyes-Manzo; 84 SAP/Robert Francis; 88 TI/Dennis Stone; 94 APA/Carlos Reyes-Manzo; SAP/Marion Morrison; 100–1 SAP/Tony Morrison; 102 ICL/Rhonda Klevansky; 104 ICL/Charles Coates; 106 RH/Charles Bowman; 108 SAP/Tony morrison; 110–1 APA/Carlos Reyes-Manzo; 112 TI/Abbie Enock; 114 TI/Brian Garrett; 118 ICL/Robert Gibbs; 120 SAP/Robert Francis; 123 SAP/Tony Morrison; 126 SAP/Tony Morrison; 128 ICL/Rhonda Klevansky; 130–1 ICL/Neil Morrison; 134 SAP/Chris Sharp; 136 FY; 140 ICL/Simon Shepheard; 142 ICL/Robert Gibbs; 144 ICL/Robert Gibbs; 146 SAP/Jason P. Howe; 148 SAP/Chris Sharp; 150 ICL/Sergio Dorantes; 156(b) SAP/Mike Harding; 160 SAP/Jason P. Howe; 162–3 SAP/Tony Morrison; 166(b) FY; 168 APA/Carlos Reyes-Manzo; 170 SAP/Chris Sharp; 172 SAP/Mike Harding; 174 ICL/Christopher Pillittz; 176 ICL/Charles Coates; 180 APA/Carlos Reyes-Manzo; 182(t) SAP/Tony Morrison; 184 SAP/Chris Sharp; 186 SAP/Tony Morrison; 190(br) APA/Carlos Reyes-Manzo; 192 SAP/Chris Sharp; 194(l) SAP/Tony Morrison; 196 Sally Maltby; 197 ICL/Sally Fean; 200–1 TI/Brian Garrett; 202 FY; 204 ICL/Alain le Garsmeur; 206 ICL/Cristina Pawel); 208 SAP/Tony Morrison; 210 APA/Carlos Reyes-Manzo; 212 APA/Carlos Reyes-Manzo; 214(bl) SAP/Mike Harding; 216 TI/Brian Garrett; 218(t) SAP/Mike Harding; 218(b) SAP/Tony Morrison; 220 APA/Carlos Reyes-Manzo; 220 GPL/Lamontagne; 224(m) APA/Carlos Reyes-Manzo; 224(b) ICL/Michael Mirecki; 226 SAP/Rolando Pujol; 228 APA/Carlos Reyes-Manzo